Classical and Modern Interactions

KARL GALINSKY

Classical and Modern Interactions

Postmodern Architecture

Multiculturalism

Decline

and Other Issues

UNIVERSITY OF TEXAS PRESS, AUSTIN

Grateful acknowledgment is made to the following for permission to quote from certain materials:

From *THE AENEID* by Virgil, trans. by Robert Fitzgerald. Translation copyright © 1980, 1982, 1983 by Robert Fitzgerald. Reprinted by permission of Random House, Inc.

From *THE AENEID* by Virgil, trans. by Cecil Day Lewis. Copyright © 1952 by Cecil Day Lewis. Reprinted by permission of Sterling Lord Literistic, Inc.

Requests for permission to reproduce material from this work should be sent to Permissions, University of Texas Press, Box 7819, Austin, TX 78713-7819.

∞ The paper used in this publication meets the minimum requirements of American National Standard for Information Sciences—Permanence of Paper for Printed Library Materials, ANSI Z39.48-1984.

Library of Congress Cataloging-in-Publication Data
Galinsky, Karl, 1942–
    Classical and modern interactions : postmodern architecture,
    multiculturalism, decline, and other issues / Karl Galinsky.—1st ed.
        p.   cm.
    Includes bibliographical references and index.
    ISBN 0-292-77053-7
    1. Civilization, Classical.   2. United States—Civilization—1970–
I. Title.
DE60.G35   1992
938—dc20   92-11516
                                                              CIP

To the memory of Hans Galinsky

Contents

IV Leadership, Values, and the Question of Ideology: The Reign of Augustus

V Multiculturalism in Greece and Rome

VI Rome, America, and the Classics in America Today

Preface

Postmodernism, the alleged decline of the United States, multiculturalism, deconstruction, and ideology—these are topics that have been in the forefront of the current discussion and are likely to retain their actuality in this decade. They can be illuminated usefully from wider than contemporary perspectives. One such perspective is the classical world, a connection that is anything but extraneous: classicism, in fact, has made its reappearance in postmodern architecture; discussions of the decline of nations inevitably lead back to Rome; the Greco-Roman world was multicultural in the literal sense of the word; the Augustan reign has often been viewed as a precursor of modern, ideologically oriented regimes; and much of the current criticism of Vergil's *Aeneid* is de facto deconstructionist. Besides, there is a long tradition of using the ancient world for purposes of analogy.

One of the aims of this book is to define the validity, and the boundaries, of such approaches and comparisons. They are, in their own way, an important aspect of the continuing vitality of the classical tradition. Because of their many facets, their richness, and their extensiveness, the Greek and Roman civilizations have provided not only continuing models, such as in architecture and literature, for conscious adaptation but also a wide frame of resonance for modern issues and approaches. The process is reciprocal, as it applies both to the projection of contemporary issues into the past and to the discussion of aspects of the ancient world in terms of current approaches. The danger, as always, is anachronism. There are striking commonalities as well as profound differences. By concentrating on specific examples, this book, I hope, will provide some guidance for arriving at a proper balance. Decline, for instance, is a relative notion, and we can learn, perhaps, less from the Roman experience than from the excesses of previous interpretations. Or, to give a different example, the application of concepts from modern political science and cultural anthropology can result in a better understanding, respectively, of the nature of Augustus' leadership and the behavior of Aeneas without any forcing of the argument.

Another principal theme is the creativity required to maintain the vitality of cultural traditions (and, apropos of the topic of decline, the life of nations). I will assess, therefore, on several occasions and in several settings, the dynamics of the relationship between existing traditions and their adaptations, and the issues suggested by that process of renewal, whether in postmodern American architecture or by Hellenism in the Roman world. Early in this century, T. S. Eliot wrote a perceptive and justly famous essay on this subject, entitled "Tradition and the Individual Talent." He asserted that in such a creative and organic continuum, as exemplified by European literature, it would not be preposterous for us to find "that the past should be altered by the present as much as the present is directed by the past."[1] This apt formulation also applies to the reciprocity I have outlined in the preceding paragraph.

I have chosen deliberately a diversity of topics to which these perspectives apply, and I have made due allowance for their individual nature instead of subordinating the discussion to the same schema of exposition each time. This is meant to illustrate both the breadth and the flexibility of the classical tradition without impeding thematic interconnections between the various chapters. A few comments are in order on each.

The purpose of the first chapter is to combine a concise survey of postmodern architectural classicism in America with a discussion of its meaning. It aims, therefore, to familiarize classicists and others with the phenomenon while contributing another point of view to the debate among architects and architectural historians, a debate that has many similarities with the current argument about the classical tradition in the curriculum. As for chapter 2, the supposed parallels between Rome's decline and America's, I feel as if I were saying goodbye to an old friend. I have lectured on this subject well over fifty times in the past four years, and the publication of this presentation will, I almost hope, mean the end of continuing invitations to address the topic. It obviously struck a responsive chord with many different audiences, including radio call-in shows. My treatment of it evolved and underwent several stages of *aggiornamento*, especially after the appearance of Paul Kennedy's book. I am pleased to note, however, that subsequent world events required no modification of any of my conclusions.

Vergil's *Aeneid* (chapter 3) and the reign of Augustus (chapter 4) have been scholarly concerns of mine for over two decades. They exemplify what is true of many of the most central areas of classical scholarship: so far from having been treated in a definitive fashion that would leave room only for quiet regurgitation and revisionist nibbling around the edges, they are still in need of considerable study and scholarly and interpretive initiatives. Part of the reason is their complexity and sophistication, which our age is increasingly beginning to appreciate. In a survey article I published five years ago,[2] I briefly suggested the applicability of James MacGregor Burns' definition of leadership to Augustus; I am pleased with the response this suggestion has received and therefore decided to expand on it more fully. I have also incorporated into that chapter a few revised paragraphs adapted from a paper I gave at the international conference in Italy on the occasion of the bimillenary of Vergil's death and am grateful to the publisher, Arnoldo Mondadori, for permission to reprint them.[3]

My chapter on multiculturalism in the Greek and Roman world (chapter 5) illustrates a procedure I have followed throughout this book: I have concentrated on identifying the main salient issues—and on seeing the forest for the trees—and I have provided a representative number of examples instead of treating each topic exhaustively. This is an invitation to the readers—reader response is a major aspect of literature, after all—to continue to work on their own; if they wish, for instance, to explore the validity, or its lack, of further parallels between the late Roman Empire and the United States today they can use the Appendix to chapter 2. My main purposes in writing on Greek and Roman multiculturalism have been to address the misconception that these societies were monocultural and monoethnic, to provide an impetus for future work in this area, and to suggest some implications that are useful for the current debate.

Instead of conforming to the time-honored academic genres of the theoretical manifesto or the call to action without any follow-through, most of the last chapter was written from various realistic perspectives germane to my experience, such as having been chairman of the country's largest (and growing) classics department for sixteen years; directing or substantively participating in numerous projects sponsored by the National Endowment for the Humanities; serving as one of the regional chairmen for the Mellon Fellowships in the Humanities and as a panelist for NEH for several years; working extensively with clienteles outside of academe such as high school teachers and businesspeople; seeing a multitude of classics departments firsthand as a lecturer or consultant; and finally, both longer and less long ago than I care to remember, working on an assembly line in a chemical factory to earn money for college—you cannot help but notice how privileged the academic existence is by comparison. Hence my advocacy, in the light of the previous chapters and my own professional experience, of an active and positive role for classicists in America that is a far cry from solipsism. An earlier version of the second part of that chapter, entitled "Classics beyond Crisis," has appeared in *Classical World* 84 (1991).

The book was written for many other audiences besides classicists, as it owes its genesis to my appointment as a Phi Beta Kappa National Visiting Scholar in 1989–1990. This involved two-day visits at nine universities and colleges around the country, and shorter engagements at several others en route. I am grateful to the Committee on Visiting Scholars of the United Chapters of Phi Beta Kappa and its chairperson, Professor Hazel Barnes, for the initial selection and to its two staff members, Kathy Navascués and Frances Robb, for their cheerful help and patience in making the many logistical and travel arrangements. The individuals who helped with the visits on each campus are too numerous to be listed here; I simply want to thank them all for their unfailing hospitality, kindness, and courtesy. I could not have wished for livelier audiences than those provided by the individual chapters of Phi Beta Kappa. My interest in current architectural classicism was aroused by an invitation from Professors Wayne Attoe (now of Louisiana State University) and Charles Moore to serve as a panelist at a symposium they were organizing in 1985 on its manifestations in twentieth-century America. I want to thank them and Dean Hal Box of the University of Texas School of Architecture for their early encouragement. The impetus for the chapter on multiculturalism came from an invited lecture in connection with the SHARE minority recruitment program at the University of Texas at Austin in the spring of 1990, and it is my pleasure to thank Ms. Corina Fuentes in particular for her assistance. Consistent with this general orientation, I have kept notes to a reasonable minimum and appended select bibliographies for further reading.

For almost a quarter of a century, I have had the pleasure to be associated with a large, thriving, and interdisciplinary classics department, and I am grateful especially to my colleagues Michael Gagarin, Peter Green, Gwyn Morgan, and Alex Mourelatos for sharing their expertise with me and for help on several special points. I would also like to thank Dr. Stephanie Katz for critiquing an earlier version of chapter 6, and Professors Mark Morford and Alexander McKay for reading the entire manuscript and making many valuable suggestions. Our departmental staff, especially Cate Fowler and our slide librarian, Celeste Robinson, provided ready technical assistance. I also appreciate with gratitude the help I received from my editors at the University of Texas Press, in particular Frankie Westbrook and copy editors Bob Fullilove and Lisa Tippett. Finally, without the understanding and support of my wife, Harriet Harris, this project would not have materialized. Only a professional travel consultant could have put up with a travel schedule like mine and kept it from becoming too disruptive.

The dedication records my lifelong debt to someone who excelled in the area of American studies and once may have had the same in mind for me, except that I decided to focus a few centuries earlier—precisely in order to be able to remain in the United States.

Austin, November 1991

Classical and Modern Interactions

I

Classicism in
Postmodern American Architecture

Less is more.—Mies van der Rohe   *Less is a bore.*—Robert Venturi

Classicism and Modernism

To an even greater degree than literature and the arts, architecture embodies the cultural, social, and spiritual trends of a civilization. Vitruvius was fully cognizant of this, and Paul Zanker's most recent book on the Augustan age is a splendid and sensitive illustration of the phenomenon.[1] The emergence of the classical idiom in the American architecture of the 1980s, therefore, is part of a wider context. It is important to lay out some of the issues raised by the current architectural manifestations of classicism and to outline some of the ramifications before we proceed to a discussion of individual examples.

The new classicism is eclectic. We are not dealing with the conscious, earlier neoclassicism of American public and government buildings nor, in the end, with the same kind of personal adaptation, which is authentically and authoritatively classical, as practiced most successfully by Thomas Jefferson (and, for that matter, Schinkel in Prussia and Soane in England). Instead, the new classicism in American architecture came about, firstly, as a reaction against the ideology and practice of the reductionist modernism of the International Style—in other words, the "box" as championed by Mies van der Rohe and others.

Yet matters are more complex, since Mies, too, had followed classical precepts, albeit of a different order. He was, in essence, a Platonist.[2] He shared Plato's belief in universals, as manifested especially by geometric forms; the motto of Plato's Academy, Let No One Untrained in Geometry Enter, aptly applies to the buildings of Mies and his followers. At its best, Mies' and Plato's intent was to lead the beholder to a richer reality by drastically reducing the manifold variety of outer appearances. Hence a few of the more overtly classicizing contemporary architects could actually argue, as Thomas Beeby did in connection with the Sulzer Library, that "we believe what is implicit in Mies is somehow made explicit in this building."[3] Most of their confreres, however, view the break with Modernism in terms of a return to a fuller, more open, and more diverse tradition. Plato had emphasized statism. So did Mies, and both, in their own way, rejected poetry. Modern classicism, by contrast, is a celebration of the imaginative and contradictory richness of the human experience.

Secondly, therefore, the new classicism, which is far from being a uniform style, is part of the pluralism of American culture. It is a liberating and tolerant idiom whose time has come after the culture of the 1960s and the "culture of narcissism" of the 1970s.[4] It coexists with other styles and other kinds of architectural syntax.

Hence, with all due regard for precision, we are ill served by rigid taxonomies and attempts to define the term *postmodern* too closely. Postmodernism is a grab bag of creative empiricisms and reaction formations. Attempts have not been lacking to categorize it, and therefore it may mean something very different when applied to literature[5] rather than painting. I intend to use the term in a combined chronological and programmatic sense here. When applied to architecture, it is elastic enough to incorporate all sorts of responses to modernism, including the attempt to modify and continue the modernist style with decorative and classical elements. For good reasons, we are talking about *post*-modernism and not *anti*-modernism; scholars of Roman literature of the Principate, who are apt to subscribe to the facile dichotomy of pro-Augustan and anti-Augustan, could learn a great deal from this.[6] Postmodernism in the 1980s mirrors the culture at large by what the art historian Hans Sedlmayr long ago called "Verlust der Mitte,"[7] the loss of a center that would provide a spiritual and conceptual anchor amid the bewildering and very un-Platonic plurality of beliefs and perspectives. Hence the new classicism is comparable not even to the neoclassicism that we see at work in the sculpture of the similarly unsettled Hellenistic period as exemplified by the Apollo Belvedere. No such return is possible, and therefore—and because it began as a heterodoxy—the new architectural classicism is more tentative, allusive, and playful.

A second complex of relevant questions is that of form and meaning. Does the return, however idiosyncratic, to classical forms also signify an espousal of the values of the classical tradition? The answers to that question are divided and I will reassess the situation after surveying the evidence. To some architectural critics, the reemergence of classicism in American and international architecture indicates the continuity of a prevailing and meaningful tradition, broken only by the aberrant hiatus of the International Style. Others are less sanguine and identify it with poverty of imagination rather than respect for tradition. We will have to determine whether the new classical manifestations in architecture go beyond decorative aspects and beyond language, semantics, and semiotics to express substance, values, and commitment. Not surprisingly, this will vary from case to case.

Thirdly, there are critical perspectives that pertain equally to the interpretation of classical, and especially Roman, literature and architectural classicism today. One, for better or worse, is the absence of a binding hermeneutics.

The interpretation of Roman poetry, for one, in the 1970s and 1980s, exhibits the same kind of pluralism and eclecticism that we see in postmodern architecture.[8] De facto deconstructionism with its emphasis on the "infinite plurality of meanings" is part of the phenomenon, but there are limits to the equation: the exhibit at the Museum of Modern Art in New York on "Deconstructivist Architecture" in the summer of 1988, "essentially a-historical in outlook and anti-Classical in composition,"[9] is difficult to integrate even into the most elastic definition of architectural postmodernism. Another aspect is the principles of *imitatio* and *aemulatio* with which scholars of Roman literature are conversant. They are appropriate to architectural classicism as well, enabling us better to gauge the nuances of innovation and allusiveness. For an ancient author, imitation was always creative. It defined the tradition in which one was writing, but it was a tradition to whose development one contributed by modifying and surpassing the work of one's predecessors. The same process applies to classicism in architecture, including contemporary architecture.

Lastly, there is the question whether this classicism implies or ought to have a normative function. The issue runs parallel to the discussion about a canon in literature and university curricula; the postmodern uses of architectural classicism have been discussed just as intensely, and the resulting debate provides an instructive analogue that often turns out to be simultaneously more pleasurable, more sophisticated, and more original. The downside is that many of the buildings are not fully meaningful without an accompanying explication.

Three Pioneering Examples

A convenient milestone that heralded the emergence of classicism in the decade of the 1980s was the First International Exhibition of Architecture at the Venice Biennale of 1980. It was organized by Paolo Portoghesi and demonstratively entitled "The Presence of the Past." As a purposeful reaction to Modernist architecture and planning, twenty architects designed facades for an imaginary street, the Strada Novissima, which was created between two rows of columns inside the Arsenale in Venice. The facades were meant to highlight the element of historicism within Postmodernism, or, in Robert Stern's words, "to proclaim that architecture was free again to employ Classical language on a civic scale."[10]

Several American architects participated. Robert Venturi, whose writings by that time had prepared for the break with Modernism, designed a cutout classical temple facade that was suspended two meters above the floor and came complete with squat Doric columns, triglyphs, and a pediment cleverly incorporating Le Corbusier–like figures (Fig. 1). Charles Moore contributed an overlapping, polychromatic arrangement of arches and half arches, and Thomas Gordon Smith enclosed the serpentine columns of Bernini's Baldac-

1. *Strada Novissima*, Venice Biennale, 1980. Facade by Venturi, Rauch & Scott Brown. (Photograph courtesy of Venturi, Scott Brown and Associates, Inc.)

chino in St. Peter's with a Doric framework. Classical decoration was back with a flourish.

It was precisely this decorative aspect of postmodern architecture that was used by its practitioners to make their early statements. Two outstanding examples, which immediately generated copious discussion, were Michael Graves' Portland Public Services Building (1980–1982) and Philip Johnson's AT&T Building in New York City (1979–1984, in partnership with John Burgee). Graves' design, the result of a fiercely contested competition, set the tone for the ensuing eclectic pluralism in which free-style classical elements came to play a noticeable part. The significance of "The Portland" (Fig. 2) was not a return to simple neoclassicism (and we will see few examples of this sort), but to "art, ornament, and symbolism on a grand scale in a language the inhabitants understand. . . . The main role of art and ornament [was that] their presence returned architecture to the wider Western tradition of classicism, the Free-Style tradition," as Charles Jencks put it.[11] Dark, multistory pilasters are topped by three-meter-high projecting "capitals." A romantic belvedere tops out the center of a five-story "keystone," which incorporates Modernist strip windows. Yet this is no Modernist box; stylized festoon ornaments take the place of the capitals on opposite sides of the building, and the statue

2. The Portland Building. Michael Graves, architect, 1980–1982. (Photograph by William Taylor, courtesy of the architect.)

of "Portlandia," with her meaningful symbolism of trident (Port) and sheaf of corn (Land), dynamically flies over the front door of the public entrance. The Modernists initially succeeded in getting her banished, along with some classical accretions on top of the building in Graves' original design, but she was soon recalled by the *vox populi*, thus confirming the return of the traditional collaboration between artists and architects.

The mix of elements includes an art deco scheme: a black granite substructure with a cream-colored block superimposed on it. The building both related to and departed from the surrounding modernist architecture, including Portland's city hall, but above all it suggested—not in the least because of its veiled

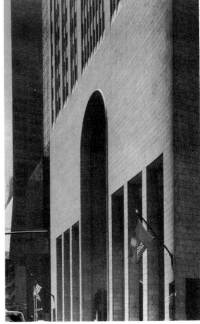

3. AT&T Building, New York. Johnson and Burgee, architects, 1978–1984. (Photograph by Richard Payne.)

4. AT&T Building, New York. View of street level and entrance. (Photograph by Richard Payne.)

references to the human body and face and because of the classical integration of sculpture and polychromy—the return to a more humanistic and civic tradition.

The same effect is achieved by Johnson and Burgee's AT&T Building through a richer and multivalent mode of associations. It has a modernist body standing on classical feet and sports a large and variously defined ornament as a head (Fig. 3). There is at once a referential anthropomorphism and a bond with the grand New York skyscraper architecture, exemplified by the Empire State and Chrysler buildings, which flourished before the nihilism of the Miesian box took over. The base (Fig. 4), moreover, is modeled deliberately on that of New York City's Municipal Building created by the classicizing firm of McKim, Mead & White in 1908 (Figs. 5a and b)—hence the large central arch (which in the earlier building spans Canal Street) and the columned arcade. In addition, the architectural decoration of the base is densely evocative of sacred building types: the oculi recall the Duomo in Florence, the arcades— besides referring to the Municipal Building—are reminiscent of San Andrea in Mantua, and the Carolingian lobby with its gilded cross vault and Romanesque capitals (cf. the Cloisters in New York) fuse into a Pazzi Chapel centering on the hilariously kitschy, gilded statue of the Genius of Electricity, "a

5a. Municipal Building, New York. McKim, Mead & White, architects, 1908. (Photograph courtesy of the Center for American Architecture and Design, The University of Texas at Austin.)

5b. Municipal Building, New York. Archway. (Photograph by David Bogle, courtesy of the Center for American Architecture and Design, The University of Texas at Austin.)

suitable icon for the new secular religion that Henry Adams predicted for America: energy equals power equals money."[12]

The pediment, another triumph of allusive eclecticism, culminates with symbolic references, depending on one's orientation, to car grilles, a grandfather clock, a Chippendale highboy, and as an in-joke, a monumental reference to the split pediment used earlier by Venturi for his mother's house (Fig. 41, p. 42). Plurality of meanings indeed! The building thrives on this very multivalency that despite all the carping—Tom Wolfe's little book is a delightful example—brought back the representational and historicizing architecture of New York's skyscrapers.

One other project belongs in the same seminal category as the Portland Building and the AT&T skyscraper because it did for the architectural shaping of place the same thing that Johnson and Burgee did for the high rise. That is Charles Moore's Piazza d'Italia in New Orleans, designed in 1976 and completed in 1979. The hallmarks of the eclectic, serious yet playful classicism that it embodies are again stylistic pluralism, civic humanism, and a multiplicity of references that "released a flood of associations that the public found woefully absent in conventional Modernist architects' urbanism."[13] In a city

6. Piazza d'Italia, New Orleans, aerial view. Charles Moore, Perez Associates, and Urban Innovations Group, 1976–1979. (Photograph © Alan Karchmer.)

dominated by other ethnic groups, Moore was asked to design an architectural center of identity for the Italian community and for its public festivals and celebrations.

The ground plan of the site is circular. A topographic map of Italy, made of stepping stones, extends from the middle of the large arcade through an eighty-foot pool; the outline of Sicily—most of the New Orleans Italians are of Sicilian descent—lies at the very center of the piazza's concentric circles (Fig. 6). The waters come from a fountain, framed by a collage of temple fronts and colonnades, replete with Latin inscriptions evocative of the great public buildings and places of Italy, and representing all five classical orders: Doric, Ionian, Corinthian, Tuscan, and Composite. This suggestion of monumental dignity, however, is permeated by humor. Neon tubing is part of the reconstruction of the Ionic and Corinthian elements of the central arcade (Fig. 7). The Doric columns really are curved sheets of stainless steel with streams of water mimicking the fluting. The metopes are actually "wetopes," as sprays are mounted in each of the cutout spaces in the entablature. In a similarly playful vein, the architect is immortalized by two water-spouting masks in

7. Piazza d'Italia, New Orleans. View northeast. (Photograph courtesy of Charles Moore.)

the central arch of the Doric colonnade. All the while, the public function of the site is kept before our eyes by the dedicatory inscription to Saint Joseph, on whose feast day the city's mayor gives his address from the podium placed atop the representation of Sicily. The edifices in the piazza with their earth tones were meant both to complement and to contrast with a backdrop, which at this point is completed only partially, of urban buildings of white stone and dark glass. At the same time, the Modernist high-rise building is picked up by the black and white paving of the piazza and its abstract planar elements, thus underscoring again the coexistence of Modernist and postmodern architecture.

The Conceptual Framework

Taken together, these three works by Graves, Johnson, and Moore form an instructive triad. They reflect the vocabulary and theoretical discussion of postmodernism that preceded and accompanied its actual implementation.

From the late 1960s on, architects like Venturi and Stern advocated inclusiveness instead of the Modernistic monopoly, and Moore, in an essay entitled "You Have to Pay for the Public Life" (1965), heterodoxically praised Disneyland for both its public spaces and its architecture: they authentically represented the public realm, and its values were accessible to the public. Disneyland thus could be considered the greatest urban project of the last two decades. Similarly, Venturi in 1973 used Las Vegas, often scorned for its brand of architecture, as the starting point of his ongoing disquisition on architecture as a "vehicle of signs." "Venturi's argument that architecture must refer to something beyond itself and represent contents other than architectonics was the first serious challenge to modern architecture";[14] this concept, of course, is thoroughly familiar from the ancient world and its classicism. With a view to semiotics, Charles Jencks and others attacked modern architecture because it was impoverished as a language, and they emphasized instead that it should be a language with multiple interpretations. This idea "became the key to the development of Post-Modern theory. Firstly, it identified the two major audiences the architect addresses; the general public and the other architects, and from this developed a further reason for double-coding: the idea that a building should be accessible to different groups in different ways with various types of architectural sign."[15]

Conceptually, there is yet more involved than mere pluralism of styles. Architecture also has a poetic and narrative function, defined in the simplest terms as invention of places. This is Moore's credo: "If architects continue to do useful work on this planet, then surely their proper concern must be their creation of place—the ordered imposition of man's self on specific locations across the face of the earth. To make a place is to make a domain that helps people know where they are, and by extension, know who they are."[16]

That notion is not new: it was articulated in the nineteenth century by Karl Friedrich Schinkel, whose liberating brand of inventive classicism has become an inspirational and undogmatic model for his American counterparts in the 1980s. Schinkel opposed radical abstraction—so akin to the functionalist formula of Modernism—and sought liberation from it by two elements: the historical and the poetical. As Heinrich Klotz has aptly commented:

> The historical enriches the spectrum of possible references and the wealth of historicizing stylistic means, in order that the poetical may emerge. The poetical is the power of imagination to picture desirable places; it is the generative power of fiction going beyond mere purpose. Fiction limits abstraction because it confronts the nonobjective directive of mere utility with the contents of imagination. Schinkel's statement reduces the maxims of modern architecture limited to functionalism and the injunctions of postmodern architecture to a common denominator. He realized that an architecture that draws its explicit visual character only from trivial purpose and from construction does not attain a satisfactory

result. His statement contains a definition of architecture that is also the definition of postmodern architecture.[17]

If we arrange these concepts hierarchically, the insistence on the fictional, poetic, and narrative character of architecture subsumes the pluralism of styles. It is in this context that classical elements have made their comeback as legitimate ingredients of an architectural statement, in contrast to the abstractness of modern architecture. The buildings I have discussed so far are informed by this context; we may also note that for these very reasons, Hadrian's Villa at Tivoli has continued to exert its inspiration for some of the most successful works of postmodern architecture, such as James Stirling's Neue Staatsgalerie in Stuttgart. We can now proceed to a survey of some other representative examples of American architecture of the decade.

Traditionally, such surveys have been grouped either by individual architects, which often results in *disiecta fragmenta,* or by generic labels that run the risk of imposing almost Linnaean classifications on a phenomenon that by its very nature is resistant to precise categories; Robert Stern's resorting to such labels as "latent classicism" points up the pitfalls inherent in any such method. True enough, in some cases the classicism is more traditional and canonical than in other more ironic and playful examples. It seems best, however, to eschew even such headings and, since the character of postmodern classicism is highly idiosyncratic, to illustrate its particular qualities in each individual case before attempting a final summation.

As Martin Filler has observed, "in the 1980s, more extensive opportunity for building in the U.S. than in Europe has made Post-Modernism largely an American phenomenon, if executed schemes are taken as a basis for discussion."[18] Besides their variety, the range of these schemes is remarkable. The spectrum reaches from private homes to commercial buildings large and small to skyscrapers and public places. It is useful, therefore, to structure the discussion on the basis of building type.

Domestic Architecture

The houses, including his own, built by Thomas Gordon Smith in California are a good example of the juxtaposition, rather than the integration, of classical and modern forms. This kind of architectural collage defies easy labels; to some it is irreverence, whereas others see in it a deep-rooted desire to go back to Mycenaean origins. So much for the aesthetic of reception in architectural criticism.[19] Smith's own Richmond Hill House is entered through a set of columns most of which are barely functional. The color scheme is Minoan, and the playful presence of bucrania enhances the Minoan allusion (Fig. 8). The living room recalls Pompeian styles of decoration (Fig. 9). On the walls, there

8. Richmond Hill House, Richmond, California. Thomas Gordon Smith, architect, 1983. (Photograph courtesy of the architect.)

10. View from Tuscan House to Laurentian House, Livermore, California. Thomas Gordon Smith, architect, 1979. (Photograph courtesy of the architect.)

9. Richmond Hill House. Interior view of living room. (Photograph © Henry Bowles, courtesy of the architect.)

11. Laurentian House, Livermore, California. Detail. (Photograph by H. Klotz, reprinted, by permission, from H. Klotz, *The History of Postmodern Architecture,* Fig. 261 [Cambridge, Mass.: MIT Press, 1987]. © 1987 by MIT Press.)

12. Monroe House, Lafayette, California. Thomas Gordon Smith, architect, 1986. (Photograph courtesy of the architect.)

are miniatures of gas stations, linking the house to its ambiance as it looks out on storage tanks and oil tankers. A circle of Roman-inspired still-life motifs forms a band above the windows, and on top of these are paintings from the myth of Persephone. Around a pseudo-oculus in the ceiling are representations of the stages of human life. The floor plan is essentially baroque while several building elements, such as aluminum windows, are solidly representative of modern technology.

With the Laurentian and Tuscan houses in Livermore Smith placed himself into a flexible classical tradition, as the exact configuration of the originals, as described by Pliny, cannot be determined. A whole range of classical architectural details creates the mood. The Tuscan house has clusters of green columns framing the courtyard on one side; the cutout type of architecture, including arches, that goes with it (Fig. 10) is reminiscent of facades at the Venice Biennale, of Charles Moore's designs for Kresge College at the University of California at Santa Cruz,[20] and of his columned facades in the Piazza d'Italia. In the Laurentian house next door, an arched entrance is set off with columns that are connected by an entablature of metopes and triglyphs. There is the classical use of polychromy, albeit on plaster, and the garages thereby receive a hint of a pediment. Their aluminum doors, demarcated by columns in the center, are modern-day vintage, as are the cheap windows in the houses. Such juxtapositions as an aluminum rain gutter with a replica of a classical acroterion (Fig. 11) play up the blend between the classical and the modern throughout.

Smith's Monroe House in Lafayette (1986) is even more overtly classical with its more functional use of columns and porticoes and the strong reference to Doric temple architecture (Fig. 12). Nor are such borrowings limited to this particular architect. In south Florida, a congenial place for Mediterranean architecture, the husband-and-wife team of Andres Duany and Elizabeth Plater-Zyberk created a villa on Key Biscayne, the Vilanova House (1984), that derives much of its multileveled inspiration from the Erechtheum (Fig. 13).

13. Vilanova House, Key Biscayne, Florida. A. Duany and E. Plater-Zyberk, architects, 1984. (Photograph © Steven Brooke, courtesy of the architects.)

There is a picturesque massing of porticoes and simple side walls that is "meant to be perceived from an oblique approach as indeed the Erechtheum is first seen."[21] Also seen from below, the tetrastyle porch in front of the main bedroom is reminiscent of the Athena Nike Temple, extending as it does to the edge of the structure. The small tetrastyle entrance, or propylaeum, continues the allusion and gives the rest of the building a gigantic scale. The dark cream entablatures mark off the massive base from the "village" of one-room temples on top.

Conceptually, much of the architectural syntax here is akin to the design of Leon Krier, "the most curious, potent and significant force in architecture today," as Jaquelin Robertson has called him.[22] Curious, we might add, because his visionary and uncompromising nature kept him from actually building most of his urbanistic schemes that are akin to Roman *insulae*. At the same time, his reconstruction of Pliny's Villa Laurentium (1982) is a positive exercise of classical and Arcadian nostalgia, and its temple-topped belvedere made its reappearance in Krier's multilevel house at Seaside, Florida (1985). Its kinship with Duany and Plater-Zyberk's Vilanova House is evident—"a frontier Erechtheum," as Stern has called it with reference to its combination of classical elements and the American vernacular wood house construction (Fig. 14).[23]

A similar combination can be observed in the somewhat more whimsical

14. House at Seaside, Florida. Leon Krier, architect, 1985. (Photograph © Steven Brooke.)

house on Long Island Sound in Connecticut, designed by Stephen Izenour of the firm of Venturi, Rauch and Scott Brown (1983). The small size of the house is ironically compensated for by four squat and grandiose clapboard columns (Fig. 15), reminiscent both of Doric temples (including those by the seaside as, e.g., at Selinus) and of Venturi's earlier facade designs for his (unbuilt) "eclectic houses" in the late 1970s, which are replete with arches, columns, entablatures, and other classical elements. The land side of the house, however, is dominated by a window shaped like a pilot's wheel; Greek temple and American icon coalesce.

Michael Graves' design for the Domaine Clos Pegase in Calistoga, California (1985–1987), may also be included here, although it works on a somewhat grander scale, as it includes a winery and private residence. The latter is

15. House on Long Island Sound. Stephen Izenour, architect, 1983. (Photograph by Tom Bernard, courtesy of Venturi, Scott Brown and Associates, Inc.)

on a hill, reminiscent of the ambiance of Tuscany, and the winery is below (Fig. 16). Both share the same architectural language and painting in earth tones. The outer building of the winery incorporates a mixture of historical references: to the Pompeian house with its massive outer wall (though broken up by narrow vertical windows here as the building is not facing a real street) insuring privacy; to the almost Minoan columns in the entrance court; and to Palladian architecture with its lunettes. From there one passes into the peristyle court, where cypresses ultimately had to take the place of columns for reason of lesser cost. At the other end is the equivalent of the *taberna,* i.e., the sales office and the storage buildings; one of the architectural puns is the barrel vaults for a facility where barrels are stored—historical reference and humor blend.

Finally, the distinction between explicit and implicit classicism does have some useful applications. Charles Moore's Rudolph House in Williamstown, Massachusetts (1979–1981), for example, involves the traditional composi-

16. Domaine Clos Pegase, Calistoga, California. Front view of winery. Michael Graves, architect, 1985–1987. (Photograph by the author.)

tion on the model of Palladio, including the symmetrical proportions, dome, and columned entrance. The Villa on the Bay in Corpus Christi, Texas, by Batey and Mack (1983) represents the opposite approach (Figs. 17a and b). In Batey's own words: "Classicism [is] used as a reference point, as a system of ordering buildings, including even axial views, courtyards, impluvium and prosceniums."[24] In addition, the architects considered the substance and age-less quality of classicism to be reflected particularly by such substantial, non-aging materials as granite. Finally, they discerned well the continuum between inner and outer space so typical especially of Roman country villas. Hence the columns actually extend down to the Gulf of Mexico and into the sea and help tie the building to its landscape. These columns do not replicate any of the classical orders, nor is the ornamentation of the building classical. Rather, the emphasis is on the bare essence of classical concepts and design.

Commercial Buildings

During the economic expansion of the 1980s, commissions for commercial structures were extensive. In this area of architecture, too, the classical and historicizing idiom made considerable inroads, often in contexts and for func-tions that seem rather banal. But it is precisely the ability of this idiom to create references beyond mere functionalism that led to its reuse.

17a. Holt House, Corpus Christi, Texas. A. Batey and M. Mack, architects, 1983. (Photograph courtesy of Mark Mack.)

17b. Holt House, Corpus Christi, Texas. Detail. (Photograph courtesy of Mark Mack.)

18. Stanley Tigerman, *The Sinking of the 'Titanic.'* Collage 1981. (Photograph courtesy of Tigerman McCurry Architects.)

A good example is provided by the Chicago architect Stanley Tigerman. Tigerman has strong modernist roots. In what is not an uncommon procedure among postmodern architects, he at first distanced himself from the legacy of Modernism not in his architectural works but by resorting to other media, such as drawings and collages. Thus, in 1981, he pictured one of the most famous—or infamous— of Mies' buildings in the Chicago area, the School of Architecture on the campus of the Illinois Institute of Technology (IIT), as the *Titanic* sinking in a calm sea with gorgeous summer clouds overhead (Fig. 18). In some of his subsequent buildings, he proceeded to adopt a more classical orientation, which adds at least a narrative dimension beyond their trivial function.

Such is the case with the Hard Rock Café in Chicago (Fig. 19), which devotees of the Ur-Café in London might have a hard time recognizing. The design goes back to the classical garden pavilion, and classical accents are used throughout: a set of freestanding columns at the entrance; arched door and windows; an entablature on part of the building; and spacing provided by pilasters along the entire outside of the structure. After the restaurant had been built in 1985, the utility company decided to remodel the electric substation next door and gave the commission to Tigerman with the understanding that the design be related to the architectural context he had created in the

19. Hard Rock Café, Chicago. Tigerman, Fugman, McCurry, architects, 1985–1986. (Photograph courtesy of the architects.)

Hard Rock Café. Sure enough, the old substation was remodeled so as to resemble an eighteenth-century Palladian villa, and the two buildings definitely harmonize.

The issue that is brought to the fore by such contextualism is the old, classical one of "decorum" and appropriateness. It has been a concern of classical architects from Vitruvius to Sir Edwin Lutyens and of many of their postmodern colleagues. Its definition is flexible and individual, but in that respect alone it goes beyond the universalist reductionism preached by the practitioners of the International Style.

Not always are the results as homogeneous as in the example we have just discussed. The tendency of postmodern architects often is to juxtapose, and not necessarily harmonize, the classical with the modernist elements. We have already observed this phenomenon in the domestic architecture of Thomas Gordon Smith. When applied to commercial buildings, the dimension is added to which we adverted earlier also—that is, the classical is to provide an ennobling effect to lift a building out of its banality. The resulting incongruity, however, can also have an ironic effect.

A good case in point is Robert Stern's Point West Place in Framingham, Massachusetts (1983–1985). The site of a former truck depot next to a toll plaza on the Massachusetts Turnpike, it was "only the quintessential non-place of the American roadside strip."[25] Yet the developers who selected the place for an office building were commendably intent on giving it some dignity. At first—and we may compare the similar concern of Batey and Mack for their seaside villa at Corpus Christi—this was to be achieved by choosing building material that conveyed permanence, e.g., stone, but considerations of cost

20. Point West Place, Framingham, Massachusetts. Robert A. M. Stern, architect, 1983–1985. (Photograph by Peter Vanderwarker, courtesy of the architect.)

doomed that noble endeavor. The subsequent course of action, in the architect's words, was this: "Rather than applying stone thinly, wrapping it around the frame like a curtain wall of glass, I chose to concentrate its use at the entrance and at the base, where its inherent solidity counterpoints the lightness of metal and glass."

The effect certainly is remarkable (Fig. 20).[26] The Miesian horizontal office block sports a monumental, classicizing entrance front. The entrance proper recalls a temple with five antae, but then deliberate classical misquotations take over: the pediment is bloated and curved; the oculus window is out of place; further up, the keystone is unnecessary; and there are four meaningless acroteria on the four corners of the roof. Inside the massive, but woefully constricted, entrance hall, four colossal architraves are piled on top of one another, and instead of directly bearing the load, they do so (apparently) by means of bulbous globes (Fig. 21). Thus the ironies abound, although Stern avows his serious intent of creating "a palace of work" with "a lavish entrance sequence" and a "tree-lined Court of Honor." And history, as so often, is about to vindicate him: unintended irony is the lesser downside compared to "lite architecture."[27] Stone, once emblematic of bulk, can now be cut into the thinnest of slices, and Stern could have given much of his building a stone veneer with the quantity he had available. But light in weight often leads to lightweight intellectual substance and aesthetic, something that Point West commendably avoids.

No other building is as suggestive in terms of American values as is a bank. It is not surprising, therefore, that banking and classical architecture were melded again in the era of Reaganomics. Of course, there was an ample tradi-

21. Point West Place, Framingham, Massachusetts. View of interior. (Photograph by Peter Van-derwarker, courtesy of the architect.)

tion to hark back to: the classicizing style for banks was in vogue from the time of the First National Bank in Philadelphia and flourished in the late nine-teenth and early twentieth centuries with such firms as McKim, Mead & White (well connected with the American Academy in Rome, for instance) taking the lead. A more homey example sharing in such aspirations is the facade of the Security Marine Bank in Wisconsin of the early 1970s—a classical ex-ample, in more ways than one, of what Venturi calls the "decorated shed" (Fig. 22). The task facing the American architect John Blatteau in remodeling a branch of the Riggs Bank in Washington, D.C., (1983–1985) arose from an interesting development: banks, too, had been cast in the Modernist Style by the 1950s, and their architecture had become indistinguishable from that of other and, presumably, more fragile enterprises. Thus the building that housed the Riggs Bank at 17th and H streets had a modernist exterior; Blatteau was commissioned to evoke the classical tradition inside. And so he did (Fig. 23). The main entrance is comprised of Corinthian marble pilasters supporting an entablature that attenuates into an architrave and runs all the way across the top of the teller windows. These, in turn, are flanked by smaller, elongated

22. Security Marine Bank, near Madison, Wisconsin, 1970s. (Photograph by Wayne Attoe.)

23. Riggs Bank, Lincoln Branch office, Washington, D.C. John Blatteau, architect, 1985. (Photograph by Matt Wargo, courtesy of John Blatteau Associates.)

Doric pilasters giving the teller bays the effect of aediculae. Underneath the teller bays runs a long marble counter, and the actual teller windows are detailed in the form of two smaller columns cum entablature, making their overall appearance similar to that of a tabernacle.

Since such facile characterizations as "ironic" and "playful" pervade so much of the literature on the classicizing element in postmodern architecture, it is easy to be tempted to view this invocation of the classical mode as ironically inappropriate for institutions that proved anything but solid in the 1980s.[28] But the intentions of the architects definitely were otherwise. The point was precisely to underline the stability and security of the Riggs as a bank (it has a classically inspired logo as well) and to use a dignified architectural metaphor, enhanced by appropriate decorative elements, that reaches back, through the earlier American tradition, to the Greek Treasuries at Delphi. A corollary is that Blatteau, quite in contrast, for example, to Moore, Stern, and Smith, consciously eschewed exploiting the contrast between the modernist exterior of the building and the classical interior for ironic purposes. Even in postmodern architecture, therefore, classicism can mean serious commitment.

In some of the buildings designed by the Chicago architect Thomas Beeby, we return to the deliberate intertextuality of the modernist and classical genres of architectural language. The American Academy of Pediatrics in Elk Grove, Illinois (1984), designed by him and his partners, combines structurally articulate steel-frame construction with varied classical elements, such as the utilization of brick bands of alternating colors for the purpose of "rustication," an entrance portico with two columns *in antis* and a modernist glass wall (Fig. 24a), the unification of the main floors of the building by means of columns and pilasters, and a loggia at the rear of the building whose columns support an exposed steel beam that takes the place of the architrave (Fig. 24b).

Similarly, in the Sulzer Library in Ravenswood, a Chicago suburb, the steel frame is rendered visible with the horizontal beam on top suggesting the equivalent of a frieze and, above the entrance, a pediment. The entrances are styled as Romanesque arches, and the glass wall above them, punctuated by steel pilasters, as a curtain wall hanging from the steel architrave (Fig. 25a). Inside, the entrance hall opens up into an oval with Doric columns. Above them, light globes suggest metopes (Fig. 25b). The Doric order continues in the reading rooms as purple columns double as ventilation shafts; they abut directly into the exposed steel trusswork of the roof. The building is characterized by this ongoing juxtaposition of the modernist and classical traditions. Beeby solidly subscribes to both—a common aspect of classical postmodernism—and the integration is more thorough, for instance, than in Stern's Point West Place. The medieval clock tower adds another element of historicism.

24a. American Academy of Pediatrics, Elk Grove, Illinois. Hammond Beeby & Babka, architects, 1984. View of entrance. (Photograph © Timothy Hursley.)

Even more boldly, Beeby worked out this process of integration in the Formica Showroom he designed for the Merchandise Mart in Chicago. The material obviously is as contemporary as any while the showroom is detailed as a Doric temple. The unifying bond is polychromy, which is an essential aspect both of formica and of the Greek temples (Fig. 26). There is even a hint of the seaside location of many of these temples as the showroom ends with a "highly lit terrace overlooking an imaginary sea, also rendered in plastic laminates."[29] More overtly whimsical and yet startlingly appropriate for the world of entertainment and fantasy is Michael Graves' new office building for the Disney Company corporate headquarters in Burbank, California. Besides classicizing hallmarks dear to Graves, such as the truncated round "tower" and intersecting barrel vaults, the main entrance facade of the building, oriented toward a pedestrian plaza, is cast in the form of a postmodern temple. In contrast to Robertson's Amvest Building and Beeby's Academy of Pediatrics and Sulzer Library, the pediment is higher and the modernist glass wall is broken up much more—by the Seven Dwarfs who hold up the pediment (Fig. 27a)! The godmother of inspiration, as in the Florida houses by Krier and Duany/Plater-Zyberk, is the Erechtheum, but female emancipation has finally arrived as the

24b. American Academy of Pediatrics, Elk Grove, Illinois. View of west elevation. (Photograph © Timothy Hursley.)

porch-supporting maidens have been replaced by the male dwarfs. The pedestrian plaza toward which this sculptural front is oriented can only bask in the good humor of this classical adaptation. It adds yet another touch to the multiple meanings Bruno Bettelheim has so delightfully discerned in this particular fairy tale.[30] In the inner courtyard, however, the organization of several tiers of stylized classical colonnades (Fig. 27b) is a great deal more rigid and almost oppressive.

Finally, analogous to Batey and Mack's Holt House in Corpus Christi, some commercial buildings represent the same kind of classical minimalism that relies not on ornament and decoration but on structural simplicity to assert its classicism. A good example is the Amvest Headquarters in Charlottesville, Virginia (1985–1987), designed by Jaquelin Robertson (Fig. 28). The regard for context is evident: both the central portico and the tripartite division into that center and two low-set wings recall eighteenth-century Virginia country houses with their classical and Palladian overtones. In the Amvest building, however, everything is reduced to the simplest outline. Present, too, is the typical postmodern blend of modernism and classicism: the glazed window wall, so typical of modernist architecture, appears behind the classical portico

25a. Sulzer Regional Library, Ravenswood, Illinois. Hammond Beeby & Babka, architects, 1983–1985. General view and entrance. (Photograph © Timothy Hursley.)

with its diagrammatic columns, a collocation similar to the entrance fronts of Beeby's Sulzer Library and Academy of Pediatrics.

Similarly understated but pervasive is the classical idiom employed by Taft Architects from Houston for the River Crest Country Club in Fort Worth, Texas (1981–1984). The mandate was to rebuild the burnt-down structure with something "classical." Since the structure functions as an enlarged country house, the Palladian inspiration is appropriate with its cross-axial plan and emphasis on the four horizons, here accentuated by four stacks that, *more moderno*, carry ventilation ducts, elevators, electrical cables, and the like (Fig. 29). On the west side, we again encounter the familiar combination of glazed window wall and a columned porch in front; both inside and outside, modern abstraction carries over into the shaping of capital-less columns (Fig. 30). Finally, as Stern well observes, "the principles, but not the ordered expression, of a Classical building are also evident in the relation between the building and the landscape, where an *allée* of trees marching across the golf course gave the architects the opportunity to tie the formal axes of their building to those in the landscape."[31] Ultimately, this is a concern that we know from Roman villas and that we saw reflected also in Batey and Mack's

25b. Sulzer Regional Library, Ravenswood, Illinois. Interior view of lobby. (Photograph by Jim Hedrick, Hedrick-Blessing.)

26. Formica Showroom, Merchandise Mart, Chicago. Hammond Beeby & Babka, architects, 1984. (Photograph by Barbara Karant; © 1984 Karant & Associates, Inc.)

27a. Disney Company Corporate Headquarters, Burbank, California. Michael Graves, architect, 1989–1991. (Photograph © Jeff Goldberg/Esto. All rights reserved.)

Corpus Christi villa. In a larger sense, it is part of the contextualism that, as we have seen, other postmodern buildings, including urban ones, reflect in their own way.

Campus Architecture

For many reasons, classical architecture found a congenial environment at American colleges and universities from the colonial period on.[32] On the other hand, few campuses, if any, escaped the ravages of the modernist multipurpose box, a style—sometimes labeled "preventive architecture" by its critics—that has become almost as synonymous with collegiate architecture as the classical style used to be. Analogous to the developments in the domestic and commercial architecture of classical postmodernism that we have surveyed, we cannot

27b. Disney Company Corporate Headquarters, Burbank, California. Interior colonnades. (Photograph © Jeff Goldberg/Esto. All rights reserved.)

28. Amvest Headquarters, Charlottesville, Virginia. Eisenman Robertson, architects, 1985–1987. (Photograph by Joseph E. Garland.)

29. River Crest Country Club, Fort Worth. Taft Architects, 1981–1984. (Photograph courtesy of the architects.)

30. River Crest Country Club, Fort Worth. Detail of interior. (Photograph courtesy of the architects.)

expect classical revivalism or neoclassicism in the campus architecture of the 1980s. It is precisely because the burden of the past weighs on this particular area of American architecture even more heavily than on others that classical idioms here are used far more tentatively. They defy a single common denominator, and their use is anything but heavy-handed.

An instructive paradigm can be found at the University of Virginia in Charlottesville, whose original, Jefferson-designed edifice Paul Goldberger, throwing usual restraint to the winds for excellent reasons, has recently pronounced to be "the most beautiful building in America."[33] This circumstance had an undeniably mitigating effect, certainly by comparison with other campuses, on the local manifestations of Modernism. The latter was represented by some science buildings (still fashioned in red brick, however) and, more starkly, by the dining hall on Observatory Hill at the end of the same street. Robert Stern was appointed to modify the hall to give it a more classical appearance consonant with the general ambiance of the campus, a notion reinforced by the Georgian-style dormitories across the street. The modification was achieved by the creation of four pavilions, echoing—but certainly not repeating—the pavilions on the main mall, with pyramidal roofs. Each pavilion is demarcated on both the outside and the inside with a set of paired Tuscan columns, while the windows combine modernist influence with classical lanterns. The appearance of four minipavilions on top of the pyramids playfully repeats the

31. University of Virginia, Charlottesville, Observatory Hill Dining Hall. Robert A. M. Stern, architect, 1982–1984. (Photograph © Whitney Cox, courtesy of the architect.)

scheme and is the light counterbalance to the heavy brick girders and arches of the lower structure that supports the piano nobile. The resulting building meets the classical criteria of decorum and appropriateness without lapsing into classical epigonism (Fig. 31).

The same process, with more emphasis on the creation of space, can be seen in Charles Moore's design of the Extension Center and Alumni House at the University of California at Irvine (1983–1985). The campus, laid out by Pereira on a "near-megalomaniacal scale"[34] a few decades earlier, lacked distinctly defined outdoor public space. Moore's clients approached him with the specific request for a building with a number of classrooms and offices that would face the public. Moore turned for inspiration to three small chapels on the Celian Hill in Rome, near San Gregorio Magno, that were designed in 1607 by Flaminio Ponzio (Fig. 32). He used fairly literal copies of them as facades for the new buildings (Fig. 33). Moore's comments on this "copying" are worth quoting because they have parallels in literary theory:

32. Three chapels on the Celian Hill, Rome, seventeenth century. (Photograph courtesy of Charles Moore.)

It seems to me (of course) that the fact that our building started life as a copy does not rob it of passion, or of legitimacy, or of authenticity. Our building has a new life for new people in a new place for a new function. It is a safe bet that few, if any, of the inhabitants have ever seen Ponzio's chapels on the Celian Hill, so the new buildings will have to stir up their own connections with the inhabitants' memories. I was delighted to be told (without asking) that, at least for some, they do.[35]

This is the equivalent in architecture to reception aesthetics and reader-response criticism. Critics like Wolfgang Iser would deemphasize a knowledge of the historical context as a primary tool for interpretation. Instead, the meaning of a literary work is considered to be an ongoing process, shaped by the reception it finds in each successive generation and century.[36] This theory intersects with the more traditional notion that classics are classics precisely because they are meaningful to each new generation, which can interpret them anew from fresh and even personal perspectives. The point of convergence is the universality of a classic, a universality quite different, as we saw earlier, from Mies' and Plato's abstractionism. As in his Piazza d'Italia, therefore, Moore's use of the classical idiom is a humanizing one, and its function is ontological rather than ironic. Similar to Stern's classical modification of a

33. Extension Center and Alumni House, University of California at Irvine. Charles Moore and Urban Innovations Group, architects, 1983–1985. (Photograph courtesy of the architects.)

modernist building on the Virginia campus, Moore "gathers together a modest group of 'vernacular' buildings to form a public space, defined in boldly scaled Classical porticos and exaggerated gable ends."[37] The style is also appropriate in the light of the Spanish and Mediterranean tradition in California architecture.

In his earlier design of Kresge College, a residential college at the University of California at Santa Cruz (1971–1974), Moore proceeded by allusion rather than outright quotation. The whole is reminiscent of an Italian hillside village. The buildings lining the street are mostly student residences, punctuated by deliberately antimonumental structures, such as a laundromat that nevertheless is adorned as a speaker's rostrum. There are historicizing references to the Spanish Steps, the Arc de Triomphe, and the cascades and waterways of the Alhambra, but the main historicizing element is the ground plan (Fig. 34). Its many buildings "set up their own axial and rhythmic systems rather like Hadrian's Villa" (Fig. 35),[38] a favorite source of inspiration, as we observed earlier, for postmodern architects with its eclecticism of sources and structural discontinuities. The manner throughout is eclectic and playful; while real and historical monumentality is debunked, the trivial is deliberately monumentalized—*et in California ego*—such as the already mentioned laundromat and, to give another example, the telephone booth that is turned into

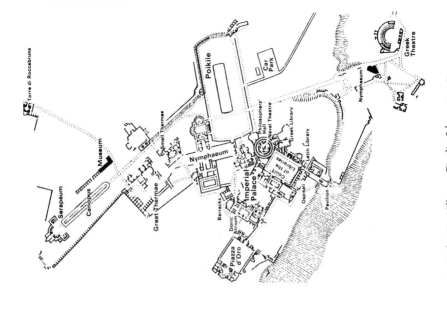

35. Hadrian's Villa at Tivoli, 2d cent. A.D. (Ground plan.)

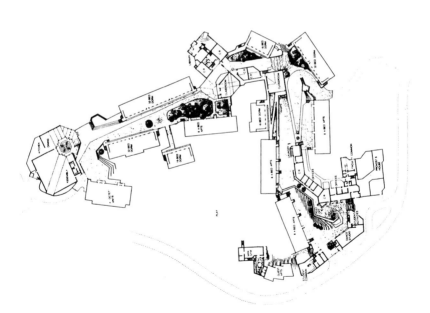

34. University of California at Santa Cruz, Kresge College. Charles Moore, architect, 1971–1974. (Ground plan, courtesy of the architect.)

36. University of California at Santa Cruz, Kresge College. Partial view. (Photograph courtesy of Charles Moore.)

a monstrous baldachin with giant ears. The cheap, cardboardlike wood cutouts (Fig. 36), a Moore trademark (necessitated often by budgetary restrictions), can be regarded either as a pervasive deflation of great pretensions or as an erosion of the meaning that is otherwise intended: hill town, community, security, civic spirit, and serious, historical, and intertextual allusion, etc. As Klotz rightly points out, however, a narrative force is there "without using a single historical form."[39] What is recaptured, above all, is a classical *humanitas* that incorporates play.

Similarly allusive is the utilization of some classical themes in his Loyola Marymount Law School in Los Angeles (1984–1986) by Frank Gehry, an architect otherwise not known for much historicizing. His "small block planning" of the Law School campus recalls the concepts of Leon Krier. Due to various constraints of the site, Gehry produced what he describes as "a pileup of buildings like an acropolis," a notion reinforced by the appearance of the two-storied, columned facade of the South Instruction Hall. The classical motifs Gehry employs are highly abstracted, though that was true, too, for instance, of the Batey and Mack house in Corpus Christi and some of Beeby's

37. Loyola Marymount University Law School, Los Angeles. Frank Gehry and Associates, architects, 1984–1986. (Photograph © Michael Moran, courtesy of the architects.)

38. Art Museum, Oberlin College, Ohio. Venturi, Rauch and Scott Brown, architects, 1973–1976. Wooden column. (Photograph by Tom Bernard, courtesy of Venturi, Scott Brown and Associates, Inc.)

buildings. They include columns without any ornamentation, both freestanding and integrated into porticos (Fig. 37), and a "pediment" suggested by a glass structure to which one ascends on an outer staircase. In his discussion of this design, Martin Filler has argued that "Gehry's reference is not to the classical tradition *per se* but the Roman origins of the western legal tradition and the typology of courthouses in America."[40] References to all three, however, are not mutually exclusive. The association noted by Filler may well have been the more immediate one for this particular architect, leading him to a more extensive frame of classical reference, as is indicated by his mention of the acropolis and his adaptation of one of the concepts of Leon Krier, one of the foremost postmodern classicists, even though this sort of historical exploration is not part of Gehry's usual style.

A wooden column in the Museum of Art at Oberlin College in Ohio (Fig. 38) may serve as a coda to this disquisition on the uses of classicism in collegiate architecture today. The museum, and the column, are the work of Robert Venturi's firm (1973–1976). The column handily illustrates two points about architectural postmodernism. It is a perfect example of Venturi's affirmation of buildings as a "decorated shed." In contradistinction to the abstract universalism of the Modernist Style, decoration is brought back as a signifier: the column signifies "Museum" with all its tradition. But it is not a portentous return to classicism: the spaces between the wooden strips of the shaft, on the one hand, which revoke the suggestion of weight, and the grotesquely exaggerated volutes, on the other, deflate any pretension of serious monumentality. There is a double coding at work here, albeit a different one from that defined by Jencks in terms of modernist/postmodern: the classical tradition is invoked without, however, the whole weight of the "burden of the past," to use W. J. Bate's analogous phrase from the area of literature.[41] Architecture is thus liberated "from the pressure of hierarchical concerns in order to bring into action the play of wit and to rupture set expectations."[42] We find the same phenomenon, for instance, in Ovid's *Metamorphoses,* which came after the classicism of Vergil's *Aeneid;* just as we have *Ovidius ludens,* so do some postmodern architects resemble Vitruvius *ludens.*

Large Public Buildings

The three buildings we used as a starting point for this discussion—the Portland Public Services Building, the AT&T skyscraper, and the Piazza d'Italia—obviously belong in this category. Two further examples may be added to illustrate the successful variety of this trend.

The first is the City Hall, or, more appropriately, civic complex for Mississauga (Fig. 39a), a suburb of Toronto. The task faced by the architects has been aptly summarized as follows:

> Perhaps the greatest challenge for the next generation will not be the reurbanization of traditional cities—a task that is now well under way—but the creation of rational focal points in the placeless sprawl of automobile-dominated suburb. . . . In undertaking the design of a city hall complex for Mississauga (1982–86), a former rural township which became a suburb of Toronto in the 1960's and 70's, Edward Jones (b. 1939) and J. Michael Kirkland (b. 1943) set out to do more than design a handful of buildings on one large lot; as they saw it, and as their clients mandated, their job was to provide an urban focus amid the suburban sprawl, to create something that would help define Mississauga as a place in its region, as a transition point between town and country.[43]

This statement has proved prophetic, as the building today is being rapidly surrounded by the crowding of an architecturally undistinguished assortment of shopping centers and mostly high-rise office buildings and apartment houses. In their midst, the civic center complex provides not only a rational focus, but a humane one as well, as is evidenced by its popularity and many uses.

As for the layout, several clearly defined components fuse into an ensemble. In the best tradition of Leon Krier, they are a mix of the vernacular and the classical. To concentrate on the latter: on one side of the complex is a reflecting pool, flanked both by trees and by porticoes, one of which extends into an apse. A capital-less column divides the main entrance, which leads to a

39a. City Hall Complex, Mississauga, Canada. Jones & Kirkland, architects, 1982–1986. (Photograph by Robert Burley, courtesy of the architects.)

39b. City Hall Complex, Mississauga, Canada. Great Hall. (Photograph by the author.)

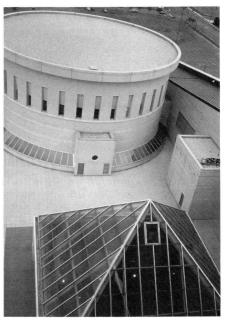

39c. City Hall Complex, Mississauga, Canada. Detail of exterior. (Photograph by the author.)

marbled atrium demarcated by a wide arch (Fig. 39b). The main administration building—fittingly styled more as a facade than backed up in depth—has a pedimental configuration with its long sloping gable but thereby is able to incorporate a grand staircase of proportions that recall ancient monuments. Behind it, a ramp leads up to an open podium, an outdoor public space, and then on axis to the *tholos,* the round council chambers; an adjacent glass pyramid, a forerunner of Pei's at the Louvre, evokes another tradition of the past (Fig. 39c). Several of these elements, of course, also have vernacular associations: the round building recalls a silo; the facade of the elongated gable of the administration building, a barn, etc.

On the exterior, ornament and narration are not in evidence in the prevailing constructionist classicism, but an obvious parallel for the concept and some of its important details is the complex of Fortuna Primigenia at Praeneste. There we find a similar choreography of space and interplay between its rectilinear and curved determinants (Fig. 40). There are ramps ascending to public spaces, apses, a pedimental facade with a center-section cut that is the remote ancestor for Venturi's house for his mother (Fig. 41)—and, by extension, the top of the AT&T Building—and a *tholos* that houses the complex's most important image. Actually, there are two complexes, as at Mississauga, upper and lower; the lower may well have had the purely civic function of a forum. And, as at Mississauga, the intent was the redefinition of focus when Praeneste, after being defeated by Sulla in 82 B.C., changed from city to colony.

On the inside of the Council Chamber there are elements of decoration and narration with classical precedents (Fig. 42). The circular wall space is punctuated by sets of double pilasters. Functioning not as triglyphs but as diglyphs, they support an entablature that has the names of the townships inscribed on it. The domed ceiling is ornamented on a grand scale with signs of the zodiac and the Indian legend of the Hunter and the Great Bear. A final classical motif is the central column in the underground car park.

The design of the Humana Building in Louisville, Kentucky (1982–1986), by Michael Graves is even more programmatic in its espousal, in the architect's own words, of the "humanist aspirations which have been too long neglected by modern architecture" and rejection of the Miesian minimalism that resulted in being "anti-urban and alienating to the human spirit."[44] Graves' proposal for the $60-million headquarters of this national health concern was the winning entry in a national competition for a building on a downtown site that faced the Ohio River, Main Street with its smaller nineteenth-century structures on one side and a modernist high-rise bank ("the box the Humana came in," as Graves put it) on another (Figs. 43, 44). Clearly, more was intended than mannerism or playful irony, and therefore it is useful to quote the beginning of the architect's statement, which accompanied the design and amounts to a creed, in full:

40. Temple Complex of Fortuna Primigenia at Praeneste (Palestrina), 1st cent. B.C. Model of restoration. (Photograph Fototeca Unione, at the American Academy in Rome; neg. no. F.U. 4348F.)

41. Vanna Venturi House, Philadelphia. Robert Venturi, architect, 1960–1962. (Photograph by Rollin LaFrance, courtesy of Venturi, Scott Brown and Associates, Inc.)

42. City Hall Complex, Mississauga, Canada. Interior of Council Chamber. (Photograph ©
Robert Burley Design Archive, courtesy of the architects.)

In accord with Humana's interest in recognizing the unique character of the
Louisville site, we have taken the presence of the Ohio River and an understanding of both the specific and the general urban context as two primary influences
in the design of our building. Our design addresses the river and the city, not
only in terms of the views that they offer, but also in terms of the thematic
associations they suggest. The formal gestures and activities of our building are,
we believe, natural and intrinsic to urban structures in general and a river city
in particular. In their figurative and thematic aspect they attempt to reaffirm and
re-establish humanist aspirations which have been too long neglected by modern
architecture. With the onset of the Modern Movement in architecture, the prevailing humanist code based on the representation of man and landscape was
supplanted by new technical interests born out of the Industrial Revolution. This
mechanical machine metaphor inspired today's steel and reflective glass towers
and their minimalist configurations—structures which, with some hindsight, we
now recognize as being anti-urban and alienating to the human spirit. With the
modernist trend, the individual's ability to identify with his place, whether it be
the city as a whole or an office within the building, has been dramatically diminished. Responsible urban architecture today must try to counteract this unfor-
tunate effect.[45]

43. Humana Building, Louisville, Kentucky. Michael Graves, architect, 1982–1985. (Photograph by Paschall & Taylor, courtesy of the architect.)

44. Humana Building, Louisville, Kentucky. View from Main Street. (Photograph by Paschall & Taylor, courtesy of the architect.)

How does all this work out in practice? Again, we must not expect the sort of literal revivalism or neoclassicism that lends itself to positivistic cataloging. The building is tripartite, following its functions as public space, office tower, and health facility. The public spaces are accommodated by a shopping mall/loggia at the base; as Johnson did in the AT&T Building, so Graves decided to build the loggia out to the end of the sidewalk. As one enters through the colonnades into the covered loggia, the effect produced by the lighting and the richly colored granites resembles that of a shrine, "thereby encompassing the connection between water and the gods of healing, or the River and the Temple—a theme reiterated in the roof garden."[46] The strong classical vocabulary comprises columns, pilasters, waterworks, and a terraced atrium. From the loggia, one passes into the lobby of the office tower. Analogous to the "chapel" in the AT&T Building, there is a rotunda (here called Rotonda) at the center where marble of various colors adorns the walls and red marble columns set off the rotunda itself, which enshrines a Roman torso (Fig. 45).

45. Humana Building, Louisville, Kentucky. Rotunda. (Photograph by Paschall & Taylor, courtesy of the architect.)

On each side of the building there is a small temple above the twentieth floor. On the river side, it is cantilevered out. The exposed trusses that are used for that purpose and correspond to the steel bridges spanning the river constitute an imaginative piece of contextualism that, with its recall of Russian constructivism earlier in this century, adds to the historical syntax of the building without negating any of the classical elements (Fig. 44). The opposite side, facing downtown, is articulated with a multistory center "column," composed of red granite with blue-glassed sun rooms curving out (Fig. 46). It continues, even with its art deco admixtures, the metaphor of the temple of healing. Back on the riverside, there is a cantilevered and apsidal open-air roof garden that frames a view of the river with a pattern of classical pilasters that have gold-leaf flutings (Fig. 47). The building culminates with the equivalent of a recessed greenhouse on top; light as it is, it also incorporates a reminiscence of the classical barrel vault.

Overall, the building suggests the classical division of a column into base,

46. Humana Building, Louisville, Kentucky. South facade. (Photograph by Paschall & Taylor, courtesy of the architect.)

47. Humana Building, Louisville, Kentucky. Roof garden. (Photograph by Paschall & Taylor, courtesy of the architect.)

shaft, and capital as well as a vague anthropomorphism, which is "clearly felt, but abstract and never explicitly stated—an apposite humanization of the Humana Corporation. The subtle use of canted 'brows' on the loggia front, or suggested 'eyes and nose' of the cantilevered garden, hint at the body image underneath. The side views of this inherent metaphor are more austere with shoulders tilting in to a neck and small head."[47] Vincent Scully has aptly remarked on the "sculptural power" of the building and the resemblance of "the whole figure" to "a colossal masked creature."[48] And in contrast to the Portland Building, Graves here was able to work with granite and marble, which further enhances the classical dimensions of the edifice.

The result, as Paul Goldberger has observed, is different from both the classically inspired towers of the eclectic period of the 1920s and the abstraction of the 1960s and 1970s.[49] While the classical idiom is clearly discernible and intentional, it is, at the same time, a liberating and undogmatic idiom, letting the beholder find ever new associations and attempt ever different interpretations—a multivalency that also is at the center of both the postmodern literary discourse and, perhaps somewhat less subjectively, the very classicism of Augustan art.[50] This is another useful reminder that, even before postmodernism, it was well recognized that a literary work is a classic precisely because it is susceptible to a variety of interpretations. In that sense,

48. Neue Staatsgalerie, Stuttgart, Germany. James Stirling and Michael Wilford, architects, 1977–1984. (Photograph by Heinz Vogelmann.)

Graves' Humana Building is one of the most successful evocations of creative classicism, surpassed only by James Stirling's Neue Staatsgalerie in Stuttgart (1977–1984; Fig. 48).

Some Implications

We can now return to some of the issues we raised at the very beginning of this discussion. How meaningful is this new, eclectic, and largely free-style classicism? Is it simply a mannerist development without adequate substance?

Conceptually it is, as many of the examples we have surveyed amply illustrate, a deliberate turning away from what Jencks has aptly called "The Protestant Inquisition" of the proponents of the International Style with its reductionism and minimalism.[51] Deviation from the prevailing Modernist orthodoxy initially necessitated the guise of humor, playfulness, and irony, but more was involved than a purely formal departure: there is concern for humanizing space, creating identity, and providing an architecture that is accessible in the various meanings of the word and transcends purely rational functionalism with a sense of poetry. All this corresponds to trends in the culture of the 1980s on which we need hardly elaborate. It suffices to mention the enthusiastic response to Bill Moyers' series of interviews with the late Joseph

Campbell on "The Power of Myth." *Mythos* provides identity, a sense of shared values, ties to the past, a more than rational, poetic expression of human values, and much more.

The analogy is appropriate and can be extended. The academy's disdain of Campbell is paralleled by the reaction not of the Miesolaters but of the classical purists, such as Demetri Porphyrios, to this new, eclectic classicism. While, interestingly enough, arguing for the mythopoeic power of architecture, Porphyrios vigorously asserts that "classicism is not a style." Rather, it is an ontological commitment. He disparages the contemporary, eclectic adaptations of classical forms as an example of industrial kitsch pandering to a consumer-oriented society lacking an authentic culture. Here is part of his indictment; the discerning reader will recognize the various polemical references:

> In a manner similar to advertisement, Modern Eclecticism, by aestheticising the process of communication, links experience to mere anagnosis, reading or decodement. Such an architecture tolerates no aesthetic surplus that would resist consumption and thereby survive as the core of experience. Instead, figurative and syntactic sensuality takes on the quality of nightmare: weightless pediments, "neon"-classical cornices, emasculated orders, metopes enfeebled by the arrogance of architects in search of fame, engrossed voussoirs, drooping garlands, frenzied volumetric articulations and androgynously historicist plans, in short all sorts of upholstered coteries degenerate into a mere "style heap"; without essential meaning other than the cult of "irony" and the illusion of a make-believe culture. This is an architecture with no discourse; simple quotations, parentheses, brackets, and a kind of disjointed, insidious whisper that spells: advertisement.[52]

The postulate, then, is that form should reflect substance. In a similar vein, Martin Filler concluded his review of some major books on architectural postmodernism by stressing that postmodernism is meaningful only if it involves changing more than "the outer garments of buildings that remained Modernist in all respects—with the same financial sponsorship, land use, structure and engineering, materials, relation to transportation, energy consumption and environmental factors,"[53] in other words, social change.

The weakness of such arguments is that they are a palpable mix of nostalgia, frustration with social factors that architects alone cannot change, and plain carping. Interestingly enough, Filler in an earlier article stressed the positive role that classicizing architecture can play in setting the tone for our society: "What better affirmation of a human-centered universe could there be than architecture that reminds us of the values that have propelled our development as a civilization from its inception up until this most multivalent of times?" "But," he continues, "let it be an architecture that demonstrates a true knowledge of our past, even as it tries to be a genuine sign of our own times";[54] he is concerned that few architects know what classicism—even technically—was and is.

Let us briefly consider these arguments in the light of the examples we have surveyed. The charge that any of these architects are ignorant of classical conventions can be dismissed first. In this context, the association of many of these architects—Venturi, Graves, Moore, Smith, Gehry, and Plater-Zyberk, to mention only a few—with the American Academy in Rome deserves to be noted. The ability of these architects and others like Thomas Beeby and Robert Stern to integrate classical elements into modern construction suggests an even surer handling of that idiom than if we were dealing with mere neoclassicism. *Imitatio* and *aemulatio* transcend mere replicating.[55] Playfulness, as exemplified by Moore and Smith, betokens anything but ignorance. Huizinga's classic study of the play element in culture is relevant here: it is through the activity of the *homo ludens* that serious and fundamental human and cultural issues are explored and refined.[56]

More fundamentally, when it comes to social and spiritual values connoted by classical architecture, both Porphyrios and Filler are short on specifics, and for good reason. Ours is neither the time nor the society of the antebellum Greek Revival with its proliferation of Athenses and Spartas; "when order collapsed into bloodshed (i.e., of the Civil War), it was impossible to reuse the same symbols"[57] or, more accurately, the same replicas. For the same reason, the sort of doctrinaire, canonical classicism demanded by Porphyrios is not suitable because we are, in essence, eclectic about the values Greco-Roman society represents. They do not include slavery, the primitive system of health care and hygiene, or the exclusion of women from the political process—all of which presented no problem to the denizens of the mid-nineteenth century and their classical revivalism. An evocation of the classical tradition is multivalent itself amidst the general cultural multivalency that is reflected by postmodern architecture. But there are some common denominators nonetheless. The classical idiom of both the most playful structures, such as the Piazza d'Italia, and the most serious, such as the Humana Building, bespeaks the desire for humaneness, identity (including the proper relationship between individual and society that is at the core of almost all of Greco-Roman civilization), "soul," and historical continuity. In others, such as Mississauga and Observatory Hill, there is the additional dimension of *civitas* and implied order. That does not mean that society ipso facto espouses all these values. It does mean, however, that these are ideals that are fittingly upheld in architecture (sometimes even with clearly programmatic emphasis as in the case of the Riggs Bank) and that the reciprocal process between architecture and society in terms of instilling values is being recognized: architecture is not merely a reflection but also can be a catalyst.[58]

It may be painful for purists like Porphyrios to see this classical idiom operate not as a hegemonic exclusive, but as part of an architectural pluralism. Two considerations are relevant here. One is that such pluralism or mixture of styles was the hallmark of one of the greatest classical ages, that of Augustus. Both its architecture and its literature exhibit a deliberate mixture of genres and styles in individual works as well as overall. The other is that this eclectic pluralism is the condition of postmodern culture in general. It is a period without a shared spiritual or metaphysical center and without any sense of totality. As defined by Jean-François Lyotard, for instance, it evolves from the conflict of "language games," and the relativization of what he calls "the grand narratives" of science, religion, progress, and social emancipation precludes a shared worldview.[59] Absolute authority is lacking.

One can view this phenomenon with nostalgic pessimism and regard it as a shortcoming even in the most successful postmodern buildings (such as the Humana Building and the Stuttgart Galerie). Even Charles Jencks, the most eloquent and sympathetic spokesman for postmodernism and free-style classicism in contemporary architecture, concludes that "in both buildings there is finally a crisis of content which leads to a confusion of form and expression: the lack of a credible symbolic programme which could pull together all this art, ornament and money and give it some greater sense. It is as unfair to fault the architects for this failure as it is the clients or contemporary society, but it helps explain why, in the end, these great and partly beautiful buildings leave something to be desired."[60]

There is a visible "loss of center," to use the term Sedlmayr employed more than thirty years ago in his melancholy analysis of modern art.[61] The Humana Building's Rotonda with its Roman torso is really a void without activity. Similarly, the central, open rotunda of Stirling's museum complex in Stuttgart—full of allusions to Piranesi, Hadrian's Villa, and other classical spaces—purposely exhibits a banality at its very center: three lids for underground electrical conduits—a deliberately antisymbolic symbol (Fig. 48).

Here again it is easy to damn an architect if he does and damn him again if he doesn't. Instead of criticizing, however, we should admire the honesty of Graves and Stirling. They do not pretend that classical architecture today can simply manufacture that sort of fully meaningful center—that will come only after society and culture do their part. The message is by no means hopeless and is analogous to the role of the classics in a genuinely pluralistic university curriculum. As we will see time and again, there is enough inherent creativity and vitality in the classical tradition and enough untrammeled demand for it in a free environment to make it flourish and be a significant and visible force in our contemporary culture, whether in architecture or academe. The vitality of the classical idiom in American architecture today is a splendid illustration of this process. Classical academicians can take heart from its resilience and learn much from its creativity.

Short Bibliography and Suggestions for Further Reading

Filler, Martin. "Building in the Past Tense." *TLS* (March 24–30, 1989) 295–297.

Jencks, Charles. *The Language of Post-Modern Architecture*, 6th ed. (New York 1991).

———. *Post-Modernism. The New Classicism in Art and Architecture* (New York 1987).

———. *What Is Post-Modernism?* (London 1987).

Klotz, Heinrich. *The History of Postmodern Architecture* (Cambridge, Mass. 1987).

Moore, Charles, and Wayne Attoe, eds. *Ah Mediterranean! Twentieth Century Classicism in America. Center* 2 (1986).

Papadakis, Andreas, ed. *The New Classicism in Architecture and Urbanism. Architectural Design Profile* 71 (London 1988).

Porphyrios, Demetri, ed. *Classicism Is Not a Style. Architectural Design* 5–6 (London 1982).

Portoghesi, Paolo. *Postmodern: The Architecture of the Post-Industrial Society* (New York 1983).

Rodiek, Thorsten. *James Stirling: Die Neue Staatsgalerie Stuttgart* (Stuttgart 1984).

Stern, Robert A. M. *Modern Classicism* (New York 1988).

Venturi, Robert. *Complexity and Contradiction in Architecture* (New York 1966).

———. *Learning from Las Vegas. The Forgotten Symbolism of Architectural Form* (Cambridge, Mass. 1977).

Wolfe, Tom. *From Bauhaus to Our House* (New York 1981).

II

The Decline and Fall of the Roman Empire: Are There Modern Parallels?

Some General Definitions and Perspectives

Several years ago, the University of Texas invited a truly distinguished expert on ancient history to lecture on the subject of the fall of Rome. I vividly remember introducing Professor Arnaldo Momigliano, who held appointments at both the Universities of London and Chicago, with the requisite eulogy and his casually shuffling to the lectern. "The Roman Empire fell," he said, "because the Germans invaded it, and there is really no more to it than that." With this he pretended to gather up his notes and leave the podium amid general exhilaration. He did go through with the lecture, of course; at state universities, we have some rather stringent regulations about paying visiting and, for that matter, tenured professors.

The point he made, however, is quite valid. The fall of Rome has proved to be of interest not only for its own sake but also for the lessons we can learn from its interpretation. It is all good and true that we can and must learn from history; those who do not know the past, as Santayana's well-known phrase goes, are condemned to repeat it. But it is equally true that when we look at historical events, and especially such a momentous one as the fall of a major civilization, we tend to project our own concerns, anxieties, and ideals into them. Under such circumstances, history all too easily becomes a set of cautionary tales supporting our own prejudices. A difference needs to be observed between broad perspectives, which can be quite instructive, and narrow analogies, which can be hazardous to one's intellectual health.

To a large extent, this second mode has been the fate of the explanations of the fall of Rome. To each their own reason for the fall. At latest count, there were 210 (see Appendix), which surely is overkill and suggests a great deal of superficiality and subjectivism, especially as many of them are totally contradictory. For the most part, as has been well demonstrated, they are the result of such factors as the expounders' religious convictions, professions, and nationalities, fanned by the adflatus of whatever Zeitgeist.[1] Economists, for instance, will single out economic problems; military historians, any military weaknesses; critics of the IRS will concentrate on the tax system;[2] and scientists will look for such reasons as lead poisoning, climatology, and disregard for the ecology. Friedrich Dürrenmatt gently made fun of such pretensions in his play *Romulus the Great* in which Caesar Rupf, who owns a trouser factory, tells the Great Romulus that "only Romans who wear trousers will be able to prevail against the German attack."

Against this background, it is hardly surprising that predictions of America's fall have been coextensive with the very existence of our Republic. In 1778, Diderot foretold the Rome-like fall of the United States, even if he allowed for a few centuries. Diverse European scholars, such as the French sociologist Gustave Le Bon and the German historian and Nobel Prize winner Theodor Mommsen, issued similar predictions, again modeled on the fall of the Roman Empire.[3] Most recently, of course, Paul Kennedy, while citing precedents other than Rome, had rekindled the debate before it was eclipsed briefly by Francis Fukuyama's diametrically opposed affirmation that U.S.-style liberal democracy was triumphant all over the globe and the declineless end of history was therefore in sight.[4] That thesis has been contradicted as much by some world events in the meantime as Mr. Kennedy's has been by others. Regardless of such vagaries in the national spotlight, however, the perennial fascination, punctuated by cyclical bursts of intensity, with the subject of decline and the analogies between Rome and a declining America continue to be the staple of many a religious and secular sermon. It is useful, therefore, to scrutinize them more closely.

The basic schema for the historiography of decline was given by Polybius, the Greek Alexis de Tocqueville, in the second century B.C. "That all existing things are subject to decay and change is a truth that scarcely needs proof," he wrote, "for the course of nature is sufficient to force that conviction on us. There are two agencies by which every kind of state is liable to decay. One is external and the other is the organic development of the state itself. We can lay down no fixed rule (*theoria*) about the former, but the latter is a regular process."[5]

"External" causes are those that do not follow a pattern, cannot be defined systematically, and are not rooted in the past. Because they defy tidy categorization, historians of decline have tended to ignore them or, at most, accord them grudging status as "catalysts." The overwhelming tendency has been to look for internal causes that can be arranged in an orderly progression.

A coalition of forces is at work here. There are the moralists, metaphysicians, and guilt seekers who aver, from the Pentateuch to contemporary columnists, that all guilt is somehow avenged on earth. They are joined by the intellectual historians descending from the chronicler of Athens' decline, Thucydides, for whom it is a mark of sophistication to look beyond the actual events for deeper causations. Lastly, the mere unavailability of source materials about the Germanic intruders prevented historians of the "decline" of Rome to look at the phenomenon from a perspective other than inside the Roman Empire where we have a relative abundance of historical and archaeological sources. This purely material shortcoming accelerated the introspective tendency of the explanations for Rome's fall. The resulting model has exerted a powerful influence on such historians as Kennedy, but it is a flawed model.

There is a clear line of succession; Kennedy's mentor was the late Sir Basil Liddell Hart, a superb military historian. In the mid-1940s, Sir Basil wrote the historian's equivalent to the recent tractates by Allan Bloom and E. D. Hirsch, entitled "Why Don't We Learn from History?" One of its central tenets is that "the downfall of civilized states tends to come, not from the direct assault of foes, but from internal decay."[6]

There is no question that this has been the prevailing approach. It is satisfying because, for all the reasons mentioned above, it provides ready meaning. Didacticism, especially of the moral sort, and historiography have had a stable marriage. But, to return to the example of Rome, the continued existence of the eastern Roman Empire suggests that we must be very open to the first of the causations mentioned by Polybius, even if it does not lend itself as readily to *theoria*. Most of the 210 conditions cited for Rome's fall could be found in the eastern as well as the western part of the empire. Even though Gibbon characterized its existence as "a tedious and uniform tale of weakness and misery," the eastern empire survived for almost another millennium. The difference was that it was not attacked by the German invaders.

The nuclear age has dimmed the prospects for the acceptance of such external factors for the fall of nations instead of those of the traditional, introspective kind. An enemy attack on one of the great powers today would mean nuclear annihilation; the loss of dominance of earlier nations pales by comparison. Seemingly, therefore, the only viable alternative for the historian is to continue the search for internal defects. They are, of course, never hard to find, especially in democracies: Hedrick Smith's recent book provides enough material in the governmental area alone for prospective obituaries.[7] Such weaknesses or, in Toynbee's terminology, challenges, can never be ignored. They should be remedied, however, for their own sake on an ongoing basis and not because they are harbingers of inexorable decline.

As is obvious from their inflated number, analyses of the decline and fall of Rome can benefit from greater differentiation and circumspection. "Decline" itself, as a current writer on international security well points out, is a misleading metaphor because "it bundles together two quite different concepts: a decrease in external power, and internal deterioration or decay."[8] The concept echoes and refines the distinction made by Polybius. Sometimes the loss of external power is linked to internal decay, but often it is purely relational: other nations and challengers may simply get stronger. On the other hand, the weakening of external rivals—such as the implosion of the Soviet Union—does not ipso facto prevent American decline in the domestic arena. Similarly, we have to differentiate between primary and secondary causes. For instance, population decline and manpower shortage are two venerable causes that have been adduced for Rome's fall, notwithstanding the extreme limitations of demographic data for antiquity. Even if accepted, however, they are not primary causes, but result from such factors as epidemics and people's choice, available even at that time, of limiting offspring for a variety of reasons.

The overriding consideration is the tremendous diversity of the Roman Empire. It has been much neglected by many explicators of Rome's "fall," as if we were dealing with a monolith that was not supposed to change. But circumstances varied. Agriculture and the economy, for instance, might prosper at a given time in some areas but be in woeful shape in others. This heterogeneity is the companion of the empire's cultural pluralism, which is the subject of another chapter.

So much for some introductory perspectives. On occasion, I will elaborate these further when we discuss specific examples. I will approach the subject in terms of some currently popular views, scrutinize a few representative single-cause scientific theories (such as lead poisoning), survey the more global hypotheses of intellectual historians like Spengler and Toynbee, and then proceed to some specific points of contact between the U.S.A. since the 1960s and the late Roman Empire. Both similarities and differences should emerge quite clearly thereby, and we will gain a better appreciation of the extent to which the so-called decline and fall of Rome can serve as a paradigm for the kind of problems that exercise us today.

"Decadence"

One fashionable and popular myth is that of decadence. It has the advantage, for both its practitioners and critics, of considerable elasticity, but the general notion envelops such symptoms as hedonism, debauchery, moral profligacy, and spiritual vacuity. One lingering misconception, reinforced by the visual media over the past four decades, is that the whole process was well under way by the first century A.D. under the so-called mad emperors. An additional factor contributing to misunderstanding is the impressionistic and ahistorical notion that Christianity must have made an impact instantly rather than developed slowly over three centuries. The result is the rogues' gallery portrayed by *I Claudius*—it should be noted that despite the impression given there, death still came to some members of the imperial family by natural causes—and an assortment of cinema epics from the 1950s and 1960s, starting with *The Robe*.

As for Nero (A.D. 54–68), nobody would argue that he was particularly normal, though the level of the debate might gain by being shifted to the problem of heredity versus environment. Suetonius starts his biography by emphasizing the depravity of Nero's father, Lucius Domitius Ahenobarbus, or "Redbeard," evidenced among other misdeeds by his distinction of being the first Roman hit-and-run driver on record. The key to Nero's personality is his pathological insecurity; it was abetted, if not created, by the pandering to his every whim on the part of the three regents, including the philosopher Seneca, during the first three years upon his accession when he was underage. But were all Romans like that? Of course not. Did his eccentricities have any effect on the life-style or the economic activities or social well-being of Rome's various subjects in North Africa, Spain, Palestine, or Egypt? Again, no. We are dealing with a limited phenomenon.

The same is true of Claudius (A.D. 41–54) and Caligula (A.D. 37–41). The combination of a first-rate mind, a debilitating illness, and an incredibly messy private life is the stuff for movies indeed, but Claudius' rule was anything but disastrous and included notable reforms in such areas as the granting of Roman citizenship, the imperial administration, and a sound foreign policy. Caligula, alas, was perceived as a living perversion very shortly into his reign even by his contemporaries, and his pathological destructiveness—he wished that the Roman Empire had but a single neck, so he could sever it—is case material for the students of absolute power and its effect. His statement, however, indicates that even he realized that the fabric of the empire was sounder and more complex than to be susceptible to attack from a single quarter.

Contrary to Hollywood and some fundamentalists, the empire evidenced no moral decline in the first century A.D., and comparisons of demented emperors with today's drug culture and individual hedonism are extraneous handrailing. The counterexamples abound, led by Augustus (31 B.C.–A.D. 14), who set a standard for all times to come (see chapter 4), and Vespasian (A.D. 69–79), who solidified Rome and its administration after Nero's reign. The second century, once enthusiastically characterized by Gibbon as the period during which mankind was most happy and prosperous, saw the arrival of emperors chosen on the basis of merit and ability, a revolutionary principle even for some modern democracies. This opened the door to Hispanics such as Trajan (A.D. 98–117) and Hadrian (A.D. 117–138).[9] Trajan led the empire at the time when it was largest, whereas Hadrian comes right out of the pages of Peters and Waterman's In Search of Excellence: he used both the right and the left sides of his brain and practiced Management by Wandering Around to counteract the remoteness and centralization of the Roman government. And as late as A.D. 451, the empire could still strike back, as Attila the Hun found out when he was defeated by the able Roman commander Aetius.

So far from wallowing in the slough of perversion and debauchery, the fourth and fifth centuries were marked by increasingly spiritual tendencies, such as those exhibited by Christianity and Neoplatonic mysticism. Of homosexuality, for instance, which is used in some quarters as another index of the decline of our society and for presumed parallels with the fall of the Roman Empire, there is little evidence in the late empire and certainly no acceptance. Roman moralists had denounced it as early as the first century A.D., and later it was publicly condemned and subject to dire legal penalties—nothing less than burning alive.[10]

Conversely, moralists from Gibbon to Hugh Hefner have pointed precisely to the phenomenon of Christianity as undermining the empire's ability to survive. In the association of Christianity with the many posited symptoms of decline, new interpretive heights of elasticity have been reached; Saint Paul never intended to be all things to all men to this extent. The only arguments concerning the decline from which Christianity has been exempted seem to be those relating to soil exhaustion.

I do not intend to enter into these arguments except for observing that they provide another good illustration for the need to differentiate between cause and effect and between primary and secondary developments. Christianity, often—and this is a historical assessment and not a value judgment—followed certain tendencies of the time rather than set the tone all by itself. At a time when life in this world was precarious and faced by many threats, preoccupation with otherworldliness arose across the board; the escapist streak of Neoplatonism is a good example. What comes first is the extraordinary difficulties in the economic, social, and political life of the "Barracks" period of the third century when military madness prevailed and twenty-five emperors ruled in less than fifty years (A.D. 235–284). The result is the hope of many individuals for a better life that is not of this world. This does not mean complete indifference to the state. Contrary to the facile generalizations of modern observers, the Christians in the late Roman Empire did not speak with one, undifferentiated voice. Eusebius, for instance, following Origen and the idea of the eternity of Rome (*Roma aeterna*), viewed the empire as an order of peace willed by God, the emperor as God's deputy, and Christianization as a proof of progress on earth. In his view, even the incursion of the barbarians is not a calamity, but an opportunity to make converts.

Single-Cause Explanations

The theories that reduce the phenomenon of Rome's decline and fall to a single cause can be explained, at least in part, against the backdrop of the baffling complexity not only of the entire event, but even of its individual ramifications, such as the nuanced role of Christianity. There is a yearning amid all this multiplicity to simplify matters. Hence many of these one-shot explanations can be seen as a reaction against the perceived scholarly tendency to make things at times a great deal more complicated than they need to be. What fun, then, to sweep away the web of complex interrelationships and boldly project one single and usually natural cause as the end-all of a once mighty civilization. That is the stuff of which headlines and sound bites are made, and therefore such theories, not surprisingly, are picked up readily by today's press. It will suffice to discuss three of them briefly with a view to analyzing their structural characteristics.

The first of these explanations is that of one George Simkhovitch, first published in the *Political Science Quarterly* of 1916 and then republished, perhaps somewhat incongruously, in the author's book entitled *Towards an Understanding of Jesus.* The main thesis is that soil exhaustion caused the fall of the Roman Empire. Now it is certainly true that agriculture was in bad shape in some parts of the empire in the late stages, and fields lay uncultivated in some areas of Italy; even one-third of Campania, the traditional center of agricultural production, was affected. The Romans did not practice crop rotation, and it can certainly be argued that low agricultural productivity has soil exhaustion as one of its causes. To propound this as a general explanation, however, is inadequate even in the agricultural context, let alone the larger one of the presumed unraveling of the empire's fabric. The empire, as we stressed earlier, was very diverse; what is true of one area is not true of another. The soil was not exhausted in Egypt, for instance, and it is precisely in Egypt that we have the earliest reports of peasants' flight from the land, villages disappearing because of depopulation, and the failures of agronomy. The reason was maladministration, excessive bureaucracy, and insensitive taxation—the soil was not exhausted, but the people were.

For Professor Ellsworth Huntington, who also wrote at the time of the First World War, which generated much analogy hunting with the fall of Rome, the culprit was climatic change.[11] Huntington made up for the lack of a Roman meteorological service by looking at the annual rings in the trunks of the great sequoias and redwood trees in northern California, some of them three thousand years old. In discussing "The Secret of Big Trees," he assumed (1) that the climate of northern California was similar to that of the Mediterranean, and (2) that the climate in both areas underwent some drastic modifications, especially in terms of rainfall, from the fourth to the sixth century. The conclusion, to put it somewhat irreverently, is that if the rain did not fall, the empire had to. In terms of the intrinsic merits of the argument, we can note that it does rain more in the Mediterranean than it does in California, that increased rainfall in the first half of the third century A.D. did not lead to unusual prosperity, and that it is arguable to what extent rainfall or temperature is responsible for the trees' growth. In other words, specialist theories of this kind are susceptible to criticism on their own, intrinsic grounds, besides being unable to illuminate the larger issues.

The same is true of the most recent theory of this sort that has been given much play, i.e., lead poisoning. Analysis of forty-five skeletons from Herculaneum, for instance, revealed a high degree of lead content in eight and revived further speculation by J. Nriagu in the *New England Journal of Medicine* that the bizarre behavior of Nero and Caligula could be attributed to the Romans' daily contact with lead vessels.[12]

Roman doctors were well aware of the dangers of lead poisoning and prescribed antidotes. Nothing in their writings suggests epidemic proportions of an affliction that is anything but hidden. Vitruvius, in his standard work *On Architecture,* remarks on the danger of water being contaminated by the lead pipes in aqueducts. Unlike today, however, the water was rarely left standing in tap-regulated pipes but was allowed to circulate freely throughout the system. Besides, after a few years, the pipes were encrusted with calcium carbonate deposits, thus insulating the water from contact with lead. Mainly, however, the minimal statistics that occasion such far-reaching generalizations as lead poisoning contributing to the downfall of the Roman Empire would be totally unacceptable in any other area of scientific scholarship. In order to produce significant instead of simplistically sensational information, reliable data would be expected at regular intervals from every part of the Roman world over several centuries—not just from one small Roman town in southern Italy nearer the beginning than the end of the Roman Empire (A.D. 79). Imagine, for a moment, if scholars of history two thousand years from now were to make similarly sweeping conclusions about the demise of American civilization solely on the basis of an archaeological excavation at the Meadowlands.

The Explanations of the Intellectual Historians

Enough of beating what really should be dead horses. The essence of the requisite methodology is, as I briefly indicated earlier, a recognition of the diversity of the Roman Empire. It was one of the most enduring political systems the world has ever seen. Gibbon at one point well observed that "instead of inquiring why the Roman Empire was destroyed, we should rather be surprised that it lasted so long." It is for that reason that the fate of Rome has traditionally invited consideration as a universal paradigm. A more conceptual approach, therefore, can be useful, and that is the perspective the intellectual historians provide. The most influential in this century still is Oswald Spengler, who wrote his profoundly pessimistic two-volume study *The Decline of the West* following the end of World War I; in the United States alone, it has been reprinted more than twenty times. Spengler restated the popular analogy between the life of an individual and the life of states and empires. According to him, every state in history is subject to the organic cycle of youth, growth, maturity, and decay. The first three stages are culture, whereas the last is "civilization." Civilization, in Spengler's terminology, is simply the final conclusion to culture—"the thing become succeeding the thing becoming, death following life, rigidity following expansion . . . petrifying world city following mother earth." Everything inexorably gravitates toward decay. In Spengler's view, the ancient world reached that stage already in the fourth century B.C. Virtually all of Roman civilization, then, is only an epilogue to fifth-century Athens. Roman imperialism, so far from being a dynamic force, is a negative phenomenon; it is petrifying decay trying to perpetuate the state's lifeless existence.

A few perspectives will help us understand, though by no means share, this extreme view. The book was written in Germany under the imprint of the biggest disaster in history ever to befall that nation until that time. The result could only be boundless pessimism. Typical also of the times is the idolatry of fifth-century Athens. It is utterly romantic and lacks the scrutiny that this period has received in the past fifty years. Finally, the cyclical view of history provides a greater degree of predictability and therefore means comfort, at least in some quarters. To write off the dynamic tensions of the age of Alexander and his successors and the development of the Roman Republic and the Principate as decaying appendages to the most overrated fifty-year period in the history of Greece is, by today's standards, historical nonsense.

By contrast, Arnold Toynbee's general theory of history is more dynamic, flexible, and optimistic. He defines historical development as being shaped by challenge and response.[13] A given nation or civilization faces challenges, and if it responds to them successfully, its development, which is not cyclical, continues apace. Continued successful responses result in new challenges, which again must be met. It is only when a civilization reaches the limit of its competence in solving more complex problems—a notion akin to the Peter Principle—that stagnation and decline will set in. In his own writings on the fall of Rome, Toynbee struck a more pessimistic note, but it is useful to return to his original concept and combine it with Gibbon's answer, as it were, to the question of what the principal challenges were to which the Romans did not respond with success. In essence, Gibbon's thesis anticipates Kennedy's of the "imperial overstretch": nations engage in excessive territorial acquisition or, during prosperous times, take on commitments of a magnitude they cannot adequately support when they are afflicted by reverses. According to Gibbon, the decline of Rome, when all is said and done, was the natural and inevitable—and historians love that word "inevitable"—effect of her "immoderate greatness." "Prosperity," intones Gibbon, "ripened the principle of decay; the causes of destruction multiplied with the extent of conquest; and, as soon as time or accident had removed the artificial supports, the stupendous fabric yielded to the pressure of its own weight." Thereupon, and after hundreds of pages into *The Decline and Fall of the Roman Empire*, comes the startling revelation, which the weary reader would have welcomed in the introduction, that "the story of its ruin is simple and obvious." Then follows the sentence, which I cited earlier, that we should appreciate the empire's longevity rather than inquire into its demise.

"Immoderate Greatness" and "Imperial Overstretch"

Did Gibbon have a point? I think so. It does not, however, lend itself to pointing a simplistic moral, which would apply to both the Pax Romana and the Pax Americana, that the expansion of a nation's sphere of influence is bad per se. We should not, in the first instance, confuse Rome's territorial expansion, which is more akin to that of the later British Empire, with America's areas of influence.[14] As Kennedy's critics have pointed out, it is arguable that any gain, even for the domestic economy, would result from America's withdrawal from responsibility. And a strong case exists that the Pax Americana, defined as the extension of international influence, has for the most part been a stabilizing element in the world order since World War II. Conversely, it would be misleading to regard the United States' reduced share of the world's GNP today, as compared to the 1950s, as a sign of "decline," as Kennedy does. The time when the other major industrial powers were still barely recovering from the ravages of the war is not an appropriate benchmark for measuring decline even statistically.

It is helpful, however, to expand on both Gibbon's statement and Kennedy's concept in the Roman context. Centuries before these two historians, some good Roman emperors fully recognized that the amalgam of territorial acquisitions, which had often been made haphazardly and without any grand design, was too unwieldy. What is more, emperors like Hadrian and Diocletian (A.D. 284–305) actually remedied the imperial overstretch. The former gave up some of the conquests made by his predecessor, Trajan, under whom the empire reached its largest territorial expanse. The latter reorganized the administration of the empire by both streamlining some boundaries (with resulting territorial divestment) and decentralizing. This logical, effective system fell victim, a few decades later, to Constantine's megalomania. He did not, however, try to reconquer any of the ceded territories. Or, to give another example: Britain, which was relatively stable, was considered an overextension by A.D. 410, and its Roman garrison was withdrawn.

To redefine the issue raised by Gibbon, Toynbee, and Kennedy: it would be only partially correct to say that the challenge Rome did not meet successfully was "immoderate greatness" or territorial overstretch. Rather, since continued territorial acquisition is insufficient and even counterproductive in guaranteeing the continuing vitality of a state or nation, internal goals and visions at some point have to supersede the purely territorial and external ones. This recognition, for instance, characterized the rule of Augustus. It requires leadership or, to be more precise, the kind of transforming leadership that James MacGregor Burns has discussed so usefully in his exemplary book on the subject. He differentiates between transactional leadership and transforming leadership. Transactional leadership is the kind of leadership an executive provides almost institutionally. It consists of doing the necessary things in any office, broadly defined as transactions with followers or subordinates, from answering the mail to making patronage appointments—the necessary activities and minutiae that take up most of the day. Transforming leadership, by contrast, goes beyond this by defining the visions, shaping the values, and making the meanings that satisfy higher needs of both the leaders and the followers. "The result of transforming leadership," Burns notes, is a relationship of mutual stimulation and elevation that "converts followers into leaders and leaders into moral agents."[15]

I do not think this is asking naively for an ideal that could not be realized at the time of the late Roman Empire or, for that matter, today. Both the Roman Empire and the United States are characterized by cultural and ethnic diversity, which is desirable but needs to be balanced by a unified vision and shared ideals.[16] Otherwise, the word *united* becomes purely ritualistic. In Rome, the issue was even more pressing. The empire had been the result of conquests; in many parts, the Romanization went only skin-deep. How does one hold such an immoderately large mass together? Outstanding emperors, such as Augustus and Hadrian, had the kinds of vision and policies that were apt to create a sense of unity. Under other emperors, the centrifugal tendencies of the empire simply became too strong. It is wrong to emphasize simply the territorial aspect of this tendency, such as parts of the empire seceding and needing to be reconquered. The problem is much more of a conceptual and inner one; it consists of a lack of shared values, ideals, visions, and purpose.

America and Rome: Some Comparisons

I am not arguing that in the absence of these characteristics lies the fall of the Roman Empire. It is simply another concern that deserved attention then as it does now. This gets us squarely into the area of other analogies or, as I would prefer to call them, points of contact, between the late Roman Empire and modern America. I will explore four specific such parallels as a representative sample of both similarities and differences. The first is the excessive growth of the bureaucracy and of the role of the central government, accompanied by government's usurpation of functions the private sector could perform more effectively.

Here we can indeed learn something from the Roman experience. In the first and second centuries, effective emperors like Augustus, Claudius, and Hadrian organized the imperial staff efficiently into various bureaus, dealing with specific areas of responsibility, such as correspondence, legal petitions, fiscal affairs, records, and the like. And a vicious circle began to set in, as always: the more efficient the imperial staff and the emperors, the more delighted were provinces, regions, and cities to let them do a good job and to devolve an ever increasing number of tasks and responsibilities upon Rome. There was no federal outlook to prevent them from doing so. Accordingly, the work load at the center grew steadily, and the manner in which it was handled was subject to the preferences and competencies of various emperors. The Severan dynasty, for instance, at the beginning of the third century, marked the militarization of the system. Veterans who had served for at least twenty-five years in the military now set the tone for the civil service. "Conservatism," as one writer has aptly observed in this context, "is bred into soldiers by the nature of their dangerous occupation—deviation from tested procedures can be fatal—but this rigid dependence on precedents can also be stultifying. Furthermore, the soldier's conservatism is combined with a devotion to station that is comical when it does not frustrate all improvement."[17] The predictable lack of initiatives and innovation was compounded by the natural tendency within bureaucratic structures toward immoderate growth: "The bureaucrat's love of classification and of specialization in the name of efficiency swiftly leads to a morass of supernumeraries relentlessly multiplying tasks of an ever more petty nature." By the beginning of the fourth century, the Christian church father Lactantius could complain that the civil servants outnumbered the taxpayers.

Instead of being a means to an end, then, the bureaucracy tended to become self-serving and oppressive. This led to increased evasion of civic responsibilities by ordinary citizens, the farmers, manufacturers, and tradesmen. That, in turn, increased the work of the bureaucrats, but well past the productive stage. A related development, therefore, was the regimentation of the private sector. Whereas formerly—and parallel to today—the members of the well-to-do classes (curiales) in each town or city had contributed freely and individually to local philanthropic needs, they were made responsible for the delivery of tribute and taxes from their localities in the fourth and fifth centuries regardless of their economic condition. In other words, local independence of action was taken away, and the curiales became the servants of a central government that passed no fewer than 192 laws regulating their lives and duties between A.D. 313 and 436. They were bound to their own position regardless of their wishes or financial ability; their status became hereditary, and they could not leave their towns. It was the end of social and geographic mobility for one of the empire's most important sources of strength.

Despite occasional jeremiads, we are not looking at a sclerosis of similar magnitude today. Even if the acuteness of John Naisbitt's observations varies greatly, the shift from centralization to decentralization and from institutional help to self-help is a megatrend,[18] certainly in comparison to the late Roman Empire. This is not, however, a time for easy self-congratulation. The good news is, for instance, that between 1968 and 1980, the number of federal employees increased by only 100,000, from 2.7 million to 2.8 million. During the same period, however, the ranks of local and state employees ballooned by 4 million. As for the noninstitutional sector, we are reclaiming, as Naisbitt puts it, America's traditional sense of self-reliance after four decades of trusting in institutional help. We are, I think, at this point aware of the strengths and limits of both. No such perspective prevailed in the late Roman Empire. Had there been, to take but one concrete example, people like the Vietnamese refugees, they would not have gotten another start due to enlightened government policies, nor could they have succeeded as brilliantly as many of them have on the basis of their own initiative and excellence. America's capacity to reinvent herself is one of her greatest strengths.

We may usefully connect this with another phenomenon in the final stages of the Roman Empire. That was the policy to grant Roman citizenship to the first wave of invaders indiscriminately in the hope that, as newly designated Roman citizens, they would hold off the next series of invaders. Basically, the procedure was as follows: when, for example, Germanic warriors infiltrated the *Agri Decumates* (i.e., the area between the headwaters of the Rhine and the Danube), the Roman authorities settled them at the very border inside the Roman territory. They were given Roman citizenship without further ado and expected, wrongly of course, to turn away their Germanic brethren who tried to get through the Roman fortifications next. The policy did not work because there was, in fact, no difference whatever between the "Romans" on one side of the boundary and the "barbarians" on the other. Contrast this with our immigration procedures today: anyone who wants to become a U.S. citizen must become familiar with American history and our Constitution and system of government. The reason is the elementary need to understand the heritage and traditions of a country whose citizens we choose to be.

Another seeming parallel is the cult of the individual, which was in evidence in the third and fourth centuries. According to one contemporary observer, Christopher Lasch, it was also the very hallmark of the culture of the 1970s. In his view, the decade was characterized by a culture of narcissism, which is the result of an age of diminishing expectations. The latter certainly is a characterization that also fits the late Roman Empire. On the most general level, narcissism is a metaphor for self-absorption, although its clinical definition is far more extensive. When all is said and done, the popular bottom line is the "me" generation, although, because of the existence of a sophisticated psychiatric vocabulary without a counterpart in late antiquity, we can today be a great deal more precise about the clinical ramifications, such as manipulativeness, cultivation of emotional shallowness, the illusion of limitless options, the pathological avoidance of commitment, and much more. Nor was there an exact analogue in antiquity to the corporate gamesman, as defined by Michael Maccoby.[19]

Instead, there is the otherworldliness of a Neoplatonist, such as Plotinus, whose highest ideal is the unification, through mystic contemplation, of the holistic self with the supreme unity of the so-called One, the ground of all existence. It is the kind of ecstasy that is not alien to the evangelicals today. All these phenomena are responses to their times. When public events seem out of control, when there is a realization that the individual's role in a highly structured and bureaucratized society faces stifling obstructions, when there is a high degree of emptiness of feeling and sense of powerlessness, philosophies and cults that carry introspection to the point of absorption with the individual self are bound to arise and win followers. The uncertainty, danger, oppression, and regimentation that were part of the Roman world in the final centuries certainly were conducive to spawning trends of that kind, just as they had been in Hellenistic times, although they were not shared universally. Nor is everybody guilty today of what President Carter once castigated as "the crisis of confidence"—or, more popularly, malaise of the spirit—affecting the American people. The underlying parallels and implications, which should not be minimized, are that any culture and society, if it wants to remain vital, needs to provide a sufficient number of positive outlets for the human search for meaning in life—and Neoplatonic tenets despite their quietism seem a great deal more positive than modern pathologies or, worse, "the inclination, in our therapeutic age, to dress up moralistic platitudes in psychiatric garb"[20]— and prevent the most highly motivated and qualified individuals from withdrawing solely into their private sphere. Again, it is a phenomenon that merits our concern without being an axiomatic portent of the impending fall.

A fourth and related point of contact is the dissatisfaction with or apathy toward existing governmental institutions. If we bought into the greater causality of internal deterioration as opposed to external factors, we could say that the end of the Roman Empire or, for that matter, any civilization occurs at a point when a critical majority of the people experience psychological defeatism and apathy, when they feel that the system, the traditions, the values, and the whole structure simply are not worth maintaining any longer. Such points in time are hard to fix for ancient history, given the absence of opinion polls. One of the most palpable expressions of change in this direction during the late Roman Empire was the villa economy; that is, ministates within the state, which were commanded by nobles, strove for economic independence and kept at bay the armies of both the invaders and the central government. This development foreshadowed, as can be readily seen, the feudal system of the Middle Ages. It was the constructive alternative of the powerful nobility. An equivalent in another realm was the rise of monasticism.

The parallels today are more secular, without being secessionist in nature.

Instead, analysts point to such phenomena as low voter turnout as being indicative of apathy and de facto dropping out from meaningful participation in the political process. Our *representative* democracy, as Naisbitt and others have observed with reference to the institutions of the presidency and the Congress, does not enjoy the most vigorous popular involvement. It would be simplistic, however, to view low participation in these elections, which can be explained in a variety of ways,[21] as a sign of decline. It is amply counterbalanced by the emergence of an intensive *participatory* democracy at the grassroots level, as evinced by schoolboard and other local elections, neighborhood issues and associations, initiative and referendum, and the like. There is no evidence that the majority of the American people would prefer another system of government. It provides us, paradoxically, with the freedom not to participate. When looking for parallels between late Rome and contemporary America, it is not enough to note the superficial similarity of the ebb and flow of the relevance of public institutions. More important is the spirit of the system of governance and its adaptability at various levels. It may be more vital at any given time at some levels than at others. That is what we are seeing today in our democratic society; change is not to be equated with decline.

That indeed should be the dominant perspective on the "decline" and "fall" of the Roman Empire too. I will return to it shortly, after touching on some of the major differences between their world and ours. They add to the total context of our discussion, and they are all too easily ignored because we take them for granted today. They are, in quick order, technology, health and hygiene, and education.

While we know from our daily lives that technology, without being guided by firm values, can initiate a vicious spiral, its near total lack—at least in the sense we take it for granted today—in antiquity is the larger of the two evils. When all is said and done, the Romans had no real command of their physical environment. While we have created some environmental problems, our water is cleaner, food safer, and indoor air less contaminated than one hundred, let alone two thousand years ago. The Romans were helpless in the face of epidemics, natural disasters, problems with the management of natural resources, and the like. This is not why the empire fell; I am simply saying that if I had my choice even between living in the second century A.D., "the most happy and prosperous period of mankind," and today, I would, without hesitation, opt to live in all the ostensible turmoil of the current decades, while looking forward to the challenges of the next fifty years.

This all the more so since, by modern standards, the Roman conditions of health, medicine, and hygiene were almost totally inadequate. It was a world before Louis Pasteur, Arthur Fleming, microsurgery, vaccination, and fluoride. Life expectancy in the Roman Empire hovered between thirty and thirty-five years. Today, for men in the United States, it is around seventy-eight, and for women it is even higher. This involves more than statistics: just try to fathom

49. Stepping stones across street, Pompeii. (Photograph courtesy of Classics Slide Library, The University of Texas at Austin.)

the impact of this difference on our values, life and career expectations, and attitude toward marriage and divorce. Unquestionably, the Romans' attitude toward death was healthier than the Americans' because they could expect it anytime, starting with an infant mortality of higher than 50 percent. One serious bout with pneumonia would usually mean the journey to Hades. And while Mr. Chips might rhapsodize in the bucolic setting of the theater at Pompeii, I am struck more with the stepping stones across the streets that are palpable reminders of the lack of sewage disposal and treatment systems (Fig. 49). All this does not make us superior to the Romans in values and spirituality, but it helps remind us of the superiority of our resources, which we can put to good use at any time. It is better to live at a time when we have a baffling and complex number of options rather than none at all or pitifully few. We are moved, rightly, by the images of malnourished children in Africa; we would be appalled if we went back to the future in ancient Rome and confronted, on a daily basis, the omnipresence of fellow human beings grossly deformed and malformed by disease.

Finally, we are more resourceful today because a much higher percentage of our citizenry is educated than was the case in late Roman antiquity. I am aware, once more, that my optimism may sound a bit strange; after all, we have had one report after the other of late decrying the shortcomings of our educational system at its various levels. This criticism by itself is a sign of health; there are no corresponding critiques to be found in the fourth and fifth centuries. The severe limitations of access to education at the time gave easy rise to the theory that the fall of Rome had to be blamed on the masses or, more precisely, the masses' swallowing up the educated elite. It led to all kinds of sanctimonious comments, especially by European thinkers, about the presumed parallels of Rome's fate in this respect with that of their own countries. There is, for all its elegant phrasing, a certain lack of perception here; if anything, as Herbert Muller pointed out many years ago, the fault lay with these privileged classes, who had failed to educate or uplift the rest of the populace, "failed to maintain either the material prosperity or spiritual wealth of the nation."[22] By diffusing education to all those who can benefit from it, we are at least assuring ourselves of a large and diverse human reservoir from which the leadership and creativity essential for meeting ongoing challenges can come rather than restricting these intellectual resources to a hereditary elite in a closed system where the chances for renewal are so much more limited.

This is related to a final difference between Rome and America. It is one of mind-set. Roman sources are singularly unhelpful in sorting out the complexities of such a phenomenon as decline. According to Roman authors, decline was constant. It is a peculiarity that must have delighted the gloomy Spengler. We find it not only in the chroniclers of the late Republic, such as Sallust, but also in the writings of those who supported the Augustan restoration, such as Livy and Horace. Thus Horace concludes his cycle of odes on Roman virtues with the dire pronouncement that "our parents' age, worse than our grandparents', brought forth us who are more worthless and destined to have offspring yet more depraved."[23] It is the sentiment of a civilization that even at times of stability and consolidation would look only to the past for all of its inspiration. The past at least was a known quantity, whereas the future, in the absence of technology and the attainments we have just discussed, was a great deal less certain and never seemed preferable. The very idea of progress is largely absent from Greco-Roman antiquity. This did not preclude, as we will see in chapter 5, creative cultural evolution, but it was not identified with the modern notion of progress. Statism prevailed and so did the equation of any change, unless it was a return to a past condition, with deterioration. The preoccupation with decline, then, has very deep roots in Western thought.[24]

As any major historical juncture of the past, the so-called decline and fall of Rome can be meaningful for us. We need to resist both the initial impulse and most of the tradition of its interpretation to view it as a one-dimensional historical closure. In terms of society, culture, and economics, Rome did not fall promptly in A.D. 476; what happened is better defined as change or transformation. The significance of the demise of the empire in the west has been exaggerated by the all too frequent scholarly emphasis on it in terms of a fixed demarcation point and a sort of historical curtain call. Historians do not like empires and civilizations just to fade away; a big bang is preferred to a whimper, and dates are convenient. Life, on the other hand, is not so conveniently demarcated, and had newspapers existed in A.D. 476, the deposition of Romulus Augustulus by the German chieftain Odoacer would probably have wound up somewhere on the back pages among the ads for used sandals and black-glazed cooking ware.[25] In other words, we should not in retrospect impose a sense of firm closure on this event. Rather, an evolution of the Roman state and society had been under way for a long time, and life in the decades before and after A.D. 476 was not significantly different from life in that year itself. As always, the dynamics of change are harder to grasp and describe for the historian because they defy easy periodization.

We are on more productive ground when we look at the concerns that give meaning to individuals and the state: freedom from inhibiting constraints, a clear discernment of means and ends and of the proper relationship between them, a sense of shared values and of a shared enterprise, a management of national and international affairs that goes beyond ad hoc measures and centers on initiative rather than response, and the kind of vision and leadership that transforms both the governing and the governed. These issues are as vital today as they were then, and in that sense, we truly can learn from history.

Short Bibliography and Suggestions for Further Reading

Burns, James M. *Leadership* (New York 1978).

Chambers, Mortimer, ed. *The Fall of Rome: Can It Be Explained?* (New York 1974).

Demandt, Alexander. *Der Fall Roms* (Munich 1984).

Ferrill, Arthur. *The Fall of the Roman Empire: The Military Explanation* (New York 1986). Cf. E. Luttwak, *The Grand Strategy of the Roman Empire* (Baltimore 1976), and the rebuttal by B. Isaac, *The Limits of Empire: The Roman Army in the East* (Oxford 1990).

Kagan, Donald, ed. *End of the Roman Empire: Decline or Transformation?* 3rd ed. (Lexington, Mass. 1991).

Kennedy, Paul. *The Rise and Fall of the Great Powers* (New York 1987).

Lasch, Christopher. *The Culture of Narcissism: American Life in an Age of Diminished Expectations* (New York 1978).

Muller, Herbert J. *The Uses of the Past* (New York 1957).

Naisbitt, John. *Megatrends: Ten New Directions Transforming Our Lives* (New York 1982).

Nye, Joseph S., Jr. "The Misleading Metaphor of Decline." *Atlantic Monthly* (March 1990) 86–94.

Appendix

The following 210 reasons have been cited for the decline of the Roman Empire:

Abolition of gods
Abolition of rights
Absence of character
Absolutism
Agrarian question
Agrarian slavery
Anarchy
Anti-Germanism
Apathy
Aristocracy
Asceticism
Attack of Germans
Attack of Huns
Attack of riding nomads
Backwardness in science
Bankruptcy
Barbarization
Bastardization
Blockage of land by large landholders
Blood poisoning
Bolshevization
Bread and circuses
Bureaucracy
Byzantinism
Capillarité sociale
Capitalism
Capitals, change of
Caste system
Celibacy
Centralization
Childlessness
Christianity
Citizenship, granting of
Civil war
Climatic deterioration
Communism
Complacency
Concatenation of misfortunes
Conservatism
Corruption
Cosmopolitanism
Crisis of legitimacy

Culinary excess
Cultural neurosis
Decentralization
Decline of Nordic character
Decline of the cities
Decline of the Italic population
Deforestation
Degeneration
Degeneration of intellect
Demoralization
Depletion of mineral resources
Despotism
Destruction of environment
Destruction of peasantry
Destruction of political process
Destruction of Roman influence
Devastation
Differences in wealth
Disarmament
Disillusion with state
Division of empire
Division of labor
Earthquakes
Egoism
Egoism of the state
Emancipation of slaves
Enervation
Epidemics
Equal rights, granting of
Eradication of the best
Escapism
Ethnic dissolution
Excessive aging of population
Excessive civilization
Excessive culture
Excessive foreign infiltration
Excessive freedom
Excessive urbanization
Expansion
Exploitation
Fear of life
Female emancipation

Feudalization
Fiscalism
Gladiatorial system
Gluttony
Gout
Hedonism
Hellenization
Heresy
Homosexuality
Hothouse culture
Hubris
Hyperthermia
Immoderate greatness
Imperialism
Impotence
Impoverishment
Imprudent policy toward buffer states
Inadequate educational system
Indifference
Individualism
Indoctrination
Inertia
Inflation
Intellectualism
Integration, weakness of
Irrationality
Jewish influence
Lack of leadership
Lack of male dignity
Lack of military recruits
Lack of orderly imperial succession
Lack of qualified workers
Lack of rainfall
Lack of religiousness
Lack of seriousness
Large landed properties
Lead poisoning
Lethargy
Leveling, cultural
Leveling, social
Loss of army discipline
Loss of authority
Loss of energy
Loss of instincts
Loss of population
Luxury

Malaria
Marriages of convenience
Mercenary system
Mercury damage
Militarism
Monetary economy
Monetary greed
Money, shortage of
Moral decline
Moral idealism
Moral materialism
Mystery religions
Nationalism of Rome's subjects
Negative selection
Orientalization
Outflow of gold
Overrefinement
Pacifism
Paralysis of will
Paralyzation
Parasitism
Particularism
Pauperism
Plagues
Pleasure seeking
Plutocracy
Polytheism
Population pressure
Precociousness
Professional army
Proletarization
Prosperity
Prostitution
Psychoses
Public baths
Racial degeneration
Racial discrimination
Racial suicide
Rationalism
Refusal of military service
Religious struggles and schisms
Rentier mentality
Resignation
Restriction to profession
Restriction to the land
Rhetoric

Rise of uneducated masses	Stoicism
Romantic attitudes to peace	Stress
Ruin of middle class	Structural weakness
Rule of the world	Superstition
Semieducation	Taxation, pressure of
Sensuality	Terrorism
Servility	Tiredness of life
Sexuality	Totalitarianism
Shamelessness	Treason
Shifting of trade routes	*Tristesse*
Slavery	Two-front war
Slavic attacks	Underdevelopment
Socialism (of the state)	Useless eaters
Soil erosion	Usurpation of all powers by the state
Soil exhaustion	Vaingloriousness
Spiritual barbarism	Villa economy
Stagnation	Vulgarization

Source: A. Demandt, *Der Fall Roms* (1984) 695.

III

Reading Vergil's *Aeneid* in Modern Times

"Modern" and "Historical" Interpretation

Most of the argument in the current interpretation of literature centers on the conflict between two basic premises. One is more historically oriented (and I exclude the so-called New Historicism because it has different overtones) and linked often, though not always, with the further premise of intentionality on the part of the author. The scholar's task, therefore, is to recover, as much as possible, the historical and social context of the literary work, including the nature and cultural assumptions of the intended audience. On that basis, we can then try to make some conclusions about the meaning of the work to the audience at the time and relate that meaning to the intentions of the author. This is an important scholarly endeavor that saves us from ahistoricism.

It should not, of course, be our only task. The other perspective, greatly elaborated in contemporary theory, develops from the recognition that great literary works are classics precisely because their meaning is not immutably fixed in one time and place. Instead, they are susceptible to new interpretations by subsequent generations that, due to a changing world, may have cultural sensibilities different from those of the original audience. As teachers of classics, we don't want to treat works like the Homeric epics or Vergil's *Aeneid* as museum pieces that leave us cool and detached. We are also part of a modern audience that wants to react to them directly and find individual meaning in them.

Such meanings and readings, of course, can be very subjective, and that is the focal point of the current debate. It has been made into more theory than we actually need—theory has become an industry especially in departments of English—and the various theories can be summarized according to their essential perspectives on the problem. Reader-response criticism and, in particular, reception theory (including "aesthetics of reception") basically assert that the meaning of a literary work is concretized over time by various generations of readers.[1] In other words, different aspects of a work can be uncovered over time and their sum total, which is not necessarily a synthesis, comprises the meaning of the work. The issue that immediately arises is the hierarchy of such aspects or interpretations: on what basis can we say that one is sounder than the other? Deconstruction, as a result, obviates that issue by declaring that all such interpretations in essence are equal because a literary work has an existence, from the very beginning, independent of its maker. This puts the critic or reader in the enjoyable position of making up the rules as he or she goes along; there is no "objective" standard. Or, in Richard Rorty's words, the interpreter "simply beats the text into a shape which will serve his own purposes."[2]

This is an understandable reaction not only against excessive positivism but also against the unwarranted identification of each new interpretation of a classic with the intent of its author. To give one specific example: as a result of the Vietnam War and the sixties, it has become fashionable to interpret the final scene of the *Aeneid* as an act of irrational violence that calls into question the achievement of both Aeneas and Rome. Naively, this very personal reading is equated with a message intended by Vergil. Classical scholars can keep getting away with this sort of legerdemain because classics as a discipline has participated relatively little in the current debate about theory.[3] On the other hand, is it really necessary to resort to the deconstructionist solution that throws baby and bathwater out all at once?

Obviously, one practicable solution would be to insist more strongly on the separation between a personal, subjective response and the meaning, as best as we can establish it, of a given passage or work at Vergil's time. An ancient text or building may have meaning for us totally independent of the original historical circumstances. A useful parallel is Charles Moore's utilization, which I cited earlier,[4] of the design of three seventeenth-century chapels in Rome for the facades of buildings on the campus of the University of California at Irvine. The comments he made on that occasion are apropos: hardly any of the inhabitants at Irvine even knew of Ponzio's chapels, let alone ever saw them, "so the new buildings will have to stir up their own connections with the inhabitants' memories." That is exactly what happened; of course, such associations are purely personal. No one would argue that such connections were any part of Flaminio Ponzio's intent. Current interpreters of the *Aeneid*, who operate in a similarly associative fashion, should not make that assumption either.

If we want to explore some middle ground, another parallel is useful. The issue of interpreting a classic like the *Aeneid* in a way that has both meaning for us and is consistent with its original intent is somewhat analogous to that of interpreting the U.S. Constitution for a society different from that of our founders. The analogy is not mine. In a much-cited article, entitled "Law as Literature," Professor Sanford Levinson has applied current literary theory to constitutional analysis: "There are as many plausible readings of the United States Constitution as there are versions of *Hamlet,* even though each interpreter, like each director, might genuinely believe that he or she has stumbled onto the one best answer to the conundrums of the text."[5] In that view, no interpretation is more privileged than the other for either the Constitution or major works of literature. But it is not a compelling view. There is a *via media* between strict historicism and Nietzschean chaos. If it exists for constitutional interpretation and classicism in postmodern architecture, it can be taken even more fittingly for a classic like the *Aeneid,* which is even richer in content and more adaptable because it deals with the values of a complex civilization, with the dilemmas of human existence, and with the basic moral and existential questions that people have at all times.[6] For all these reasons, the *Aeneid* is a surprisingly modern epic. We can read it for our benefit in modern times without doing violence to the intentions of its Roman author.

Such a "historical" reading, therefore, is more than a mere exercise in positivism. As twentieth-century readers, we inevitably bring some of our own contemporary interests and assumptions to an ancient work. We saw the dangers of too unbridled an inclination of this sort in the plethora of explanations for the decline and fall of Rome. But it is possible to avoid such extremes. We may be interested in other aspects of the *Aeneid* than were its readers in the Middle Ages or the literati of Augustan France and England. Yet the aspects we prefer to explore today are not extraneous to the *Aeneid* but are immanent in it. One constant in the "reception" of the *Aeneid* is, as C. M. Bowra has well observed, that it "has succeeded in doing something that no epic has done before or since, and helped many generations of men to formulate their views on the chief problems of human existence."[7] For such reasons, classical works transcend time, place, race, and gender and are truly universal.

The complexity of our times, in fact, has been very conducive to furthering the proper appreciation of the *Aeneid,* which had suffered a great deal since the Romantic period. Aeneas is not a rebel against authority, and the world in which he has to make his choices is anything but black and white or Manichean. The other legacy the epic had to overcome is centuries of viewing Aeneas as a proto-Christian and the *Aeneid* as a school text and imperial propaganda. Take them all together and you have the "Vergil Cult" as denounced by Robert Graves: "Whenever a Golden Age of stable government, full churches, and expanding wealth dawns among western nations, Vergil always returns to supreme favor. His reputation flourished in Florence in Dante's day, Amsterdam in the day of the young republic, Paris under Louis XIV, London under Queen Anne and Queen Victoria, Baltimore in the first half of the 19th century, Boston in the second half, and Potsdam under Kaiser Wilhelm II."[8] Fortunately, and even on Mr. Graves' terms, the second half of our century is still up for definition.

Some Points of Convergence and Divergence

It is a time in which we distrust stereotypes, pat solutions, and clichés of heroism. The very first appearance of Aeneas in the epic that bears his name deliberately exemplifies these sensibilities and sets the tone for their exploration throughout the poem.

Aeneas is introduced to us not in the midst of a heroic exploit or, quite in contrast with Achilles' first appearance in the *Iliad,* a macho altercation with another warrior. He confronts death, which is the issue on which Achilles' heroism centers, but he has no control over it. He is not given an Achillean choice between a short and glorious life and a long and uneventful one; the choices he will have to make are different, less simple, and less outwardly heroic. That is why he is stripped of any of the external trappings of heroism in the poet's first direct presentation of him. With his weakening limbs and on the verge of drowning, he is the epitome of human frailty. "I sing of warfare and the man of war" is how Vergil had introduced him in the first line of the epic, but warfare now is the stuff of wishful recollection. Aeneas is thrown back on his last human and inner resources, and that will be the primary dimension of his heroism. And the first time we hear him speak, he wishes he were back at Troy (1. 92–101):

> At once Aeneas' limbs weaken with the chill of death.
> He groans and stretching out both hands to heaven
> says this: "Oh three and four times blessed you
> who met death before their fathers' eyes beneath
> Troy's lofty walls! Bravest of the Greeks,
> Diomedes! Why could I not go down on Ilium's
> battlefield and breathe out my soul at your hand,
> at Troy where fierce Hector lies struck by Achilles' spear,
> where huge Sarpedon lies, and where the river Simois
> seizes and sweeps beneath his waves so many shields
> and helmets and bodies of the brave!"

The prayer is based on Odysseus' in *Odyssey* 5.306ff., and the changes Vergil makes are significant, as always. Odysseus refers to his homecoming in Ithaca. For Aeneas, Troy is still home, and the nostalgic references to Troy are expanded; the phrase "before their fathers' eyes," for instance, has no equivalent in the Homeric model. Aeneas' plea goes beyond the warrior's wish to have died nobly in battle; it appeals to the typically Roman inclination to turn to the past especially in times of duress. The whole scene, therefore, is very programmatic. Unlike Homer, Vergil begins the events in his epic with the hero's shipwreck, thus emphasizing his being anything but a superman. And the central theme of his first utterance becomes the wish to return to the past.

In Rome, that was a powerful mind-set indeed. We saw one of its manifestations earlier in the context of the Roman view of decline.[9] What mattered in all things to the Romans was the *mos maiorum*, i.e., the custom of the ancestors. It was the quintessence of decisions not only in the realms of values and morals but also of legislation and politics. The raw challenge of it led to the assassinations of reformers like the Gracchi brothers, who often are superficially compared to John and Robert Kennedy, and Julius Caesar. The excessive appreciation of past writers frustrated even Horace; we might change Santayana's dictum by saying that the Romans worshiped the past so much that they condemned themselves to repeating it. For the Roman reader, the sounding of this theme at the very beginning of the *Aeneid* would strike more than one responsive chord.

Vergil's outlook in that regard, however, was far more modern than ancient. His orientation is part of the complex blend of tradition and innovation that informed Augustan culture, as we will see in the next chapter. He states the theme so powerfully because Aeneas and, perhaps, the Romans need to be weaned away from it. Aeneas is unique among ancient heroes in that he cannot go home again. Side by side with Vergil's extolling of such traditional Roman virtues as social responsibility is his emphasis on the impossibility of a literal return to the past. It becomes a keynote of the epic, and a few examples will suffice to illustrate it.

In Book 3, Aeneas' wish to return to the past is actually fulfilled when he encounters Hector's widow, Andromache, now married to Helenus, another Trojan. They have transformed their habitat in western Greece into a replica of Troy, a sort of Disneyland Troy, complete with the Scaean Gates and even the river Simois, the very river mentioned by Aeneas in his first speech. The architecture is only the most palpable manifestation of the inhabitants' attitude: they have retreated into the past and live there. Andromache has resolutely recreated her life before the fall of Troy. Her values, beliefs, and thinking are at home there, and everything has to conform to them. To her, Aeneas' son Ascanius is not a future ruler, but a surrogate for her own dead son, Astyanax. She gives him a gift, a Phrygian cloak, that ties him to his past, and she expresses the hope that the martial virtue of Hector will live on in Ascanius. Aeneas is strongly affected by this pull toward the past, but he recognizes its limitations and realizes that such a return is not for him although the past, to any good Roman (and even some modern politicians), is a solid symbol of felicity. His poignant farewell epitomizes the difference between their outlook and his (3.493–495):

Live happily [*felices*]; your fortune is already achieved.
We, however, are bandied from one vicissitude to the other.
For you there is quiet rest [*quies*].

"Quiet rest" is precisely the ideal that Venus had envisaged for Aeneas earlier; we will discuss that important passage shortly. The next way stations of Aeneas' progressive separation from the past are his leave-taking from Dido, who restored him to his status as an oriental prince, his encounter with the insubstantial shades of the Trojan war heroes in the underworld, and his introduction to Roman austerity by King Evander in Book 8. The culmination comes with the pact between Jupiter and Juno near the end of the epic: the Trojan nation will lose its separate identity and merge with the Latins into the Italian and Roman race. Vitality comes not from withdrawing into the past but from using it as a basis for transformation. It is the same notion that we saw at work in the classicism of current architecture.

By contrasting Venus' ideal with Jupiter's early in the epic, Vergil combines this notion with the equally significant theme of human achievement and, especially, its price. As Athena does at the beginning of the *Odyssey,* Venus pleads for Aeneas to be granted a homecoming. She understands that it cannot be a return to Troy, and therefore she asks for the next best thing, a transfer of Troy to Italy. The promised Roman world domination receives only a brief mention from her. Instead, she dwells on the hoped-for end of Aeneas' toils and his attaining a peaceful existence in Italy on the model of another Trojan refugee, Antenor. Antenor was able to retire from all his troubles and settle down in peace: (1.247–249)

> He was allowed to found Padua, make a home for
> Trojans there—could give his people a name, and nail up
> His arms, could settle down to enjoy peace and quiet.
> (C. Day Lewis trans.)

The Latin original for that last line reads as follows:

> . . . nunc placida compostus pace quiescit.

The idea of peace and tranquillity is brought out four times. *Placida* (hence English "placid") goes with *pace,* the word for peace. *Compostus* is the same as "composed"; literally, it means "put together again" and hence "quiet," "peaceful," "undisturbed," etc. *Quiescit*—think of "quiescent"—means to rest (in quiet or peace). That, then, is the core of Venus' ideal. She wants a happy, uneventful, undisturbed existence for Aeneas. Antenor hung up his Trojan arms; Aeneas should be able to do the same and enjoy the Biedermeier happiness of the Paduan angle of repose.

That, of course, is not how great nations are founded. In his reply, Jupiter forcefully reiterates the ideal that Vergil formulated in his earlier work, the *Georgics,* and that became an integral part of the Augustan ethos. It is that of ongoing effort, blood, sweat, and tears. Aeneas will reach Italy all right, but

In Italy he will fight a massive war,
Beat down fierce armies, then for the people there
Establish city walls and a way of life.
                    (1.263–264; Fitzgerald trans.)

There is no grandeur without exertion and sacrifice. It is all going to be worth it: ultimately, wars will come to an end and harsh centuries will soften (1.291), but that will not happen until hundreds of years later. No instant gratification here. The effort will culminate with the age of Augustus and all its blessings; but there is a long road to be traveled, and Aeneas' travails will be only the beginning. This is a long perspective indeed. It accentuates not only the long and ongoing effort that goes into building a great civilization, but also the selflessness that is demanded in the process.

Related to this perspective is the reorientation of the time frame of the *Aeneid*. In line with the earlier Roman epic tradition and contemporary expectations, Vergil could have written an epic centering on Augustus and incorporating the story of Aeneas by flashbacks. The essential difference would have been the vantage point: Roman history as seen from the pinnacle, i.e., the reign of Augustus. In other words, there would have been the notion that the goal had been attained and the high point reached, with the rest of the story appearing as mere preliminaries to that final achievement. Instead, Vergil turned the perspective inside out. Chronologically, we are at the beginning of the journey, and it is a well-known aphorism that the journey is better than the arrival. The dynamics of getting there give a more vivid sense of the required effort than the more static nature of the culmination. Life is a process, characterized by steady toil and struggle, rather than restful repose at a fixed point. It is more meaningful to work toward a goal than to enjoy the fruits of reaching it. Renewal is more important than fruition that leads to stagnation. The simple fact is that the reorientation of the time perspective in the *Aeneid*—it is an *Aeneid* rather than an *Augusteid*—has implications that are more than chronological: they reflect an ethos, which Vergil outlined in the *Georgics* and which permeates much of the Augustan age.[10]

All this provides a good illustration of the relation between a "historical" and a "modern" reading. One important historical factor for Vergil's insistence on divesting Aeneas of his Trojan home is that at the time of the composition of the *Aeneid*, any associations with the East were problematic to the point of disrepute. In the preceding decade, Octavian and Maecenas had waged a clamorous propaganda war against Cleopatra and Mark Antony, portraying the latter as a feckless prisoner of both her and Eastern decadence, and as a traitor to anything Roman. This was not the time to play up Aeneas' Eastern descent, which in fact is ridiculed by the African suitor of Dido (4.215–217). In addition, there is the Homeric perspective. Vergil well recognized that at the heart of the *Iliad* lay Achilles' existential dilemma: the choice, which we mentioned earlier, between a short and glorious life and a long and uneventful one. In the end, it is a choice Achilles makes as an individual for himself, without any regard for society. After a century of civil wars, from the assassination of Tiberius Gracchus in 132 B.C. to the battle of Actium in 31 B.C., that was an unacceptable ethos for the hero of Rome's national epic: rank individualism, egotism, and megalomania of Achillean proportions had played a major part in fomenting the civil wars and bringing Rome close to disintegration. One aspect of Vergil's redefinition of the heroic ideal, therefore, is the return to the Roman ethos of social responsibility, which we will discuss shortly. Related to it is the other and more existential dimension: the meaningful life exhausts itself in neither of the Achillean alternatives but is long and laborious. It is the process, and not the achievement itself, that provides the true meaning. It is a concept familiar to us from existentialism; even Sartre's famous definition of hell (*l'enfer, ce sont les autres*) is applicable to Aeneas. The reason the *Aeneid* allows of such interpretation is that Vergil, instead of writing an epic about the triumphs of Aeneas, let alone Augustus, chose the timeless moment of the *labores* of his hero. Aeneas is literally suspended in time: he cannot return to Troy, and the completion of the journey begun by him will not take place until centuries later. Thus we have the apparent paradox that Vergil's hero, who was so inextricably woven into the fabric of the Roman and Augustan experience that no later writer dared to adapt him to his own time—quite in contrast to Achilles, Ulysses, and Herakles, for instance[11]—turns out to be one of the most timeless, if not the most timeless, of the ancient heroes.

Modern readers of the *Aeneid,* therefore, should both make every effort to inform themselves properly about the historical circumstances of the epic and, at the same time, be open to the poem's transcendence of them. As we know from the study of heroic myths, their quintessence is the journey, whether literal or figurative, and that almost archetypal aspect makes them so meaningful to us.[12] Or, to give another example of a historical element in the characterization of Aeneas and its extension into our time: Aeneas is a refugee. That again would find a receptive audience in Rome after the end of the civil wars when many people had similarly been torn from the land. It met with a similar response in a Europe full of "displaced persons" after World War II and even now, and the notion can be transferred, without forcing any premises, to human spiritual existence too; one of the Vergilian exhibits during the bimillenary of his death bore the appropriate title: Man Is Only a Refugee on Earth. Not coincidentally, perhaps, the location was a West German town not far from the Iron Curtain at the time.[13]

Similar considerations apply to the notion of the *Aeneid* as an imperial or even imperialistic poem. Emphasis on that perspective, for instance, has led to the juxtaposition of the *Aeneid* in modern curricula with the writings of Frantz Fanon, the African anticolonialist who died in 1961. This can make for lively contrast, but it can also perpetuate stereotyped antinomies and prevent a more nuanced approach to the text. Interpretation of that aspect of the poem, in fact, has given rise to several polarities of this sort. Several passages predict the greatness of Rome: Jupiter's pronouncement "I have given them [i.e., the Romans] empire without end" (1.279) is a stellar example, and there are others. Hence the time-honored notion, traceable even to the early centuries after Vergil, that his epic was essentially a glorification of Rome. In our century, glorification is equated with uncritical adulation, and the concept of propaganda was injected into the discussion under the influence of the model of modern authoritarian regimes, a situation that cast a long shadow on the historiography of the Augustan age.[14] It became obvious, of course, that Vergil's view of the Roman achievement is more complex, and as a result several influential, but basically reductionist, antitheses were created to cope with the phenomenon. When Vergil emphasizes suffering, alienation, and loss, he could not be a good propagandist and therefore was quickly transformed into an anti-Augustan and anti-imperialist. To explain the existence of both aspects in the poem, critics resorted to such labels as the two voices of the *Aeneid* (quite a few more have been discovered by now), the tension between public and private, and the contrast between optimism and pessimism, the latter pair really being a sort of poor man's deconstructionism.

In actuality, Vergil's attitude to human and national achievement is utterly realistic and hardly needs to be defined with such straitjackets to be accessible to our modern sensibilities. As we know all too well, loss and achievement are complementary. There is a price to be paid for any great and exacting accomplishment, including suffering, agony, dilemma, isolation, and even death. It is because Vergil takes a balanced view of the human condition, and because the *Aeneid* really is about the human condition rather than just Rome, that these themes are reiterated with poignant honesty at important junctures of the epic.

The death of Marcellus at the end of Book 6 is a good example of the balance that this dimension provides. It comes after the lengthy preview of Rome's future leaders and her greatness, culminating in the succinct summary of the Roman national character (847–853). It is not chauvinistic, but it is undeniably one of the high points of the epic. Vergil, however, does not end on that note. Instead he opens up the other aspect of the life of a proud nation: there is sadness due to the loss of human potential. Rome is not a nation of supermen; Rome has had and will continue to have her share of grief and losses. Hence Vergil dwells on the death of young Marcellus (860–886). It was not even a death on the battlefield, in the line of duty to extend the Roman *imperium,* and therefore no moral is being pointed out nor is the connection between empire and young men having to die for it. Instead, Marcellus' death was a personal tragedy for Augustus, who was his uncle and had him in mind for the succession. The depiction of Rome and her glory is complemented by the evocation of the purely human feeling of loss and helplessness.

Another remarkably evocative description of both the inevitability and the wastefulness of the death of young people is the account of the death of Lausus near the end of Book 10. Lausus dies at the hands of Aeneas, and the scene is meant to contrast with Turnus' insolent behavior after the slaying of Pallas (10.490–505); but that is not our primary concern here. In its own right, the episode does enough to evoke our sympathy with Lausus. Vergil pointedly introduced him in Book 7 as a son who would be better off without the kind of father he had (653–654), and his father, Mezentius, comes closest to being the one truly villainous character in the *Aeneid*. Yet in battle, Lausus interposes his own body for his father (10.794–802) and he dares to take on the much superior Aeneas. Aeneas tries to warn him away—"Filial piety makes you lose your head," he says (812), and Aeneas is an expert on filial piety—but Lausus presses on. He is dispatched in two lines; infinitely more time is spent on the pity of his death and Aeneas' reaction. First there is a pathetic reminiscence of his home as Aeneas' sword pierces both his shield "and the shirt his mother had woven him, soft cloth of gold, so blood filled up the folds of it" (818–819). Then we see Aeneas' response, which has no parallel in previous epic (821–830):

> But seeing the look
> On the young man's face in death, a face so pale
> As to be awesome, then Anchises' son
> Groaned in profound pity. He held out
> His hand as filial piety, mirrored here,
> Wrung his own heart, and said:
> "O poor young soldier,
> How will Aeneas reward your splendid fight?
> How honor you, in keeping with your nature?
> Keep the arms you loved to use, for I
> Return you to your forebears, ash and shades,
> If this concerns you now. Unlucky boy,
> One consolation for sad death is this:
> You die by the sword-thrust of great Aeneas." (Fitzgerald trans.)

Again Vergil does not point to a schematic moral in terms of imperialism and anti-imperialism or optimism and pessimism. He states a fact of life: warriors, even young ones, have their own destiny and often even control it. The end result still is the loss of yet another promising human life. It is not a senseless loss, for it certainly made sense to Lausus. It reinforces, with the depiction of the deaths of many other young people especially in the second half of the *Aeneid* (and the Marcellus episode at the end of the first half can be seen as a prelude to this theme), the basic notion that such losses, whatever their cause, are as much a part of life as are success and triumph. Nor are they a total waste for civilization because they can raise civilization to a higher level of sensibility by the kind of response Aeneas exemplifies, a response that is characterized by humaneness, decency, chivalry, sensitivity, and grace. By contrast, Priam had to make an elaborate trip to Achilles to get Hector's corpse back, and Turnus kept the armor of the slain Pallas while wishing that Pallas' father, Evander, could have been present at the carnage. Aeneas' behavior is very different and illustrates that the loss of one person's potential can bring out the best in others. That is the intrinsic balance in this scene besides its function within the poem's overall balance of loss and attainment. It would be wildly unrealistic, of course, to expect Aeneas to behave like this in every battle scene of the *Aeneid*.

The sentiment Aeneas expresses in the last two lines, incidentally, should put us on our guard against anachronisms. To the modern reader, it may sound a bit presumptuous—"at least you were run over by a Mercedes and not a Volkswagen," as we might put it somewhat irreverently—but in Greco-Roman civilization, especially before the arrival of Christianity, the way you left this world really made a big difference. It was your final statement by which you would be remembered; this explains, for instance, Dido's elaborate preparations for her death by which she regains her initiative and pride. To have been slain by a lesser warrior than Aeneas indeed would have brought Lausus less glory.

There is no one-sidedness in the *Aeneid*, nor should there be any in its interpretation. The *Aeneid* is not a simple, jingoistic epic; conversely, it would be wrong to interpret Vergil's emphasis on the sacrifice and suffering with which Aeneas' path is strewn as a critique of the hero and his mission. It has often been noted that Vergil pays far more attention to the plight and grief of the civilians in the *Aeneid* than was customary in heroic epic. We see how the war affects the warriors' relatives, especially their mothers, and we even see Aeneas attack a civilian target, the Latin city, to force his opponents' hand. For us, all this is all too familiar. One of the real strengths of Vergil's presentation is that it is honest, avoids clichés, and is true to life without lacking in vision and idealism. To connect this with our theme of "historical" and "modern": while the *Aeneid* was strongly influenced by its times, its primary purpose was to portray the human condition in general. The Roman experience, which Vergil knew best and which was anything but homogeneous, was the means to that end. Some of the most incisive and useful remarks on this have been made by R. W. B. Lewis, a professor of English:

> In telling the story of the beginnings of Roman history, Virgil wanted to establish something about the peculiar character of Rome in a way which would explain something about the peculiar character of life itself. He sought to make Rome coextensive with the world: not merely as physically large as the visible cosmos (which Jupiter predicts it will be early in the first book), but of the very nature and essence of human experience. If, in so doing, he has seemed instead to

reverse his order and to make life a reflection of Rome, it may be because the task he set himself was beyond the powers even of Virgil . . . What else there is which appears inadequate in the conception of empire is not the fault of the poet; it is the inadequacy of experience. Virgil's view of Rome was identified with his view of life.[15]

Aeneas and Modern Concepts of Masculinity

Vergil's realistic perspective on Rome and the human condition deeply influenced the characterization of Aeneas, which is decidedly unromantic. Where others throw tantrums and emote, he maintains self-control. Where others look out for themselves, he looks out for others. At times he sacrifices his personal happiness and represses gratification to the point where, as some critics contend, he sacrifices any personality he otherwise might have. An anecdote attributed to William Butler Yeats is one of the kinder expressions of this perceived shortcoming: "A plain sailor man took a notion to study Latin and his teacher tried him with Vergil; after many lessons he asked him something about the hero. Said the sailor: 'What hero?' 'Why, Aeneas, the hero.' Said the sailor: 'Ach, a hero, him a hero? Bigob, I thought he was a priest.'"[16] The list of outright condemnations of Aeneas' behavior is a long one and tells us a great deal about cultural norms and prejudices at various times in history.

Should we simply settle for an aesthetic of reception at this point and say all of these interpretations are equally valid and constitute the whole spectrum of Aeneas' character? I think not. Instead, we have another good example of the convergence of the actual Vergilian Aeneas with modern perspectives that are less subjective. Recent work by David Gilmore, for instance, on the cultural construct of masculinity[17] in essence is an affirmation of the qualities of Aeneas that have led to so many misperceptions especially from the Romantic period on.

On the basis of fieldwork in various cultures around the globe, Gilmore, an anthropologist, well illustrates that manhood, properly defined, has little to do with machismo, aggression, and other such stereotypes. When he embarked on his research, he "was prepared to discover the old saw that conventional femininity is nurturing and passive and that masculinity is self-serving, egotistical, and uncaring. But I did not find this. One of my findings here is that manhood ideologies always include a criterion of selfless generosity even to the point of sacrifice. Again and again we find that 'real men' are those who give more than they take; they serve others" instead of following an "inconsequential path of personal self-fulfillment." Men nurture, too, but "this male giving is different from, and less demonstrative and more obscure than, the female. It is less direct, less immediate, more involved with externals; the 'other' involved may be society in general rather than specific persons." One principal male role, therefore, is "to reinvent and perpetuate the social order by will, to create something of value from nothing." Male sternness, tough-ness, and aggressiveness result from and are expected in conditions of threat and scarcity but, like female tenderness and gentleness, are directed to the same social end: the brave, altruistic, devoted, and industrious care of those who need protection and help.

The applicability of all these definitions to Aeneas needs no detailed dem-onstration. The underlying reason for the concurrence of the modern and the historical perspectives in this case is that manliness, the literal equivalent of the Latin *virtus,* is a result of the prevailing culture rather than of biological factors. One of the cardinal Roman virtues was social responsibility. Early Roman history in particular abounds with examples that drive the point home again and again, ranging from Horatius at the bridge to the Roman general Torquatus' having his son executed because, contrary to the orders governing the army, he vaingloriously fought in single combat against the commander of the enemy. Meritorious service to one's society was the highest ideal. Personal gratification of whatever kind was secondary: when Scipio, the conqueror of Carthage, has a dream vision in Cicero's *Republic* and, overcome with emotion, wants to join his father in the celestial regions immediately by committing suicide, his father admonishes him that he must serve his duty to the com-monwealth first. Real men, such as the *pater familias,* heroes, and statesmen, were supposed indeed to give more than take. The attitude was further refined by the concept of *pietas,* which means devoted responsibility to family, nation, and gods.

Social Responsibility: Vergil, Aeneas, and Vaclav Havel

Without engaging in the analogy hunting that we decried in connection with the relevance of Rome's decline and fall to our times, we do not have to look far for a similar appeal by the leader of a modern nation that is undergoing a renascence. The culmination of Czechoslovakian president Vaclav Havel's ad-dress to the U.S. Congress centered on the idea and ideal of responsibility, which he defined in terms that are almost Vergilian in their combination of morality, metaphysics, and call to action.[18] He prefaced this part of his speech by saying that "the salvation of this human world lies nowhere else than in the human heart, in the human power to reflect, in human meekness and in human responsibility." Then he condemned countervailing "interests of all kinds," including "personal" and "selfish" ones. He went on to make a refer-ence to metaphysics that is as old as the most famous play of another play-wright, the *Oedipus* of Sophocles: "We are still under the sway of the destruc-tive and vain belief that man is the pinnacle of creation, and not just a part of it, and therefore everything is permitted." This was followed by the central notion of Vergil's epic: "We are still incapable of understanding that the only genuine backbone of all our actions—if they are to be moral—is responsibility." Instead of a Roman hierarchy of responsibilities, Havel focused on that responsibility from which the others emanate, as they do in the *Aeneid*: "Responsibility to the Order of Being, where all our actions are indelibly recorded and where, and only where, they will be properly judged. The interpreter and mediator between us and this higher authority is what is traditionally referred to as human conscience." The corollary is, just as in the *Aeneid*, that individuals with high sensibilities cannot afford to shirk their responsibility while they know full well that the world, and the world of actual implementation, is far from perfect. "If the hope of the world lies in human consciousness, then it is obvious that the intellectuals cannot go on forever avoiding their share of responsibility for the world and their distaste for politics under an alleged need to be independent." You cannot simply be out for yourself.

Distrust of Rhetoric in the *Aeneid* and Today

It is not, of course, that the Romans always lived by these ideals,[19] and one of the purposes of the *Aeneid* was precisely to revive them. Therefore we have a hero who is anything but selfish and who, while always having free will, heeds, to use Havel's words, the higher authority's appeal to his responsibility for others and leaves Dido with whom he was supremely happy. Aeneas' behavior on that occasion and, in particular, the speeches he and Dido exchange have given occasion to endless debate. I do not wish to prolong it but want to call attention briefly to some nuances that we today may appreciate better than did the denizens of other ages.

One is the notion of complexity and dilemma as it extends into interpersonal relationships. While "communication" has become a buzzword, the reason for its overuse is the plain fact that it is so essential. Paradoxically, communication sometimes is most problematic with those to whom we are closest because we can be overprotective or mask with protectiveness our refusal to bring up difficult problems. So it is with Aeneas when he decides to part with Dido. There is no good way to tell her of his decision; any alternative has its drawbacks. He means well because he tells himself that he doesn't want to hurt her, and he tells himself, again, that he is not looking for the easy way out, but for the most gentle way and the right opportunity to tell her, as if there were any (4.291–294):

> In the meantime, assuming that Dido, who was the best,
> did not know and could not imagine that such great love could be broken,
> he would try for a way to approach her and for the gentlest times
> to speak to her, and for a suitable way to deal with these matters.

It is wishful thinking; the opportunity never presents itself, and when she finds out, the scene is a great deal worse than if he had told her at once—or is it? And when the time comes for speeches, he, in contrast to Dido, who speaks eloquently and impressively, does not resort to rhetorical power. This does not imply that his case is the weaker. Rather, it evinces a mistrust of powerful language, which tends to distort reality and exploit without restraint the emotions of speaker and audience alike.[20] By contrast with his Homeric predecessors, Aeneas is taciturn, and we even have statistics to back it up: Odysseus' speeches account for 18 percent of the *Odyssey*, Achilles' for 13 percent of the *Iliad*, Aeneas' for 6 percent of the *Aeneid*.[21] The Roman historian Tacitus, who mourned the passing of the Republic because he never had to live under it, bemoaned the decrease, which he equated with decline, of rhetoric during the reign of Augustus and his successors. That decrease, however, was not simply due to lack of talent but, as the *Aeneid* and even Roman treatises on rhetoric suggest, to a distrust of high-powered language as a tool to whip up emotions and thwart sound judgment. Cicero himself gave this advice to the prospective orator: "Nothing is more important in oratory than that the listener should sympathize with the speaker, and be moved himself in such a way that he is ruled by mental excitement and disturbance rather than by prudence and judgment. For men make more judgments through hate, love, desire, anger, joy, hope, fear, error, or some excitement of the mind, than through truth or prescription or any rule of the court, or formula of judgment, or laws."[22] The Romans had seen plenty of this kind of manipulation during the last decades of the Republic. The *Aeneid* reacts against that excess as it does against others of that period. Overwhelming rhetoric is suspect because it serves baser ends than genuinely furthering human interchange.[23]

Modern American attitudes are strikingly similar. With the exception of John Kennedy on occasion, no American president since Franklin Roosevelt has relied on commanding oratory.[24] That particular skill is distrusted because it conjures up the demagoguery of a Hitler or a Huey Long, as is well borne out, for instance, by Robert Penn Warren's *All the King's Men*. The rise of the visual media is only one factor in the decline of American public oratory to which British observers in particular, because they are used to the cut and thrust of verbal rapiers from their own politicians, habitually advert at the time of the presidential candidates' debates. The other is the basic distrust, akin to that of Romans, of high-powered, not to say highfalutin, language as being alien to meaningful communication. It connotes the ability to score points at the expense of substance and therefore commands the same credibility as photo opportunities and sound bites. The other extreme, of course, is represented by Chance the gardener in Jerzy Kosinski's *Being There* who parlays a two-hundred-word vocabulary, which he acquired entirely by watching television, into his prominence as a presidential adviser.

Internal Heroism and Strong Emotions

The other reason Vergil curtails such external skills as strong communication for his hero is the general shift from external to internal heroism.[25] Even more than the Homeric epics, the *Aeneid* focuses on the psychology, motivations, quandaries, and complexities of the characters. It is not that Aeneas lacks emotion; he tries to walk the fine line between repression and self-control by internalizing his feelings instead of expressing them openly. The tone is set again in the extended prologue to the epic where we see him cheer up his companions only to have the poet comment (1.208–209):

> So spoke Aeneas; and though his heart was sick with immense cares,
> he outwardly projected hope and repressed his deep anguish in his heart.

The sequel to the inefficacy of the speeches in Book 4, therefore, is a powerful simile that makes palpable the inner dimension of Aeneas and the depth of his emotion and self-control (441–449):

> As when some stalwart oak-tree, veteran of the Alps,
> Is assailed by a wintry wind whose veering gusts tear at it,
> Trying to root it up; wildly whistle the branches,
> The leaves come flocking down from aloft as the bole is battered;
> But the tree stands firm on its crag, for high as its head is carried
> Into the sky, so deep do its roots go down towards Hades:
> Even thus was the hero buffeted for long with every kind of
> Pleading, and in his great heart he felt cares through and through;
> His mind remained unchanged; the tears fall in vain.[26]

The psychological state of the hero is exquisitely rendered by the corresponding details in the world of the simile. The tears are those of Aeneas, but may be those of others too.

But Vergil was careful again not to portray his hero in too schematic a fashion. Throughout the battle scenes of the last four books in particular, Aeneas repeatedly bursts into anger and vents it openly. The *Aeneid*, in fact, culminates with such a scene. Because of the traditional—and un-Vergilian—emphasis on the first six books, this aspect of Aeneas used to receive scant attention. When it finally did, it obviously did not fit the established interpretation with its heavy emphasis on Aeneas as a proto-Christian or Stoic, who was making the pilgrim's progress toward a charitable and imperturbable disposition that was not to be debased by strong emotions. The thesis, therefore, was amended by the supposition that Aeneas' nonconformance to his posited behavior as a Stoic saint indicated a character flaw. What is more, this was authorial intention and a strong indication that Vergil called into question the achievement of his hero, Augustus, and Rome. Variants of this argument have dominated the discussion of the *Aeneid* for the past quarter century.

What the presence of the strong emotional element in Aeneas' behavior suggests, however, is that it should be discussed in its own right and that the previous thesis should be discarded rather than be supplemented by more extraneous moralizing. When it comes to the evaluation of anger in particular, we are again looking at a remarkable convergence between Vergil's time and ours. Anger was one of the most frequent topics in ancient ethics, and it was rarely treated in a reductionist fashion, especially when directed against someone, like Turnus, who has committed a manifest wrong.[27] "In dealing with the man who is totally perverse and wicked and cannot be entreated one must give free course to wrath," writes Plato. "Therefore we affirm that it is fitting that the good man should be both passionate and gentle each time" (*Laws* 731D). Punishment should not be administered in cold blood, but with angry emotion; that is a notion we frequently find in Greek and Roman orators who practiced in the courts. Aristotle goes into a great deal more detail and lists various categories of circumstance and human behavior when anger is appropriate. "In respect to anger," he concludes, "we have excess, deficiency, and observance of the mean" (*Nic. Ethics* 1108a4). The three characters in the *Aeneid* who are in complete conformity with these categories are, respectively, Turnus, Latinus, and Aeneas. Even the Epicureans allowed for anger on the part of the wise man. It is only the Stoics who condemned anger summarily, and there is no indication that most Romans lived by Stoic precepts.

What about anger today? Its assessment is summed up best by the following sentence from one of the many books on the subject: "The arousal of anger clearly has a multi-faceted role in human behavior."[28] Similar to Milton, who characterized anger as one of the two most rational faculties of man,[29] several modern psychologists equate it with emotional maturity—as distinguished from hate and hostility, which are considered indicative of emotional immaturity—or, at any rate, regard it as a constructive phenomenon. Due attention is given, as in the ancient tradition, to both the positive and negative aspects of anger. In related discussions, theoreticians like Norbert Elias would argue that the essential element in the "process of civilization" is a change in the structure of emotions in the direction of tighter controls; this concept is close to what the sociologist Talcott Parsons has described as the institutionalization of the neutralizing of affects.[30]

There was no consensus about anger in antiquity, nor is there now except for the recognition, which has escaped many Vergilian scholars, that it is a complex phenomenon. For that very reason—and, as we know from Cicero and others, there was a plethora of popular treatises on how to deal with anger—Vergil chose it as the keynote for the conclusion of his epic when Aeneas kills Turnus "inflamed by fury and terrible in his anger" (12.945–946). Different responses are possible, depending on such factors as cultural and philosophical orientation, and not all will have the same merit. But, as Jasper Griffin has put it so well in commenting on the multilayered and contradictory nature of Vergil's characters, "this complexity of response is a vital part of the poet's intention and of the greatness of the poem."[31] In the case of Aeneas' anger, it is not cultural or psychological anachronisms that lead to misinterpretations today, but reductionisms. They stem in part, as we have seen, from the tradition that made Aeneas into an unduly monolithic character. They also result from the tendency of the old New Criticism to regard a poem as a self-contained entity without regard for the historical context and, at times, to treat even within that framework all occurrences of a theme like anger—Juno's, Aeneas', and Turnus'—as equivalents instead of seeing them like the musical procedure of *tema con variazioni*. What is remarkable in the final scene is not just Aeneas' full-blooded and justified anger but also his humane sensibility: "Touched in his inmost being, Aeneas hesitates . . . an extraordinary moment of humanity; for the epic warrior never hesitates."[32] The humanity of the hero—he listens to Turnus' appeal, whereas Turnus earlier in the book simply rages at Latinus'—leads to his dilemma, and that dilemma, in turn, reinforces the hero's humanity. To the end, and quite in contrast to the merely aesthetic completion that the ending of the *Iliad* represents, Aeneas has to make difficult and agonizing choices. He is a hero who is true to real life.

As we have seen, all this encourages the easy assimilation of such a character to our own times, which appreciate complexity, dilemmas, and internal heroism. In terms of literary models, some of these characteristics, without the grand meaning, vision of the future, or redeeming social aspects we find in the *Aeneid*, already apply to Jason, the hero of the *Argonautica*, a product of Hellenistic times, which again were not unlike ours; much of what Lyotard says about the postmodern condition[33] has its parallels in the Hellenistic period. So far from being a superman, Jason is no different from a Hellenistic citizen and in no way is up to the task of heading up a mythical exploit. The countervailing matrix in Vergil's multilayered characterization of Aeneas is that of Hercules, the premier Greek hero whose own characterization by that time had become highly diverse. A Herculean pattern runs through the entire *Aeneid*, ranging from Juno's unjust persecution and the hero's labors to allusions to Roman cult and Hercules' popularity in Italy.[34] But there is a further dimension. Hercules, "the best of men," even more than Achilles, "the best of the Achaeans," is the quintessential hero because there is a certain isolation and rugged grandeur about him, and while he is not hostile to such civilizing virtues as moderation and consideration, he is also capable of extraordinary passions. And that is the Aeneas we see after the death of Pallas in Book 10, which evokes the story of Achilles' rage after the death of Patroclus. Not every opponent is treated like Lausus. Aeneas mows down enemies, including two suppliants and a priest, and he cruelly disparages their supplications. I leave the moralizing to others, although I suspect that even Christian soldiers fought that way in the Crusades and on other occasions.

Rather, such passages should alert us to the important aspect of the "otherness" of literary works from cultures and periods other than our own. Deconstruction, by allowing us to make everything over in our own image, deprives literature of this essential characteristic or, in John Updike's words: "It is in the nature of deconstruction to rob literary works of their intended content, substituting instead the subliminal messages the author did not intend."[35] We have seen that an appreciation of the intended content, so far from being purely philological and historical, can be enhanced by our own experiences with present-day society and culture without our resorting to forced premises. The *Aeneid* is an epic that appeals greatly to modern sensibilities. But there is that "otherness" too, and we should be mindful of it.

Short Bibliography and Suggestions for Further Reading

Anderson, W. S. *The Art of the "Aeneid"* (Englewood Cliffs 1969).

Cairns, Francis. *Virgil's Augustan Epic* (Cambridge 1989).

Commager, Steele, ed. *Virgil: A Collection of Critical Essays* (Englewood Cliffs 1966).

Griffin, Jasper. *Virgil* (Oxford 1986).

Harrison, S. J., ed. *Oxford Readings in Vergil's "Aeneid"* (Oxford 1990).

Johnson, W. R. *Darkness Visible: A Study of Vergil's "Aeneid"* (Berkeley 1976).

Pöschl, Viktor. *The Art of Virgil: Image and Symbol in the "Aeneid"* (Ann Arbor 1962).

Putnam, M. C. J. *The Poetry of the "Aeneid"* (Cambridge, Mass. 1965).

Stahl, H. P. "The Death of Turnus." In Raaflaub and Toher (see Bibliography to ch. 4) 174–211.

Williams, R. D. *The "Aeneid"* (London 1987).

IV

Leadership, Values, and the Question of Ideology: The Reign of Augustus

Some Views of Augustus

Every age, as we saw in the previous chapters, has a tendency to reinterpret antiquity in its own image, whether we are dealing with architectural adaptations, hortatory uses of Rome's fall, or the tailoring of literary works and characters to contemporary concerns. At its best, this is an ongoing process of keeping the classical tradition vital; at their worst, such efforts lapse into cultural and psychological anachronisms. The appraisal of the age of Augustus, arguably the most influential period of Roman history, is no exception. It is a period in need of considerable reassessment[1] and can benefit from being discussed in terms of issues that are at the center of the political discourse today, such as leadership, values, and ideology, because these issues were central to the age itself. A brief look at two major views of the Augustan age, that of the eighteenth century and the dominant interpretation of the last fifty years, will explain why other perspectives are needed and timely and, at the same time, are true to the spirit of that important historical period.

Many of our notions of Augustanism go back to eighteenth-century England and France or, more precisely, to the view scholars have developed of that century and its literature. Then as now, "Augustan" implied a variety of characteristics, most of them positive, although that does not necessarily apply to eighteenth-century views of Augustus himself. Briefly, the main connotations are: restoration of political stability, stable government by an enlightened monarch, nurturing of the arts, refinement of literary style, and patronage of great authors, artists, and architects. In that context, Augustanism is the corollary of royalism and absolutism, especially in France; when republican government prevails, Augustanism recedes. Perceptions like these are at the base of Robert Graves' famous harangue about the "Vergil Cult," which I cited earlier.[2]

The peace of the Augustans, however, died some years ago at the hands of the inevitable revisionism that started to scrutinize the phenomenon of English Augustanism more closely.[3] Scholars have been arguing about the precise meaning of the term and whether it is prescriptive or descriptive. There has been the increasing recognition that, certainly, Augustus himself was a controversial figure in Augustan England. Criticism of him by eighteenth-century writers runs the whole gamut of human vices coupled with the unbridled power to exert them. In that vein, he was considered a butcher, a torturer, a pathic, a lecher, as incestuous, as a legacy hunter, a censor, or even a book burner. Of course, as one astute observer has noted, "nobody is perfect, as the nation successively ruled by Oliver Cromwell and Charles Stuart no doubt remembered," and all these characteristics were not even considered his main faults. Rather, the dominant objections—largely stemming from the admiration for the Roman historian Tacitus—"were to his perceived destruction of the balanced constitution of the Roman Republic, the fatal precedent he set for other rulers, and the establishment of an empire whose slavery and fall were inherent in its creation." In the equivalent of reception aesthetics in political and historical thought, Augustus' reputation became no more than a cork tossed by the tide of different ideologies of government. Antiroyal ideology influenced the views of Pope, Swift, and others, whereas, to shift countries, Augustus once more emerged as a revered role model in the France of Napoleon Bonaparte.

The view that has prevailed over the past half century was similarly influenced by contemporary history. Otto von Premerstein's influential *Vom Wesen und Werden des Prinzipats* and Sir Ronald Syme's classic *The Roman Revolution* were written in the late 1930s when the shadows of Hitler and Mussolini loomed large. The *duce* cultivated association with Rome's mightiest ruler, and therefore the bimillennium of Augustus' birth was celebrated with all pomp and circumstance in 1937, amidst a program of archaeological excavation demonstrating the grandeur of Augustan Rome. Syme, who dedicated his book to his parents and fatherland, continued the analogy in his own way. The point was implicit, but not to be missed: Augustus was indeed the forerunner of the dictators of the 1930s. Like them, he was basically a successful party leader and *condottiere* who wound up in power. The top-down model of governance was extended to the literature of the age as the poets basically followed the wishes of the Roman Goebbels, Maecenas, and became the emperor's propagandists for "the national programme." In this and subsequent publications, Syme enlarged on his thesis with an impressive amount of research in prosopography, i.e., the study of individuals—who they were, to whom they were related, what their relations were with the emperor. But as Arnaldo Momigliano observed in a fundamental review of *The Roman Revolution* in 1940, while prosopographical research has the great virtue of identifying individuals and small groups, it does not explain their spiritual needs: it simply presupposes them[4]—which is a polite way of saying that it leaves them unaccounted for. It is precisely, of course, the attention to these issues that kept the Augustan age vital and inspirational in its own time and for later ages. They have begun to be addressed in a more nuanced fashion in recent discussions of Augustan literature and art;[5] it is useful to do the same for the interrelated concepts of leadership, values, and ideology.

Leadership: The Moral Dimension

It is fashionable today to hype leadership, in inverse proportion to its actual manifestations, in contexts ranging from presidential campaigns to the related concern about America's decline. In the process, it has become an eminently elastic and sometimes meaningless concept. Still, while it obviously includes many intangibles, it has been discussed perceptively over the past decade by political scientists. The preeminent study, distinguished for its documentation from modern though not ancient history and for its insightful definitions, is that by James MacGregor Burns, a well-known American historian and biographer of Franklin Roosevelt and John Kennedy. He criticizes earlier students of leadership for their fascination with power and argues that emphasis has led them to ignore the far more important task of a leader to inculcate purpose. The two basic types of leadership he identifies coincide easily with the views of historians, both modern and ancient, of Augustus. One is the category of transactional leadership. Leaders approach followers with an eye to exchanging one thing for another; this involves rewards for political support or, to give a specific example, such favors as the remission, after Augustus' consolidation of power in 31 B.C., of certain sums that the tax farmers, the publicans, owed the treasury. In addition, the normal everyday activities of simply carrying out the government's business comprise transactional leadership. They are well documented in Syme's book and in Fergus Millar's exhaustive study on *The Emperor in the Roman World*.

More important is what Burns defines as "transforming leadership," which transcends all that. It seeks to instill values and to satisfy needs that are more than material, and it may convert leaders into moral agents:

> [Transforming leadership] occurs when one or more persons engage with others in such a way that leaders and followers raise one another to higher levels of motivation and morality. . . . Various names are used for such leadership: elevating, mobilizing, inspiring, uplifting, exhorting, evangelizing. The relationship can be moralistic, of course. But transforming leadership ultimately becomes *moral* in the sense that it raises the level of human conduct and ethical aspiration of both the leader and the led, and thus has a transforming effect on both. . . . The fundamental process is an elusive one; it is, in large part, to make conscious what lies unconscious among followers.[6]

Condensing some of Burns' illustrative discussion, Thomas Peters and Robert Waterman list a set of concrete characteristics of transforming leaders and their agenda:

The transforming leader is concerned with minutiae, as well. But he is concerned with a different kind of minutiae; he is concerned with the tricks of the pedagogue, the mentor, the linguist—the more successfully to become the value shaper, the exemplar, the maker of meanings. His job is much tougher than that of the transactional leader, for he is the true artist, the true pathfinder. After all, he is both calling forth and exemplifying the urge for transcendence that unites us all. At the same time, he exhibits almost boorish consistency over long periods of time in support of his one or two transcending values. No opportunity is too small, no forum too insignificant, no audience too junior.[7]

All these characteristics are singularly present in Augustus. To turn to the most important, the outstanding quality of the reign of Augustus was precisely this concern for moral transformation. He was not content with merely restabilizing the mechanics of government. After one hundred years of civil war, the last and bloodiest chapter coming in Octavian's struggle against Mark Antony and Cleopatra, the Romans probably would have been satisfied with a good transactional leader; so far from being the victorious head of a political party, Augustus had his true base of support in the nonpolitical classes of Italy who had no higher ambitions than to get on with their lives and businesses without seeing them disrupted by selfish Roman politicos in the name of liberty (*libertas*) in which they did not share. But Augustus went beyond this. He sounded the note of moral revitalization and followed through on it; it was a time for rededicating the state to values, virtues, ideas, and ideals. Especially in the arts and literature, the phenomenon is more complex than mere propaganda and instead is a reciprocal process in which the emperor's role is hard to pin down precisely. Therefore it is better to look first at the so-called moral legislation of Augustus where the degree of his participation is clearly discernible.

Throughout his reign, and possibly from the very beginning, Augustus made a determined effort (in which he succeeded by 18 B.C.) to enact laws governing marriage and marital conduct.[8] Marriage was made a duty for men between the ages of twenty-five and sixty and for women between twenty and fifty. In the case of divorce or death of a spouse, remarriage within two years or less was compulsory. Adultery was not left any longer to be handled privately within the family but became a matter for the public courts. And there were incentives and penalties. Career advancement was faster if a man had three children or more; unmarried men and women were forbidden to attend the ever popular shows and spectacles; and inheritances of the unmarried would revert to the state. Though aimed primarily at the nobility, this amounted to massive interference with the private life of virtually every Roman not just by modern standards but by contemporary ones as well: there were howls of protest and massive resistance.

Augustus did not relent. In the post-Watergate era, we increasingly hear the cant, swelling again during and after the Reagan eighties, that the government sets the moral tone for society. In Augustus, we have an example of one leader's response to this postulate. Many different explanations have been suggested for Augustus' moral legislation, from stimulation of the birthrate to a crackdown on the nobles, but in essence his motives were profoundly moral. Two basic reasons were involved. One was the equation of morality with social responsibility, whose importance we already discussed in connection with Vergil's Aeneas, and especially with responsibility for a family. Augustus himself developed this point at length in a temperamental speech to the unmarried equestrians,[9] and we find a further elaboration of the theme in Horace's *Odes* (3.6, 3.24), where the decline of married life is causally linked with the Roman civil wars. The message in all three is that if individuals live only for their own benefit, society will suffer. Marriage and children, therefore, are the moral remedy for selfishness.

The emperor's concern with morality, however, was hardly that of a simplistic zealot. The reason is that ethical superiority was viewed as a prerequisite for Rome's imperial mission. When Rome had involved herself in the internal affairs of Greece and ultimately conquered all of her in 146 B.C., questions had naturally arisen about Roman imperialism and its justification. The principle that might makes right was not one advocates of Rome's expansion wished to cite, and the utilitarian argument was rejected also. Instead, pro-Roman Greek philosophers were instrumental in shaping the following conceptual framework: to the best—and the term has a strong ethical connotation—rule was given by nature herself for the benefit of the weak. The latter benefited because the license of committing injustices was taken away from the indigenous evildoers. Consequently, the peoples conquered by the Romans were much better off because they came to share in a higher standard of civilization and justice. Instead of anarchy, instead of constant strife of one part of the population against the other, there now were peace and order and the rule of law. The Roman rule, then, was based not on the law of the stronger, but on the right of the better and of the morally superior.[10]

We may regard the notion with utter cynicism due to the plethora of historical exemplars who since then have advanced similar arguments with total disingenuousness. That should not blind us to the fact that, at the time, such justifications were taken quite seriously and were expressed by several Roman and Greek authors. It is precisely the failure of the Romans to live up to this moral basis of their imperial mission that made Augustus so insistent on instilling a sense of morality into his people by means of the last resort, legislation. The behavior of the Roman state during the last century of the Republic had given the lie to any Roman claims to moral superiority; we are, again, not talking about "decadence" in the same loose way as moralists have done in connection with the decline and fall of Rome. Instead, Roman authors like Sallust single out the mistreatment of Rome's subjects as the epitome of moral decline. Concern about this loss is a standard theme in the first generation of

Augustan writers, i.e., those who had lived through the final decades of the Republic. Besides Horace and Vergil, we find its most concise formulation in Livy's preface to his monumental history of Rome where he reiterates the nexus between morality and empire. The keynote of his work, he writes, will be to demonstrate "what the life, what the *mores* were, by what kind of men and by what moral character, as shown in their actions at home and in war, the Roman dominion was brought forth and increased." That is all the more important as the mores by now have reached their nadir: in our times, Livy continues, "we can endure neither our vices nor their remedies."

The writers' voicing of these concerns was hardly the result of heavy-handed pressure by Augustus; the posited top-down model is simply inadequate. Instead, we see a perfect example of several of Burns' definitions of transforming leadership: the conscious articulation of purposes shared by both leaders and followers; the shaping of values; and the mobilization of institutional, political, and psychological resources to arouse the motives of the followers—all in terms of a moralistic relationship. "Transforming leadership," to repeat one of Burns' central formulations, "ultimately becomes *moral* in that it raises the level of human conduct and ethical aspiration of both the leader and the led, and thus has a transforming effect on both."

As we have seen, Augustus did not leave that transforming effect to chance or charisma but prodded it with the help of legislation. The legislation was aimed primarily at his strongest followers, the new senatorial majority from the small towns of Italy. Understandably, these new men (*novi homines*) at first had a social inferiority complex vis-à-vis the established Roman aristocracy. In the course of time—and we see this already at the time of Cicero—they compensated for their lack of inherited nobility by stressing their superiority in the moral realm.[11] They had *virtus* instead of the degenerate noble's descent, and they had *labor* and *industria* instead of the *nobilitas* of a bloodline. As time went on, they went even further: they claimed they had *nobilitas* also. That *nobilitas*, however, was not an inherited, external characteristic; it was a spiritual and moral *nobilitas*—a superiority they had earned by means of *virtus* and *industria*. They, and not the hereditary nobility, were in that sense the true heirs of the virtuous ancestors like Aeneas on whom the greatness of Rome was founded.

There is quite a bit of evidence, despite the usual attrition that afflicts documentation from ancient times, that Augustus' new aristocracy did not overwhelmingly live up to their claims of pristine virtue and devoted self-denial. He therefore decided to hold their feet to the fire of their own rhetoric. With the boorish consistency that is characteristic of Burns' transforming leader, he missed no opportunity, no forum to remind them of their moral responsibilities not only in their own right but also because they were the precondition for Rome's claim to empire—and while Augustus was the prince of peace domestically, he added more territory to the Roman state than anyone before him. The moral tone and direction were definitely set by him; we may argue, as the Romans did, about the implementation, but about the sincerity of his moral legislation there can be little doubt.

The same perspective informed his literary preferences. Although he enjoyed Roman popular entertainment, such as the mime and the pantomime—subliterary genres, really—his criteria for serious literature were unequivocal: "In reading the writers of both tongues there was nothing for which he looked so carefully as precepts and examples that were wholesome for the public and individuals; these he would often copy word for word and send to members of his household, or to his generals and provincial governors, whenever any of them required admonition."[12]

Nor was he alone in this. The time-honored view in Rome of poetry in particular was that it existed to inculcate morality. We find a good example in Horace's *Art of Poetry,* and the specific area of morals once more is that of marriage and marital conduct.[13] Song and poetry, according to Horace, first taught men "the wisdom to distinguish public from private property, to forbid random sexual intercourse and impose the laws of marriage" (*A.P.* 396–398). Unsympathetic as it may be to us moderns, the moral purpose of poetry was perfectly legitimate in Greece and Rome, although the result did not have to be overt moralizing. The basic fact is that "the Augustan poets found a source of inspiration in reflection on moral ideals, and some of their greatest poetry takes its origin from it."[14] Moreover, there was, to return to Burns' model, a definite reciprocity of inspiration in terms of values and ideals between them and their ruler. The relationship is quite unique and fundamentally different from Augustan England and Augustan France. The editors of a recent collection of essays on "Poetry and Politics in the Age of Augustus" summarize this aspect of the original Augustan age with acute insight when they state: "There can have been few ages in which poets were so intimately and affectionately connected with the holders of political power, few regimes with a richer iconography, few poets so profoundly moved by a political ideal and so equipped to sing its praises with subtlety, humor, learning, and rapture."[15] We can even go beyond this and say that the poets not only expressed the Augustan ethos—a truer term than ideology—but actually helped in shaping it.

"Ideology" versus Pragmatism with an Ethos

As a result of viewing the Augustan age in retrospect, it has often been overlooked that Octavian was a mere 19-year-old youth when, much to his and everybody else's surprise, he was named Julius Caesar's heir upon the latter's assassination in 44 B.C. There are precocious 19-year-olds, but it is unlikely to assume that his entire political, let alone cultural, program was firmly fixed in his mind at that time. Quite on the contrary, even his purely political operations for several decades were characterized by pragmatism, experimentation, and flexibility rather than doctrinaire planning.[16] There is no trace of an ideology in the modern sense of the word.[17] The woes of the Roman state were apparent to all, including the poets. When they expressed themselves on the deeper causations of these problems and their remedies, they were not mouthpieces of the struggling Octavian in the 30s B.C., but contributed to an ongoing discussion that provided Augustus with the tenets of the ensuing moral transformation.

One of the earliest (it was written in the 30s) and most influential formulations of the Augustan ethos is a programmatic passage near the beginning of the first book of Vergil's *Georgics* (118–159) where the poet justifies God's making man's existence one of unending toil and struggle. This is, of course, as we saw earlier, one of the central concepts of the *Aeneid*, too. Vergil does not view the legendary Golden Age as a fall from grace and the object of a nostalgic return. Rather, it was good for man to be divested of the indolence of paradise, to have to get used to hard work, and thus bring fulfillment to his existence. As in the *Aeneid, labor* is man's lot in this world and, at the same time, it is through *labor* that man can regain the Golden Age. It is not, to be sure, a Golden Age of stagnation and divine handouts, nor is the invention of skills attributed to such godlike figures as Prometheus. Instead, there is the dynamic process of our daily struggle to achieve the ideal; blood, sweat, and tears are the indispensable precondition for the ultimate reward. The Golden Age is based on daily human effort; the fulfillment in part comes from the incessant effort that is required to get us there rather than the actual arrival, and of course, we might as well forget about instant gratification. Obviously, a long-term perspective is more important than one for the short haul. At the same time, Vergil's vision is that all this amounts not to a cruel and harsh world for its own sake, but man's fate of unceasing labor is part of divine providence and dispensation.

The core of this important passage is worth quoting in full (1.121–133, 143–146):

The Father himself did not wish the way of cultivation to be easy, and first caused the fields to be worked with skill, sharpening the wits of mortals by care and not suffering his realm to lapse into gross sluggishness. Before Jupiter no tillers tried to subdue the land; even to mark it with private boundaries was wrong: men worked for the common store, and earth herself, without anyone's asking, yielded everything up more fully. He put the deadly venom into black serpents, he bade the wolves to prowl and made the ocean swell, shook honey from the leaves, hid fire away, and stopped the wine that ran everywhere in streams, so that practice, with the use of thought, might step by step hammer out the various crafts. . . . Then came hardened iron and the shrill saw-blade (for early man split wood with wedges); then came the various arts. Toil [*labor*] conquered the world, unrelenting toil, and necessity that impels when life is hard.

The important point is that this ethos did not die out with the 30s B.C. but became emblematic of the Augustan spirit even after the consolidation of his power and is basic to the Augustan quest for moral transformation. The Augustan age did not view itself as a period of complete fulfillment, attainment, and especially, contentment and self-satisfaction—quite in contrast to Augustanism in England and France. A twentieth-century observer has defined the phenomenon of the fullness of time, the *felicitas saeculi,* by saying that "there have been various periods in history which have felt themselves as having attained a full, definitive height, periods in which it was thought that the end of the journey had been reached, a long-felt desire obtained, a hope completely filled."[18] But he goes on to conclude, quite rightly, that this famous plenitude is in fact an illusion, and that genuine vital integrity does not consist in satisfaction, attainment, or arrival. The philosophical ancestor of this view is Hegel's philosophy of history—a very different one, evidently, from Mr. Fukuyama's—where Hegel differentiates between endeavor and actualization. Another antinomy that Hegel sets up in a different context is the "real capacity for change, the impulse of perfectibility," as opposed to nature in its largest sense, which Hegel, like a good Stoic, considers to be cyclical.[19]

The passage in the *Georgics* is a poetic version of this worldview. Taken together with the total context of that poem, the passage contains all the essential aspects of Vergil's definition of the ethos of human existence, which as we have seen, also pervades the *Aeneid.* They are the impossibility and even undesirability of returning to a stagnating past; the emphasis on unceasing human effort that, more often than not, is not rewarded by immediate fulfillment; the avoidance of materialistic excess; and the sanctioned place of human effort within a providential universe. In both the *Aeneid* and the *Georgics,* it is ongoing human exertion, a striving for fulfillment rather than fulfillment itself, that characterizes the human existence and makes it vital and worthwhile.

We encounter the same attitude in other Augustan poets, even in Ovid's *Art of Love,* the work officially cited for his banishment. The problem was that Ovid, as always, understood only too well the intentions of Vergil, Horace, and Augustus, who belonged to a different generation. The *Art* can be aptly characterized as a glorification, however perverse, of the Augustan way of life. Refracted in the Ovidian mirror, the ethos we have just discussed is suitably adapted to its special context. For in the *Art,* quite in contrast to modern manuals on the subject, the emphasis again is not on fulfillment or gratification but on incessant effort, the pursuit of a special kind of happiness, and the journey rather than the arrival.

A more imposing literary reflection of this ethos, which leads us back to the emperor, is Horace's *Letter to Augustus.* It is one of Horace's last works and a summation of many of the concerns he voiced throughout his earlier poetry. Rather than being a forced eulogy of Augustus, as Suetonius would have it, or a political and social document in the eighteenth-century view, it is a thoughtful if discursive statement about the state of literary and intellectual life at the time. Quite purposefully, therefore, the emphasis from the very beginning is not on achievement but on struggle, and especially on the difficulty with which the new and modern Augustan poetry has to contend. While Augustus, though following in the footsteps of the toiling Hercules, is receiving due recognition, the same cannot be said of the contemporary poets—Horace, of course, in particular. They are victimized by the Romans' inordinate craving for the literary tradition of the past and by the axiomatic equation of the good with the old. The tension to which Horace is pointing, between outward traditionalism and actual, experimental innovation, was another hallmark of the Augustan age related to the complex of ideas we are discussing.

Tradition and Innovation

It is well capsulized by Burns' other major criterion for leadership. "The cardinal responsibility of leadership" he writes, "is to identify the dominant contradiction at each point in history."[20] That is again a much truer and richer description of the Augustan system than the attempt to make it fit the matrix of modern authoritarian or self-satisfied eighteenth-century regimes. On the face of it, the emperor was ever the traditionalist. In contrast to his adoptive father, who became a victim of his desire to change things overtly and radically,[21] Augustus left the traditional Republican machinery intact: consuls were duly elected, the Senate and the assemblies kept meeting, and not one political office was abolished—nay, Augustus could claim in the very first sentence of the account of his achievements that he had restored and liberated the state, if not the Republic, from the clutches of the tyranny of a faction. Old customs were revived, priesthoods and rituals were restored, and temples were rebuilt. Rededication to the virtues and values that had made Rome great was a large writ: "By new laws passed on my proposal I brought back into use many exemplary practices of our ancestors which were disappearing in our time" reads another phrase from Augustus' account of his accomplishments, the *Res Gestae* (8.5), clearly referring to his moral legislation.

Deliberately, however, the sentence goes on: "And in many ways I myself transmitted exemplary practices to posterity for their imitation." In other words, there was innovation as well. It profoundly characterized Augustus' governmental modus operandi. He was the monarch de facto and came up with the requisite paraconstitutional terminology to have it both ways, as all these terms had a traditional, good ring to them. He did not style himself dictator in perpetuity like Caesar, let alone king, but first citizen, *princeps*, just as the senior member of the Senate had been called *princeps senatus*. The stated basis of his power was not the army but *auctoritas*, the respect that one commanded by one's deeds and that translated into influence. He took exceptional care to celebrate one of the most hallowed Roman festivals, which occurred only once every one hundred years, the Secular Games, but made many changes in its ritual, including the addition of a hymn by Horace. Or, in the rebuilding of the city of Rome, Augustus went far beyond the literal restoration of past edifices. The very change of the building materials for temples from wood and stone to marble produced a momentous new appearance. The increasing association of many of the rebuilt structures with him or members of his family led to a perceptible change in the character of the city.[22] Renewal was not simply a return to the past but, in effect, its transformation.

It was a point that because of its subtlety could be missed or ignored by the less discerning. That is precisely the predicament to which Horace is adverting in the *Letter to Augustus*. Because of Augustus' emphasis on the past, the Roman populace is unthinkingly given to imitating and praising past models and in the process ignores the vitality of the present, with the result that they do not appreciate contemporary poets like Horace. The dominant contradiction, to return to Burns' terminology, was that the Augustan reform program recalled the past but in reality was a great deal more. The issue is not dissimilar to the one we observed in the classical "imitations" in modern architecture: they were more than a simple replication, revival, or even celebration of the past; instead they offered their own reformulation and rearticulation. What, Horace continues, stands in the way of the Romans' appreciating such an effort? His answer is: mental inertia and an obsession with the past to the point where the Roman populace lacks any understanding of creative innovation and modernity that makes a tradition possible in the first place. Witness the Greeks, says Horace; if they had been inhibited by popular taste, as Horace and his contemporaries are, no literary tradition would have arisen in the first place: what would there be now that could be called old? (*A.P.* 91) And he goes on to single out as an egregious example of the excessive deadweight of traditionalism the revered Hymn of the Salian Priests. It continued to be performed under Augustus and was piously celebrated in Book 8 of the *Aeneid,* but Horace points out that even admirers of the poem are not able to figure out what it means.

So much for this particular burden of the past.[23] It is compounded by the burden of the present, which paradoxically turns out to be the very Pax Augusta. Peace is a condition in which the arts can flourish, but it also leads to the inertia of a sated Roman public. Tacitus, the archcritic of Augustus, would summarize this state of affairs succinctly by saying of Augustus that "he enticed all by the sweetness of leisure,"[24] and Alexander Pope picks up on this in his adaptation of Horace's *Letter* when he makes George II the spiritual father of the Queen of Dullness (400–401):

How, when you nodded, over land and deep,
Peace stole her wing, and wrapped the world in sleep.

The mood of awakening and the sense of departure, then, which were characteristic of the Augustan culture, were in danger of yielding to stagnation. Hence Horace concludes his discussion of the contrast between traditionalism and modernism in Augustan Rome with the extensive example of an endeavor that is far from complete, i.e., the state of the Roman theater. It is backward; it has not advanced over its state a century or more earlier; if anything, it has regressed in sophistication and artistry. The only progress that has been made is in the area of material opulence. The shows are now replete with chariots, bears, camels, and even the proverbial white elephant. Peacetime prosperity has resulted both in this new lavishness and the concomitant loss of literary taste. The double tide of materialism and traditionalism is an obstacle to further attainment in the dramatic arts. And although Horace does not say it, Augustus seemed to be quite content with this situation. As I mentioned earlier, theatrical spectacles that had scant literary value were among the things that delighted him most.

In the final part of the poem, Horace acknowledges the success of epic poetry on the Augustan literary scene but concludes with the vignette of his own poetic sheets being used as wrapping paper in the neighborhood grocery store. It is not as abrasive a picture as that presented earlier, but even with its visual amiability it recalls the earlier argument on the plight of the modern innovator amid the sea of misguided antiquarian preferences.

I have spent so much time discussing the *Letter to Augustus* because it is an instructive example of several major aspects of and perspectives on the Augustan culture. First, it again illustrates the greater insightfulness of Burns' model than of those approaches that view leadership and Augustus' attainments mostly in terms of power. Since the latter has been the ruling view, discussion of the Augustan poets' role has tended to focus on their freedom or restraint of expression, and with the usual bipolarity dear to academic investigation, lengthy discussions have centered on their pro- or anti-Augustanism. The real point of any disagreement or reservation Horace might have thus was given a skewed interpretation, ranging from amazement that his head did not roll forthwith to discovery of subtle messages between the lines. The proper issue, as can be seen, is not the poets' freedom to agree or disagree but their participation in an ongoing discussion about the direction of the culture of which they were a part. Horace feels perfectly free to explore the relevant issues with his emperor.

Second, reflecting the true ethos of the age, the *Letter to Augustus* is not an exercise in self-satisfaction but a call to continued effort. It is typical that he, like Vergil—and we need to think only of all the difficulties in which Aeneas is constantly placed—calls attention to the dilemmas and the incomplete state of affairs requiring ongoing effort, rather than to finite solutions and contentment even with the Augustan cultural milieu. The *Letter* was one of the last works, if not the last work of Horace, who died in 8 B.C., and its spiritual affinity with the thematic tenor of the *Georgics* and the *Aeneid* confirms the continuity of this ethos for at least three decades in Augustan literature.

Third, while the very notion of noncontentment and ongoing effort has a moral dimension in its own right, it was further elaborated—by Augustus in his moral legislation, by Vergil in his *Aeneid*, and by Horace in some of his *Odes*—into the concept of nonselfish, social responsibility, a traditional Roman virtue, but one in dire need of revival. This concern, as we have seen, was linked with the moral justification for Roman imperialism, but even if we remove that particular association, it remains the touchstone of a superior civilization. It is, therefore, not surprising to hear that concern being voiced today also. President Havel's speech to the U.S. Congress is one example,[25] and so is, to cite but one other instance, Derek Bok's discussion of it in his recent book *Universities and the Future of America.*[26] His conclusion is that "there is disturbing evidence to suggest that most forms of responsibility toward others have eroded." While we are dealing with perceptions, there is, as always, statistical support: "The percentage of people who feel that most individuals in power try to take advantage of others has doubled over the last two decades and now exceeds sixty percent." After the soul-searching, if not narcissism, of the 1970s, the argument goes, there came the self-consuming materialism of the 1980s, to be followed by the cynical, dispirited mood of the 1990s. It may be somewhat early to place a label on the current decade, but the issue of moral and spiritual leadership, its desirability, and its connection with political office is as acute as ever and provides a useful perspective on the Augustan age. Augustus vigorously addressed, to paraphrase President Carter, the malaise of the Roman spirit, and even Ovid gave him credit for guiding the Romans' mores by his own example.[27] That alone was not enough, however, and hence the recourse to legislation, which, besides being inconceivable in this form today, opens up the much-debated question whether morality can, in fact, be legislated. Legislation certainly cannot be the only means for moral transformation, and it was far from that in Augustan Rome where this concern resonated through art and literature too.

It would be inaccurate to label this resonance as ideology, especially in the sense in which it is applied to totalitarian regimes and party doctrines. Ideology can be an elusive term,[28] and it is more precise to define Augustanism in terms of an ethos and some guiding values and ideas. There is a shared vision, and it affects both the creation and the manifestation of some of the cardinal ideas. The emphatic occurrence, for instance, in Vergil's *Georgics* of the ethos of human toil, challenge, achievement, and divine tutelage was a significant contribution to the formation of the Augustan ideal, which, in contrast to eighteenth-century Augustanism, was dynamic rather than static. It was not a Vergilian invention in the sense that Augustus and others had never thought of it before, but it was the poetic creation of a vision that proved to be one of the lasting and most fundamental aspects of the Augustan culture. Augustanism incorporated such ideas and values without making them into ideological tenets.

There is a strong affinity between this ethos and Augustus' mode of government, in particular the experimental nature of the constitution of his powers. So far from being static and fixed definitively like those of an eighteenth-century Augustan monarch, they underwent a dynamic and evolutionary process with several stages; scholars have identified no fewer than four such "settlements."[29] His foreign policy, too, which had long been considered as aiming at stationary frontiers, was anything but that[30] and was characterized by both the setbacks and successes that comprise ongoing effort. The same is true of his main domestic policy, the legislation on marriage and morals. All this is even consonant with Pliny the Elder's famous psychohistorical sketch of Augustus, which dwells not on his achievements but enumerates an almost unbearable number of crises.[31] After reading it, one is tempted to paraphrase Gibbon's dictum, which we encountered earlier,[32] about the fall of the Roman Empire: "Instead of inquiring why Augustus was worn down, we should rather be surprised that he subsisted so long." The idea and practice of unceasing toil were anything but unfamiliar to him. He personified the ethos of the age: "By his own example he will guide men's *mores*," as Ovid put it (*Met.* 15.834).

Rather than the mere accumulation of power on which Syme and other historians have focused, it is the spiritual qualities or transforming leadership that gave Augustus' "Roman revolution" much of its lasting and inspirational significance. And there was, as in the case of any such leader of the moral kind, a mutuality between him and the "followers." We already saw several examples of this relationship in Augustan poetry; I want to conclude with a few observations on art and architecture.

The Moral Culture: Architecture and Art

Paul Zanker, whose study of Augustan culture is the most significant since Syme's, has conclusively demonstrated that Augustan art and architecture were not value-free, but an integral component of Augustus' "moral culture." As in literature and politics, there is a rejection of the excesses, modeled on Hellenistic precedents, of the late Republican period in the arts. A good example is the monumental complex of Fortuna at Praeneste (Fig. 40), which I discussed from a different perspective in connection with Mississauga City Hall.[33] It is baroque, ostentatious, and grandiose; it was composed of actually two sanctuaries built on stepped terraces, and while some symmetry controlled the swirl of centrifugal and centripetal forces, it was an uninhibited monument to flaunting the material wealth and power of the builder. The

50. Arch at Susa, Italy, 8 B.C. (Photograph Fototeca Unione, at the American Academy in Rome; neg. no. F.U. 6035.)

51. Arch of Titus, Rome. Built in the 80s A.D. (Photograph courtesy of Classics Slide Library, The University of Texas at Austin.)

Augustan age, by contrast, marked a return to classical simplicity. The showy abode of one of the richest men in Rome, Vedius Pollio, was razed after he had bequeathed his urban mansion and the surrounding land—it was the size of several small towns, says Ovid (probably with some exaggeration)—to the Princeps, who replaced it with public gardens and the tasteful Portico of Livia. Augustus did so, explains Ovid, because luxury of this sort set a bad example, and he comments on the emperor's action: "That is the way to set examples when the judge himself does what he asks others to do" (*Fasti* 6.647–648).

The same is true of Augustus' house, which was far less palatial than many private Republican villas on the one hand and the palaces of his successors on the other. A visually explicit example of the same contrast is the progression of arches, which tend to be better preserved than imperial habitats, from Augustus to Constantine. The arch of Augustus at Susa, a town in the foothills of the Alps, is classic in its simplicity: there is a single arch between pilasters, Corinthian columns are at the corners, and the structure on top of the vault is low (Fig. 50). By the time of Titus (A.D. 79–81), we are already in a world of greater display (Fig. 51). The pillars have become bulkier, the upperstructure is so huge that some scholars surmised that Titus was actually laid to his eternal rest there, and the sculptural decoration flaunts his destruction of the Temple at Jerusalem. The structure stretches the confines of the single arch to the limit. With Septimius Severus (A.D. 193–211), therefore, begins the era of the triple arch, replete with relief decoration celebrating several of the victories won by him and his sons (Fig. 52). More elaborate yet is the Arch of Constantine (built in A.D. 315), which so captivated Joseph Mankiewicz that he had Elizabeth Taylor enter Rome as Cleopatra through it in the correct expectation that few viewers would notice and fewer yet object; classical simplicity has gone by the boards completely, and it is the decorative mishmash, some of its elements coming from earlier monuments, that triumphs even more than the emperor (Fig. 53). This is not to imply a linear development in architectural form—Augustus' (lost) Parthian arch on the Forum Romanum had a triple configuration—but rather an evolution in terms of ostentatious taste.

The Augustan return to classicism was more than a matter of aesthetics; now we can understand all the better Demetri Porphyrios' impassioned affirmation that classicism is more than a style.[34] In contrast to contemporary architecture, however, the connotations of the classical style in both Augustan art and architecture were more precise. It signified, above all, a higher morality.

We find the clearest articulation of this attitude in a related area of the arts, that of rhetoric. When the Greek orator and historian Dionysius of Halicarnassus, who lived in Rome at the time, discusses the parallel phenomenon of the rejection of the Hellenistic, or Asian, style of rhetoric in favor of the classical, or Attic, he uses an imagery that recalls the visual arts. The Asian, baroque style is personified by a profligate harlot who wallows in wealth and luxury. Contrast her with the freeborn, restrained, and chaste woman, full of wisdom and sanity, who stands for the classical mode. The restoration of the latter to her rightful place has come about as part of the revolution (*metabole*) wrought by Augustus, who put in place leaders who "govern the state on the basis of excellence. They are highly cultured and they are high-minded in their decision-making, so that under their orderly rule the sensible part of the population has attained more power and the mindless have been compelled to conduct themselves rationally."[35] That is the real Roman revolution, then, brought about by a morally oriented, cultured leadership.

It is in those terms that the revival of classical art and architecture under Augustus must be understood. Instead of the excessive self-representations of the late Republic, often in the form of male statues with their teeming "Hellenistic" musculature, the Roman nobility now concurred in a preference for measured and togaed honorific statues that shared in the moral claim of the classical form. For the same reason, classical and even archaic originals of

52. Arch of Septimius Severus, Rome. First decade of the 3d cent. A.D. (Photograph Fototeca Unione, at the American Academy in Rome; neg. no. F.U. 739.)

53. Arch of Constantine, Rome. Second decade of the 4th cent. A.D. (Photograph Fototeca Unione, at the American Academy in Rome; neg. no. F.U. 736.)

54b. Archaizing head of Priapus statue. Capitoline Museums, Rome, Mon. Arc. Inv. 980. (Photograph Archivi Alinari.)

54a. Archaizing statue of Priapus, Augustan period. Capitoline Museums, Rome, Museo Nuovo Inv. 1873. (Photograph 1991 Archivi Alinari.)

Greek sculpture were prominently reutilized and displayed, and these styles were incorporated into statues produced under Augustus.[36] The Augustan version of the phallic and randy god Priapus, for instance, is done in an archaizing manner in terms of drapery, head, and posture (Figs. 54a and b). Furthermore, the god is decently dressed and, most importantly, is adorned with little children who climb all over him. They are testimony to his reproductive powers—a Priapus in tune with the legislation on marriage and morals.

This was not the end of Hellenistic art and architecture in Rome; in fact, they continued both in their own right and as part of a hybrid style, but that would be the subject for another discussion. Nor would any analogies be warranted between the Augustan artistic preferences and the current controversy over the policies of the National Endowment for the Arts; at best, such comparisons would tend to be as superficial as the bulk of the parallels between Rome's decline and contemporary America.

Of greater concern to students of leadership is the question of where the initiative rested in the creation of a cultural and political program that laid a strong emphasis on values. The answer is, once more, that we are dealing not with an ideological system but with a texture of interactions and multiple inspirations that have the Princeps at their center.[37] The ethos of unceasing effort and social responsibility was broadly shared and variously articulated, and even its specific application to responsibility for a family was not only Augustus' brainchild, though the particular legislative recourse he took may well have been; there is, to recall the earlier definition, both the urge for transcendence and his boorish consistency in pursuing it. As for mutuality, we see a leader set the tone and provide the direction on the basis of ideas or values that are not imposed extraneously, but to which followers are receptive because he made explicit and conscious what had been dormant and hoped for.

Therefore, as Zanker has shown with example after example from the visual arts, themes from the "official" art found their way into private art where they are further developed and elaborated.[38] This is a realm beyond imperial coercion, if we were still to posit such a model, and it can also be documented more fully than the populace's literary preferences. The artifacts range from oil lamps to wall paintings and from furniture to gladiatorial helmets. I will limit myself to two representative examples that illustrate the underlying mentality.

"Some eighty silver statues of me," Augustus writes in his *Res Gestae* (24.2), "on foot, on horse, and in chariots, had been set up in Rome; I myself removed them, and with the money that they realized I set golden offerings in the temple of Apollo, in my own name and in the names of those who had honored me with statues." The Temple of Apollo on the Palatine, next door to Augustus' house, was dedicated in 28 B.C., and the dedication was preceded by Augustus' action against an ostentatious personality cult. Instead, by doing

55. Arretine cup with tripod, c. 25 B.C. Museum of Fine Arts, Boston, Inv. 60316. (H. L. Pierce Fund, photograph courtesy Museum of Fine Arts, Boston.)

what he did, he presented himself as the very model of *pietas*: his honor was subordinated to that of the gods (with whom, however, he was yet associated more closely), and a plethora of statues in the showy Hellenistic style, which was not appropriate any longer for his image and aspirations, disappeared from display in the city. The resonance of this emblematic, moral act was extraordinary. The results of the transformation, tripods that were fashioned from the melted-down statues and dedicated to the god Apollo, appear, for instance, on utilitarian pottery (Fig. 55) and in Pompeian painting, where they are integrated somewhat incongruously into the prevailing style of extravagant architectural fantasy (Fig. 56). Similarly, emblems closely associated with the emperor, such as the god Mars from Augustus' Forum, the floral scrolls from the Augustan Altar of Peace, the Apolline laurel, and the oak leaves denoting his civic achievements, are found on the helmets and greaves of Pompeian gladiators. The connection is the ethos of struggle as a precondition for a blessed life. These values were proclaimed both publicly and privately, finding their true meaning in people's individual lives, as was the case with the values

56. Wall painting with tripod in center. Torre Annunziata, c. 25 B.C. (Photograph courtesy of Classics Slide Library, The University of Texas at Austin.)

reflected by Vergil's *Georgics*. The dichotomy between public and private voices, which scholars have so assiduously been trying to establish in Augustan poetry,[39] is often superseded by such realities.

Conclusion

The true Augustan revolution, as we have seen on several occasions, lay not in his successful acquisition of power and prolonged management of it, nor in a concomitant system of ideology. The concept of transforming leadership, with its emphasis on the mutually energizing relationship between leaders and followers and, especially, on its moral aspect, provides a far more suitable framework for doing justice to the spirit of the Augustan age, and to its richness and vitality. Augustan culture, for the most part, was far removed from both the solidity and stolidity of eighteenth-century Augustanism. Instead, true to itself, it was an ongoing process and a dynamic, evolving continuum. It was an Augustan evolution rather than a Roman revolution. Therefore it was not without its contradictions, a characteristic for which Burns' definition of leadership, in contrast to more rigid models, again makes due allowance. For it is precisely such tensions that kept the age of Augustus from becoming self-satisfied and stagnating and that, together with the moral and spiritual quality of transforming leadership, gave Augustan culture its enduring legacy.

One final such tension, to locate the Augustan age again within the framework of a current debate, was that between the restoration of unprecedented security and tranquillity and the effort to avoid their all too common consequences of cultural and intellectual lethargy, self-absorption, and loss of vitality. The theme is basic to Francis Fukuyama's analysis of the contemporary world situation after the dissolution of the Soviet Union, although his thesis of the near absolute triumph of Western-style freedom, democracy, and economics in all parts of the globe is more than extravagant.[40] The basic concern, however, is well taken and echoes the perspectives of challenge and decline that we considered in chapter 2. The "boredom of peace and prosperity," as Fukuyama puts it, can well lead to the loss of the "striving spirit" that imparts to humanity a sense of purpose and direction. The same concern was voiced by a plethora of Greek and Roman writers who saw in protracted peace and bliss the ever-present danger of cultural decline. Precisely in the times that Gibbon considered "the most happy and prosperous period of mankind" Juvenal wrote pithily: "We now suffer the ills of a long peace (*longae pacis mala*); luxury presses on us more fiercely than arms and avenges the world we conquered" (*Satire* 6.292f.). It is clear from the writings of Dionysius of Halicarnassus that these issues were debated at Augustus' time also.[41] The resulting realization, which was well articulated by Vergil and other Augustan writers and was reflective of the culture in general, was that *pax* and unceasing effort could be meaningful complements indeed.

Short Bibliography and Suggestions for Further Reading

Augustus. *Res Gestae Divi Augusti: The Achievements of the Divine Augustus.* Edited, with introduction and commentary, by P. A. Brunt and J. M. Moore (Oxford 1967).

Burns, James M. *Leadership* (New York 1978).

Gabba, E. "The Historians and Augustus." In Millar and Segal (see below) 61–88.

Galinsky, K. "Augustus' Legislation on Morals and Marriage." *Philologus* 125 (1981) 126–144.

Griffin, J. "Augustus and the Poets: 'Caesar qui cogere posset.'" In Millar and Segal 189–218.

Millar, F., and E. Segal, eds. *Caesar Augustus: Seven Aspects* (Oxford 1984).

Raaflaub, K. A., and M. Toher, eds. *Between Republic and Empire: Interpretations of Augustus and His Principate* (Berkeley and Los Angeles 1990).

Salmon, E. T. "The Evolution of Augustus' Principate." *Historia* 5 (1956) 456–478.

Syme, R. *The Roman Revolution*, 2d ed. (Oxford 1956).

Wallace-Hadrill, A. "The Golden Age and Sin in Augustan Ideology." *Past and Present* 95 (1982) 19–36.

Wilkinson, L. P. *The Georgics of Virgil: A Critical Survey* (Cambridge 1969).

Woodman, T., and D. West, eds. *Poetry and Politics in the Age of Augustus* (Cambridge 1984).

Zanker, P. *The Power of Images in the Time of Augustus* (Ann Arbor 1988).

V

Multiculturalism in Greece and Rome

Some Definitions

The Greco-Roman world, certainly from the time of Alexander the Great onward, was multicultural in the literal sense of the word: it was a composite of diverse cultures and ethnicities. So far from being Eurocentric, it encompassed all of the Mediterranean, including North Africa and Egypt, much of the Near East, and at times, sizable portions of the Middle East extending as far as Afghanistan and the Indus Valley. The current catchphrase about "dead white European males" is as inaccurate as it is racist and sexist: with reference to Greece and Rome, it is more precise to speak about light- to dark-brown Near Eastern and Mediterranean people whose cultural traditions have remained vital and lively for reasons related to their adaptability.

Given the fairly loose current definitions of "multiculturalism," the experience of Greco-Roman civilization provides some useful perspectives for the academic, though perhaps not the political, dimensions of the concept. An overview of Greek and Roman multiculturalism, broadly defined as the interaction between various cultures and their mutual awareness, is helpful in two basic respects. First, it will, I hope, clear away some misconceptions about the ancient world, which was neither homogeneous nor monolithic in its culture. Second, it provides a good opportunity to discuss some of the issues essential to the contemporary debate, such as cultural identity and assimilation, in a context that is reasonably free from the excessive emotionalism and, for that matter, total ahistoricism that characterizes much of the prevailing discussion. When Oliver Wendell Holmes proclaimed that "we (i.e., the Americans) are the Romans of the modern world, the great assimilating people," he was aware of historical precedent, but, to give only one other example, a study of the cultural interaction of Arabs, Jews, and Spaniards in pre-Inquisition Spain could be equally enlightening. Cultural conflict, coexistence, and assimilation are a constant theme in history, and few civilizations have been so insular as to be unaffected by them. That, in the end, is what multiculturalism, or at least the study of multiculturalism, is about.

Before we look at some of the Greek and Roman evidence, a few basic aspects deserve comment. One is the essential distinction between cultural indebtedness, or inheriting a tradition, and continuing it by changing it and thereby assuring its vitality. We saw a good illustration of this process and its underlying issues in the adaptations of the classical tradition in postmodern architecture. On an even grander scale, the question of originality versus imitation has been debated endlessly by scholars of Roman civilization. The simplistic notion that the Romans were merely imitators finally died a post-Romantic death and yielded to a more sophisticated assessment. A similar perspective is called for in determining, for example, any Egyptian influence on Greece, which is most palpable in architecture and sculpture. The real criterion for the quality of a people's cultural contribution is the degree of creative adaptation and development of preexisting traditions. In that sense, as T. S. Eliot put it in his most relevant essay on "Tradition and the Individual Talent," "the past [is] altered by the present as much as the present is directed by the past." Not much of the present discourse on multiculturalism is so elegant or discerning, and therefore we may put the argument more bluntly by saying that conclusions, such as Greek culture being essentially Egyptian because of some borrowings, are simplistic nonsense.[1]

Secondly, the issue of culture and race was not nearly as intense in Greco-Roman antiquity as it is today. Color prejudice, in terms of racial and biological assumptions, existed neither in the ancient world nor until the eighteenth century.[2] One result is that the contributions of people of color to Greek and Roman civilization are well established. They included, as we will see, leading philosophers, writers, and rulers. The focus, however, has never been on their nationality but on their merits as individuals. The reasons for that are not to be sought in a concerted effort to present Greco-Roman culture as lily-white, but in the perception that any such leading figures, especially writers and thinkers, transcend race, gender, and even history. Terence's much-quoted dictum "I am human and nothing human, I believe, is foreign to me" is all the more poignant as he originally was a North African slave, possibly even negroid, who became one of Rome's leading playwrights by adapting Greek comedies—an exemplar of multiculturalism, if any, who saw human commonality surpass any cultural distinctions. But since the prevailing image of classical antiquity is almost as erroneously white as the remnants of its sculpture and architecture, which used to be brightly colored, it is not inappropriate to call attention to the existence of leading nonwhites and their active participation in the development of the Western tradition.

A third overriding issue is that of acculturation. For instance, does the general laissez-faire policy toward the cultures of subject peoples in Hellenistic and Roman times indicate indifference, tolerance, or respect? A related point is that "Hellenism" and "Romanization" are terms of convenience and do not connote a uniform degree of cultural penetration, let alone imposition.

Finally, we need to be careful, again, not to impose modern notions on past ages but to view Greco-Roman antiquity in the context of world history. As a reviewer of Bernard Lewis' *Muslim Discovery of Europe* sadly observed, curiosity about other peoples, their beliefs and way of life has hardly been the norm in the relations of one civilization to the other, whereas the pattern of ignorance, suspicion, and xenophobia has.[3] That is not to say that all this has drastically changed today—witness some of the excesses of the multiculturalism debate—but the information alone that modern communication constantly puts at our disposal about other cultures is unprecedented. As in the discussion of the parallels between the United States today and the decline of Rome, it is the wider context and perspectives, and not the narrow analogies, that relate the subject of Greek and Roman multiculturalism to the current discussion of the topic in the United States, and I will return to that point at the end.

Greece before Alexander

Conventional wisdom has it that the Greeks ruthlessly differentiated themselves from all other cultures who were simply labeled "barbarians." We find this national awareness particularly in the fifth century B.C., heightened as it was by the threat of the Persian invasion. The overall picture, however, is more diverse and begins with the Greeks' explanations of their origins.

In these, their multiracial descent is freely acknowledged. The Greeks considered themselves a relatively young race, descended from Hellen, the son of Deucalion. They were by no means the original settlers of the country: Greece had been largely inhabited by pre-Greek, barbarian populations, notably the Pelasgians, who were gradually absorbed and assimilated. Among others, the Pelasgians included the Athenians and all the inhabitants of the Peloponnesus before the Dorians. We cannot expect a sophisticated and scientific explanation from Herodotus, one of our main sources, for anything as complex as cultural assimilation: he simply says that the non-Greek inhabitants of the land underwent a change (*metabole*) and came to "be reckoned as Greeks."[4] In the subsequent mixed culture, the Greeks predominated in language and the non-Greeks in religion; the origin of many cults is ascribed to the Pelasgians.

There were other traditions besides the Helleno-Pelasgian theory of the origin of the Greek nation. One of the strongest is the one centering on Argos, which lists several generations antedating Deucalion and Hellen. At its center is Io, whose children are scattered over Egypt, Phoenicia, Asia, and Crete, as well as Argos and Thebes in Greece. Danaus and his daughters, pursued by their Egyptian suitors, returned to Greece, and the settlers of the Peloponnesus therefore were called Danaans. The result of the Egyptian sojourn of the descendants of Io was a partially foreign ancestry in the lineage of the Argive and

Dorian kings, which was never denied. Herodotus (6.53) simply lists the upper generations of the Dorians as Egyptian and the lower as Greek. The turning point is Perseus; while he is the son of the Egyptian Danae, his father was Zeus and it is patrilineal descent that counts. Other myths, such as that of Cadmus and Thebes, also trace descent to foreign invaders.

All this goes along with an important distinction drawn by Herodotus and others. The difference between Greeks and barbarians is not biological or racial, but lies in specific intellectual attitudes and attributes: "What differentiates the Hellenic race from the barbarian since olden times is that it is more skillful and more removed from foolish simplemindedness" (Hdt. 1.60.3). Defining the Greek mentality for the Persian king Xerxes, therefore, the Spartan king Demaratus does not simply leave it with the cardinal virtue of the Greek character, *arete* (virtue and excellence), but specifies that this *arete* is the product of *sophia,* i.e., wisdom and intelligence (Hdt. 7.102.1).

Of course, such qualities can be shared by people regardless of nationality, and from this perception originates the not inconsiderable tradition in Greek thought that by meeting these criteria, barbarians can become Greeks or, by not meeting them, Greeks can be assimilated to barbarians.[5] Instead of occurring in an isolated context, the issue was part of the larger debate, anticipating quite a few modern ones, whether virtue and intellectual skill could be taught or resulted from noble genes (again, it should be emphasized that genetic ability in Greek and Roman thought is not defined in terms of race). The Sophists, of course, who made a living by teaching such skills, strongly asserted that by nature all men were equal, and that any subsequent distinctions, such as ethnic ones, were man-made rather than natural. Thus Antiphon in the fifth century:

> [Those] of more familiar societies we understand and respect, but those of distant societies we neither understand nor respect. In this we have become barbarous towards each other, since by nature we are all equally equipped in every respect to be both barbarians and Greeks. This we may perceive from the circumstances of those things which are by nature necessary for all men and can be shared by all on the same terms; it is in these very things that none of us is differentiated as a barbarian or a Greek, for we all breathe into the air with our mouths and with our nostrils and we all laugh when there is joy in our mind, or we weep when suffering pain; we receive sounds through our hearing; we see in daylight with our sight; we work with our hands and we walk with our feet.[6]

Antiphon does not say that Greeks and barbarians are the same, only that they were born the same; and yet, in acquired habits like the lack of understanding of faraway peoples there is no difference between Greeks and barbarians either—such attitudes, according to Herodotus (1.134.2–3), were typical of the Persians. Still, the view that there was no natural difference between Greeks and barbarians was not shared by Plato and Aristotle; the latter's pronouncement (*Politics* 1252b5–6; cf. 1254b7–13) that barbarians were slaves by nature and therefore ought to be ruled has been brought up often enough in the contemporary multiculturalism debate and needs to be seen in the light of such statements as Antiphon's. A basic social reality in the Greece of the period we are surveying is that most Greeks were acquainted with barbarians as slaves. While the system was color blind, the obvious *class* distinction did not engender a deep respect at that level for other cultures. Due to restrictive citizenship laws, which were passed mostly for economic reasons, few of these slaves could ever aspire to being freed and becoming citizens; we will see that the situation in Rome was vastly different.

Besides allowing for the possibility of crossing the line between Greeks and barbarians, the Hellenic self-definition in terms of inventive intelligence had another corollary: "It was these qualities of intelligence and discernment that let the Greeks take over so many good things from older civilizations, especially Egypt. By contrast, the Scythians, for instance, who are an even younger people than the Greeks, killed and denied those of their kings who wanted to learn from the Greeks."[7]

The distinction, then, between Greeks and barbarians was nonbiological. The very term *barbaros* is linguistic, aping foreign speech; we may note that the Egyptians, too, had a similar blanket term, "those of another language" (*alloglossoi;* Herodotus 2.158), for foreigners. In due course, especially as a result of heightened national consciousness and hostility to the Persians and other outsiders during the fifth century, it could suggest the superiority of Greek customs to barbarian ones. No personal baseness was implied; in fact, Herodotus has barbarians like Croesus and Xerxes intelligently discuss problems that were of fundamental importance to the Greeks at the time, such as the relation of intentional and unintentional behavior to guilt, because these are general human concerns. All at the same time, Herodotus speaks of the "Greek nation, of one blood and one language" (8.144) pitted against the Persians—both attitudes coexist. Similarly, Euripides can have Achilles pronounce that "it is right for Greeks to rule barbarians, and not for barbarians to rule Greeks. For they are slaves and we, the Greeks, are free" (*Iphigenia in Aulis* 1400–1401) and yet portray the barbarian Medea as in every way superior to her Greek husband, Jason.

One other prevailing explanation for cultural differences also was extrinsic in essence. That was the view that they were caused by climate. A good example comes from the Hippocratic treatise on *Airs, Waters, Places,* which probably dates from the late fifth century:

> The small variations of climate to which the Asians are subject, extremes both of heat and cold being avoided, account for their mental flabbiness and cowardice as well. They are less warlike than Europeans and tamer of spirit, for they are not subject to those physical changes and the mental stimulation which

sharpen tempers and induce recklessness and hot-headedness. Instead they live under unvarying conditions. Where there are always changes, men's minds are roused so they cannot stagnate. Such things appear to me to be the cause of the feebleness of the Asiatic race, but a contributory cause lies in their customs; for the greater part is under monarchical rule. . . . Such men lose their highspiritedness through unfamiliarity with war and through sloth, so that even if a man be born brave and of stout heart, his character is ruined by this form of government. A good proof of this is that the most warlike men in Asia, whether Greeks or barbarians, are those who are not subject races but rule themselves and labor on their own behalf. Running risks only for themselves, they reap for themselves the rewards of bravery or the penalties of cowardice. You will also find that the Asiatics differ greatly among themselves, some being better and some worse. This follows from the variations of climate to which they are subject, as I explained before.[8]

While adducing climate as a major factor, the passage is typically undogmatic. Neither the Asian nor the European climate produces perfection: while one may make men prone to indolence, the other can lead to intemperate behavior. Climatic causes are not irreversible, but can be overcome by social ones; the form of government one lives under ultimately makes an even greater difference. Nor is there a convenient breakdown along the line of a Greek/barbarian antithesis: both Greeks and barbarians respond in the same way to climate and political institutions. And finally, allowance is made for differences among Asiatics. The recognition of such diversity is characteristic of Greek attitudes even at that time.

Still, there was the rage for order. The ensuing systematization again is best viewed in the context of Greek thought and philosophy where preoccupation with the problem of diversity and unity is a major theme, but there is a component of cultural pride as well. I am referring to the process by which Greek historians integrated the ever increasing number of places with which the Greeks made contact especially in the West into a framework that was thoroughly Hellenic. They routinely ascribed the beginnings of any of these to a Greek founding hero.[9] Traditional culture heroes or wanderers, such as Herakles, Odysseus, and various refugees from the Trojan War, thus came to roam even more extensively, and the number of myths associated with them grew accordingly. No heed was paid to local traditions, and the resulting world and attitude can best be defined as Hellenocentric. So far from rejecting such traditions, the natives who were endowed with such pedigrees were mostly intent on maintaining them because they provided an instant entrée into the sphere of a recognized culture. Nor did this lead to a suppression of the local legends; Rome, for instance, is a good example of this kind of multiculturalism from early on.

It remains to highlight briefly some of the cultural interactions between Greece and other civilizations from the eighth century to the fourth. Detailed discussions are not in short supply, which again contradicts the assertion that classical scholars have been inattentive to such evidence, let alone wanted to suppress it. In his edition of Hesiod's *Theogony*, for instance, M. L. West, one of the leading Greek scholars of his generation, exuberantly declared that "Greece is part of Asia. Greek literature is a Near Eastern literature."[10] The reference more specifically is to the influences, such as we can ascertain them, of Near Eastern myths on Greek mythology.

Absolute certainty, of course, is hard to come by. Instead, we are dealing with an accumulation of affinities, and it is a matter of individual judgment at what point they reach the degree of specificity that will enable us to posit a concrete instance of influence or borrowing. Modern readers need to keep in mind that scholars of classical antiquity are blessed with anything but abundant documentation. Accordingly, one critical issue that constantly divides us is whether one find or document is an isolated example or stands for many more that simply did not survive. Therefore, while the probability of extensive contact between the Near East and Greece in the area of mythology is generally acknowledged, there is a great deal of disagreement about specifics. The case of Herakles is a useful paradigm.

He was the pan-Hellenic hero par excellence and from the eighth century on, his attestations in both literature and cult are copious. Given the range of Herakles' exploits, it is not surprising that there are oriental affinities.[11] Heroes who tame animals—many of them the same as those tamed by Herakles, including a multiheaded hydra—appear as early as the fourth and third millennia B.C. on pre-Sargonic cylinder seals of Mesopotamia and continue in Hittite representations of the second half of the second millennium B.C. One of Herakles' chief exploits was the strangling of a lion whose skin became his emblem ever after—but were there ever lions in Greece? The principal limitation is that the evidence is almost exclusively iconographic, and while there must have been a continuity of texts too, they are not available. The same, of course, applies to the oral tradition. Other similarities, concerning Herakles' birth for instance, extend to Egypt, Babylonia, and pre-Greek Asia Minor. For other aspects, such as the descent to the underworld, patterns found in Indo-European mythology provide parallels. This background "makes us realize that Herakles is, basically, not a heroic figure in the Homeric sense: he is not a warrior fighting warriors, he is mainly concerned with animals, just as he is a savage clad in a skin. . . . In this perspective, it is clear that there is not one myth of Herakles, there is not a character to start from, but a set of different stories involving the same name, some of them variations upon the same pattern, some of them apparently unrelated."

All a scholar can do, and Walter Burkert does it very well, is make the strongest possible case, and even he admits that much of the argument must remain speculative. I am inclined to assume that Herakles, in terms of the genesis of his myth, is a multicultural product; the gods Apollo and Dionysus, too, were imports. What matters even more, however, is the Greeks' creative adaptation of this hero from archaic to Roman times. He did not remain a savage clad in a skin; the inherent theme of the quest he represented was ever more expanded not only in physical terms but also in cultural and metaphysical ones. He became the culture hero who cleared away both human and animal monstrosities ahead of Greek colonists. On the tragic stage, he became an exemplar of the grandeur of internal heroism while his excesses simultaneously made him the favorite and most riotous subject of Greek comedy. He was sublimated by the philosophers as a protagonist of the choice between good and evil and as a model of enduring the iniquities of this world. Finally, there were his divine parentage and his deification; it is for reasons like these that Alexander assimilated his image to Herakles' on his coins.

In short, we cannot simply measure a cultural tradition by its origins but by the degree it avoids stagnation and takes on fresh stimuli for its evolution. One resultant, salutary perspective on the contemporary debate on multiculturalism is that one culture can make another its own, regardless of race, and creatively continue it. A similar pattern emerges from Greece's debt to Egyptian architecture and sculpture.

Again, I can be brief because full documentation exists on the subject. A. W. Lawrence's standard work on Greek architecture contains no fewer than thirty references to Egyptian precedents; this completely contradicts the assertion even of the usually informed Charles Jencks that they are suppressed in discussions of classical architecture. Jencks correctly sees the roots of the "free-style" classical tradition in Egypt.[12] A good example is the Anubis shrine and north colonnade of Hatshepsut's mortuary temple at Deir al-Bahri of c. 1500 B.C. with their proto-Doric columns and cavetto mouldings (Fig. 57). The Egyptian architectural influence on Greece was multiple. It began with the Minoan palaces in Crete and continued in Mycenaean times. Since both these civilizations had been lying in ruins for several centuries by the time the Greeks started building stone temples in the seventh century, it is questionable how much the Greeks were inspired by any of those remnants (the most relevant models had been built in wood and had probably long disappeared) instead of the Egyptian stone architecture directly. There is no doubt about close familiarity: even small details, such as terra-cotta gutter drains, have Egyptian precursors. But despite all these borrowings, the Greek temples were not simply replicas of the Egyptian ones. The loaned elements of architectural grammar were utilized for a new syntax and over time the specific "canonical" styles developed: Doric, Ionic, and Corinthian. Parallel to the myth of Herakles, continuous evolution became the hallmark of the classical architectural tradition. Because "the classical language [of architecture] has been transformed over time and tied generations together in a common pursuit,"[13] it became multicultural in Greek and Roman times, even more so in the Renaissance, and yet more so in the postmodern period; while I restricted my dis-

57. Hatshepsut's mortuary temple, Deir al-Bahri, c. 1500 B.C. Anubis shrine and part of north colonnade. (Photograph by C. Jencks; reprinted from C. Jencks, *Post-Modernism: The New Classicism in Art and Architecture* [London: Academy Group Ltd., 1987]. © 1987 by Academy Group Ltd.)

cussion to North American examples, the phenomenon is worldwide and includes architects of Japanese and Chinese descent.

As for Greek sculpture, the earliest statues (seventh century), both male and female, clearly are modeled on Egyptian types. This includes details such as the wiglike coiffure of the females, best preserved in the so-called Auxerre Maiden in the Louvre (Fig. 58). Again, we can turn simply to the standard history of Greek art for an appropriate characterization of the early male statues or *kouroi:* "The most conspicuous example of Egyptian influence on this earliest phase of Greek monumental art is found in the pose of the *kouros* type: the naked youth standing with arms at sides and left foot forward,"[14] well exemplified by two statues in the Delphi Museum (Fig. 59). But even here, the stirrings of a new aesthetic are already discernible in such details as the nudity of the males and the distribution of the weight over both legs. The direction of the ensuing evolution is characterized precisely by a turning away from the blocklike monumentality of the Egyptian models toward greater individualization—there are similar developments in Greek lyric poetry at the time—and ultimately, idealization. By the end of the fifth century that process, from which Egyptian statuary remained largely immune, is complete.

58. Female figure, c. 650–625 B.C. Limestone; Musée de Louvre; Louvre Inv. 3098. (Photograph © Cliché des Musées Nationaux–Paris.)

59. Kouroi from Delphi, c. 600 B.C. Delphi Museum Inv. 467 and 1524. (Photograph courtesy of the Delphi Museum.)

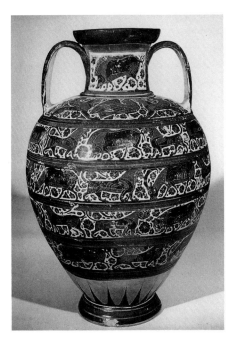

60. Corinthian amphora in the orientalizing style, 7th cent. B.C. British Museum, London, Inv. 1914.10-30.1. (Photograph © Trustees of the British Museum.)

Whereas in this case Greek artists could rid themselves of the tyranny of a tradition on their own, they relied on foreign aid in doing the same in another field of art, i.e., vase painting. There the predominant mode, through the ninth century, had been the fairly rigid Geometric style, which yielded, especially in Corinth, Greece's leading city in the eighth and seventh centuries, to the "orientalizing" style. The term speaks for itself; the decoration includes, but is not limited to, animals and floral motifs, such as griffins, sphinxes, and lotus palmettes. Art followed trade, in this case the trade in scented oils. A new, smallish vase shape was devised for these, and it is precisely on these *aryballoi* that oriental influence appears first. The style then spread both to larger vases, which combine regard for the inherited organization of a vase by way of clearly delineated friezes with the new subjects (Fig. 60), and to other locales, such as Athens. "Oriental influence on Greek vase painting," as Martin Robertson sums it up well, "consists in the impulse given by the revelation of a new way of looking at things, and in the borrowing of certain types and stylizations of animal and vegetable forms. It is never a matter of slavish imitation."[15]

Other attempts to discern oriental influences, such as on early Greek phi-losophy, have been more problematic,[16] although they underscore once more the lack of reluctance on the part of classicists to pursue such investigations. What is clear from our survey especially of archaic Greece, however, is that at the crossroads of the Mediterranean and at a time when the Greeks came into intensive contact with other peoples due to colonization and trade, they had an open window especially to the Near East and Egypt. They received and actively sought a variety of impulses from there; at the same time, they did so confidently and developed their own culture and consciousness of it. That is as much as one can expect at a time when the systematic study of other peoples, the learning of foreign languages, and the translation of literary works from one language into the other were anything but the rule. It should be clear also that the assimilation of such techniques as vase painting does not neces-sarily imply a real understanding between two civilizations; a systematic study of each other's culture was a concept alien to both Greeks and Egyptians. For political reasons, to which we will turn momentarily, foreigners in Greek states were rarely granted citizenship, and they were excluded from such fes-tivals as the Olympic Games in the same way that Greeks were from Egyptian priesthoods, but even "barbarians" could frequent Greek oracular shrines and did so. Barbarians were not considered inferior on the basis of race, but the overall worldview, especially in the fifth and fourth centuries, was comfortably Hellenocentric. It was to be challenged by the mere geographic explosion of Alexander's conquests.

Alexander the Great and the Hellenistic Period

One of the major differences between the ancient world and ours is accurate maps. Had they existed and had Alexander shown his Macedonians how far he intended to take them, they would have stayed home in the first place instead of mutinying eight and a half years later in India and forcing him to turn back. By that time, the expansion of horizons was a fait accompli as it became once more in 1492, and that involves both geographic and cultural horizons. The dynamic, uneasy, and restless character of Hellenistic civiliza-tion is a direct result of the loss of the safety of the old dimensions. A massive number of new populations came under the rule of Alexander and his succes-sors, producing a truly multicultural environment, and the resulting inter-actions were anything but uniform.

In one of their rare instances of agreement, Plato (*Laws* 12.950a) and Aristotle (*Pol.* 5.3.1303a) strongly counseled against granting citizenship to strangers and letting them intermarry. To do so, in their view, invites confu-sion and revolution. Such "strangers," in fact, are other Greeks; the possibility of granting such rights to barbarians is not even considered (although it was not an uncommon practice even in pre-Alexandrian times especially in outlying Greek colonies) because Aristotle, as has been mentioned before, considered barbarians to be born to servitude. For all we know, Alexander probably was Aristotle's best student and, like some of our best students today, went on to discard his teacher's advice; that is, of course, what often makes such students the best. While the ostensible justification for Alexander's expedition against Persia was a pan-Hellenic cause, he realized soon enough that Macedonian and Greek manpower would never suffice to rule the conquered territories. Hence he left the civil administration pretty much in the hands of the natives, especially the Iranians, but made sure to reserve the military control to trusted Macedonians and Greeks. He came not as a colonizer but intent on the fusion between Greeks and Achaemenids. He kept the ceremonial system of the Persian kings the same and made it mandatory for Persians *and* Greeks, rebuilt two major Babylonian shrines, took a Persian wife and had ten thousand of his Greek and Macedonian troops do the same, and publicly prayed for "harmony and partnership in rule (*homonoia*) between Macedonians and Persians." At the same time, he founded numerous cities, often named after him, that served a variety of purposes—military, economic, and political—and had a mixed population.

On that basis, much has been made both of the "fusion" of cultures and the "diffusion" of Greek culture in the Hellenistic East. Either notion needs to be carefully defined and seriously qualified.[17] As for programmatic racial fusion, Alexander's successors stopped it immediately after his death in 323 B.C., but intermarriages between Greeks and foreigners became a great deal more frequent. This involved common folk as well as rulers, notably the Seleucids who were the dynasts of the largest of three successor kingdoms. Totally absent, however, in both the Seleucid kingdom and in Ptolemaic Egypt was an aggressive imperial cultural policy with the aim of "Hellenizing" the natives. While historians of late have come at least to recognize this fact, proper appreciation of it is not universal, and the lack of a sweeping triumph of Greek culture over the Orient is viewed almost as a failure.

This is one exemplary instance where the substitution of some larger multicultural and historical perspectives for a Eurocentric focus is helpful. In such a context, it is beside the point to discuss Hellenistic civilization in terms of the success or failure of Hellenization (*Hellenismos*), a term whose first recorded use occurs in an unfriendly passage in the Second Book of Maccabees (4.13) that leaves no doubt about the natives' feelings. The limiting Eurocentric approach also is evident, for example, in expressions of regret, which track the sneers of Greeks residing in the homeland at the time, that acculturation often went the other way as especially Greeks in Egypt "succumbed" to Eastern traditions, religious cults in particular. Or, to comment on another issue: the indifference of the Greek or Hellenized ruling class toward native cultures needs to be placed within the larger perspective of similar situations in world history before we fault the denizens of the ancient world on the basis of relatively modern notions. For instance, Bernard Lewis has well observed that "even the astute and highly competent makers and rulers of the Ottoman Empire showed only minimal interest in the history and the languages of the peoples they had conquered or were planning to conquer,"[18] and only worse could be said about the American settlers' attitude to the Indians.

What is important is not the success or nonsuccess of Hellenism but the creation of a multicultural environment where the Greeks did not try to destroy other cultures—quite in contrast to many conquerors in earlier and later history—with the resultant cultural coexistence, juxtaposition, hybridization, and varying kinds of mutual respect and disrespect. What applied to the discussion of the decline and fall of the Roman Empire holds true here also: there was a tremendous variety of local and regional differences. Cultural interaction and even the very presence of Greek culture were considerable in some areas and nonexistent in others. Before we look at some examples, we need to remind ourselves about the true significance of the Hellenistic period: far too many windows were opened between East and West to be closed again for centuries, if at all. It is during this time, for example, that the Greeks discovered Judaism and the Jews Hellenism.[19]

Cosmopolitanism was one result. Greek literature and philosophy were enriched by natives of Phoenicia (combining parts of today's Lebanon, Syria, and Palestine) and North Africa. A triad of Phoenician poets stands out, and the epitaphs of one of them, Meleager (late 2d–early 1st cent. B.C.), tell us a great deal about his cultural attitudes:

> Tyre was my nurse, and Gadara, which is Attic but lies in Syria, gave birth to me. From Eucrates I sprung, Meleager, who first by the help of the Muses ran abreast of the Graces of Menippus. If I am a Syrian, what wonder? Stranger, we dwell in one country, the world [*kosmos*]; one Chaos gave birth to all mortals.
> This is Meleager, the son of Eucrates, who linked sweet tearful love and the Muses with merry Graces. Heavenborn Tyre and Gadara's holy soil reared him to manhood, and beloved Cos of the Meropes tended his old age. If you are a Syrian, *Salam!* If you are a Phoenician, *Naidius!* If you are a Greek, *Chaire!* and say the same yourself.　　　　　(A.P. 7.417, 419 [Loeb transl.])

Meleager is aware of and relishes his belonging to different cultures, hence his trilingual "hail" in the final stanza. He was born in Syria, though in a city that he considered Hellenized, and then moved to Tyre before retiring in the city of Cos on the island of the same name. His acknowledged model was Menippus, a poet of the third century who also was born in Gadara, was a slave at first, then acquired his freedom and became one of the great innovators of the iambic and satirical genre, mixing prose with poetry and serious, philosophical views with humor and fantasy. As a product of different cultures Meleager, like Terence and others, emphasizes our common humanity, which transcends such divisions. It is not necessary to deny one's cultural identities in order to be part of the more universal evolution from chaos to *kosmos*, which implies order.

Meleager did not simply become acculturated in the sense that he continued Hellenistic love poetry along traditional paths. Like any innovative, vital keeper of a cultural tradition, he infused it with his own, different sensibilities: "Well versed in Greek poetry, a master of the lyre himself, a Greek in his love habits, one might take Meleager as a prototype of the Hellenized Asiatic. Yet his sensitivity to suffering, and his romantic and nervous attitude to love, stamp him as an alien. The common Hellenistic view that love was an infantile disease, not to be taken seriously, was beyond him."[20] Meleager further left his mark on Greek letters by editing one of the major collections of Greek poetry, with works of various poets, the *Garland*.

It includes much of the poetic oeuvre of his countrymen Antipater of Sidon (2d cent. B.C.) and Philodemus, also born at Gadara (1st cent. B.C.), and illustrates once more the diversity of such poets and the freedom the Hellenic tradition afforded them. The sensitivities, viewpoints, and approaches of all three are quite varied; certainly, there is nothing like a Syrian or Phoenician "school" or uniform mentality. Multiculturalism—although the point seems to be lost at times in the current debate—is exactly that and has nothing to do with cultural tribalism. One distinctive aspect of Antipater's poetry is his interest in nature, and his facility with the Greek language must have been extraordinary as Cicero singled him out as a fluent improviser. Philodemus' interests were yet more varied. He was a protofeminist, writing some of his poems from the woman's point of view (e.g., *A.P.* 5.120, 306), and he could bear his multiculturalism lightly. After a passionate enumeration of the various charms and body parts of one of his loves, he mock-justifies falling for a non-Greek by reference to Perseus, who loved the Indian-born Andromeda (*A.P.* 5.132): "If she is Oscan and her name is Flora and she does not sing Sappho, even Perseus was in love with Indian Andromeda." The Oscans lived in southern Italy, and Philodemus settled in Herculaneum, achieving fame as a prolific Epicurean philosopher whose wide-ranging writings included literary criticism, aesthetics, theology, and psychology. He gathered some of the most brilliant young Romans around him and influenced some of the most influential and distinguished Romans of the time, including Vergil and Horace.

His career as a philosopher bears witness to the fact that the Hellenistic philosophies broke down the antithesis between Greek and barbarian in actuality as well as theory. Zeno, the founder of the Stoic school, himself came from a Phoenician family on Cyprus and relegated differences of nationality to the broad category of "things that do not matter" (*adiaphora*); what really mattered for a Stoic was to live in accordance with reason (*logos*). Several of his successors also were from the East, including Diogenes of Babylon in the second century. Despite his general opinion about barbarians, even Aristotle is reported once to have recognized a non-Greek, a Jew, as an equal because he was "a Greek in his soul" (Josephus, *Contra Apionem* 176–180), and Theophrastus, who succeeded him as head of the Peripatetic school, explicitly pronounced the kinship of all peoples. The Cynics in their usual fashion acknowledged only one true fatherland, i.e., poverty and obscurity, and to the Epicureans, whose goal was tranquillity of mind, such matters as nationality were too insignificant to get worked up about. In the meantime, the geographers, especially Agatharchides (2d cent. B.C.), revised the earth's climatic zones with the result that Greeks and most of the "barbarians" came to inhabit the temperate zone, as opposed to the zones that were too hot and too cold. The old distinctions between the two races, based on geographic environment, therefore became meaningless.

It is not surprising, therefore, to see a North African native from Carthage become one of Plato's successors as head of the Academy in Athens in 127 B.C. His native name was Hasdrubal and his Greek name, Cleitomachos. While being the chief exponent, in his more than four hundred writings, of the new and less dogmatic orientation that his predecessor Carneades imparted to the Academy, he showed enough independence to found his own school in the Palladium in Athens, which he maintained for more than ten years before his appointment to the headship of the Academy. Despite his foreign origin, he also became a member of the council that ruled Athens, and despite being from Carthage—a city that Romans destroyed during his lifetime—he was highly praised by Roman writers. Cicero singled out precisely his Punic acumen and his diligence and industry. Cleitomachos' cultural attitudes were similarly transcending: while being one of the leading lights of Greek philosophy in Athens, he maintained his ties with Carthage, sending a *Consolation* to its citizens amid their misfortunes, but also dedicated two of his treatises to the Roman poet Lucilius and the former consul Lucius Censorinus; both were used extensively by Cicero in his extant works.

Hellenistic religion illustrates that the process of acculturation was a two-way street. Whereas there is no inspiration from Egyptian culture, for example, in the works of major Alexandrian poets, such as Callimachus and Theocritus, Greek and oriental cults provided a significant meeting point between the various cultures. The result was that the different deities increasingly "became understood as aspects of a common Hellenistic religious system rather than as expressions of historically discrete traditions."[21] The term for this well-known phenomenon is syncretism (from the Greek word for "to mix together").

As for the preponderant direction of influence, it was, as I noted earlier, the oriental cults that made the Greek cults assimilate rather than the other way around. This development was prepared for by a tradition of openmindedness that equated the gods of other nations, however "barbarian," with those of the Greeks. Herodotus provides numerous instances, and in actual practice the phenomenon had flourished for several centuries at one of the major shrines

61. Statue of the Artemis of Ephesus, Hellenistic period. (Photograph courtesy of Classics Slide Library, The University of Texas at Austin.)

of the Greek world, that of Artemis at Ephesus, where the goddess (Fig. 61) looked like anything but a chaste Artemis and clearly was an Asiatic deity of fertility, earth, and nature. This "Greek interpretation" (*interpretatio Graeca*) not only reached new heights in the Hellenistic period—the oriental god Melquart, e.g., was identified with Herakles in Phoenicia, North Africa, and Spain; Astarte (the Babylonian Ishtar) and the Syrian Atargatis with Aphrodite; the Egyptian Osiris with Dionysus; and Isis with Demeter, Aphrodite, and Hera, to give only a few examples—but actually entered into the syncretistic stage. The result was that "the more essentially Hellenic deities lost ground; those better suited for syncretistic equations gained."[22] Conversely, in the major shift that took place during the Hellenistic period, oriental cults that satisfied needs left unfulfilled by the Greek religion were adopted by Greeks and non-Greeks alike while the "Greek interpretation" eased their acceptance without changing much of their character.

A prominent example is the cult of Isis, whose diffusion throughout the

Hellenistic and Roman world was second to none. She was the Egyptian manifestation of the "Great Mother" goddess; then was associated, through the story of her husband, Osiris, with the cult of the dead; and finally became a universal deity who represented each and every aspect of the divine. The ritual, part of which involved water from the Nile, largely remained Egyptian and even in Greece and Rome was in the hands of an Egyptian priesthood including blacks from Ethiopia, as a fresco from Herculaneum (Fig. 62) and other artifacts attest. On the other hand, the specific initiation mysteries, which are a Hellenistic development, seem to have been modeled on those of Demeter at Eleusis, with whom the Greeks identified Isis. In addition, most of the shrines and statues of the goddess followed Greek traditions, the language of the cult was Greek, and there were no national barriers for her worshipers. About the cultural inclusiveness of this cult and others there can be no question.

Once again, it is important not to view this phenomenon from the limiting perspective in which the discussion of Hellenism has often been framed since the time of its seminal history by J. G. Droysen (1836), i.e., its success or failure in making the world, the East in particular, thoroughly Greek. Rather, by its very inclusiveness and fusion of religious traditions, Hellenism provided a loose and yet unifying and universally intelligible commonality, which was one of the major reasons for the long survival and popularity of pagan religion into late antiquity. This common cultural medium, in turn, influenced both Christianity and Islam.[23]

A similar commingling of traditions—Mesopotamian, Iranian, and Greek— is observable in some of the art and architecture especially of the eastern part of the Hellenistic world by the second century B.C.[24] I would like to focus, however, on the even more important development of the appearance of non-Greeks in art and their representation. An indicative example is the so-called Alexander Sarcophagus from the late fourth century, which was probably made for the king of Sidon who was appointed by Alexander. Two of the sculptural panels on the long and short sides depict Greeks and Persians battling one another (Fig. 63a), whereas the other two show Persians and Greeks jointly engaged in a royal hunt of lions (Fig. 63b). Alexander prominently participates in both. The classical aesthetic of the opposition and resolution of tensions, which underlies, for example, the architecture of the Parthenon, is now applied to the subject matter of the reliefs: while Persians and Greeks started out as enemies, they join together under Alexander's leadership and participate in the hunt on equal terms. This is both in the spirit of Alexander's *homonoia* and in the artistic and monumental tradition, which was Eastern rather than Greek, of the royal hunt. We saw earlier that the precedents of Herakles as a lion slayer were Near Eastern, and there may be a subtle allusion to this, too, as Alexander identified himself with Herakles.

Another group of statues makes it clear that "barbarians" now could be

62. Isiac ceremony. Wall painting from Herculaneum, 1st cent. A.D. Museo Nazionale, Naples. (Photograph Archivi Alinari.)

63a. Alexander Sarcophagus, late 4th cent. B.C. Battle of Greeks and Persians. Archaeological Museum, Istanbul. (Photograph courtesy of the Archaeological Museum.)

63b. Alexander Sarcophagus. Greeks and Persians at lion hunt. Archaeological Museum, Istanbul. (Photograph courtesy of the Archaeological Museum.)

64. Dying Gaul. Roman copy of original dating from c. 230–220 B.C. Capitoline Museums, Rome. (Photograph Archivi Alinari)

portrayed with respect and even empathy. Since the beginning of the fourth century B.C., when they sacked Rome, the Gauls had made their presence felt in many parts of the Mediterranean. Their threat to Delphi in 278 B.C. stirred deep emotions throughout the Hellenistic world and led, upon their withdrawal, to the foundation of the *Soteria*, the Festival of Salvation, which became one of the most important of Hellenistic times. One would not expect marauders like these to be treated kindly—and the Greeks, while having a flourishing colony at Marseilles since the early sixth century, never bothered to acquaint themselves with Celtic culture—but their representation, after their defeat by King Attalos I of Pergamum in the early 230s B.C., comes from a nobler spirit. Attalos commissioned several statues of dying Gauls as victory monuments (Figs. 64 and 65), and their pathos is compelling: "In the faces of both, a kind of animal ferocity has been infused with an unusual sort of dignity, not the dignity of the traditional Greek intellectual or hero but the dignity of the fanatical and fearless opponent whom one both fears and respects. . . . Empathy for his physical anguish as his strength ebbs away is stimulated not only by the lines of pain in his face, but also by a taut and tortured feeling in the musculature."[25] Instead of using the term "victory," two major inscriptions from Pergamum refer to the conflict with the Gauls as an

65. Gaul and wife. Roman copy of Greek original of c. 230–220 B.C. Rome, National Museum of the Terme. (Photograph courtesy of German Archaeological Institute, Rome.)

agon (a contest or struggle), which recalls a concept central to the Greek ethos. It was used, for example, for contests at the Olympic Games and implies that the opponent is one's equal. There is, of course, no glory in overcoming an opponent inferior in strength, but the sympathy evident especially in the rendition of the Gaul who is committing suicide and his wife whom he has just killed (Fig. 65) goes beyond such considerations. As a monument to human pain, they transcend nationality and individuality. It is interesting to note that the representation of such pathos, which is totally absent from classical art but found frequently in subsequent Hellenistic art, perhaps was made palatable first by showing it in people other than Greeks.[26]

The genres of Hellenistic art cut across the boundaries of race and culture. The subjects of burlesque and grotesque, for example, are drawn predominantly from the lower and bourgeois classes but do not differentiate on the

66. Balsamarium of bronze, 3d or 2d cent. B.C. Archaeological Museum of Florence, Inv. 2288. (Photograph courtesy of Soprintendenza alle Antichità, Firenze.)

basis of skin color. Quite on the contrary, as Frank Snowden's careful and comprehensive work on the iconography of blacks in antiquity has shown, all the salient characteristics of Hellenistic art are found in works that represent Negroes—"the expressive modelling, the anguish of features, the naturalistic portrayal of subjects in a variety of moods and movements, the engaging studies of children and single figures, the deeper understanding of the people. The result is that several portraits of blacks carefully and sympathetically executed, are among the finest specimens of the period."[27] Far from being a minority and stereotype, blacks were a frequent and extremely varied subject in Hellenistic sculpture and also occur in various decorative arts, such as jewelry, perfume vases, and lamps.

None of these art forms was considered degrading, and they often attracted the most accomplished artists. An outstanding example is a balsam vase with the delicate features of a young girl (Fig. 66); black is beautiful here indeed. One of the best-known statuettes is that of a young black entertainer (Figs. 67a and b), found in France. He holds a musical instrument and his pose is vivid and graceful. The attention given to the meticulous styling of his locks will not be lost on modern audiences. Two of the finest bronze statuettes from the entire Hellenistic period are that of a boy, expressive in its tense dynamism (Fig. 68), and a young orator who appropriately controls the gestures of his hands and arms (Fig. 69). One of the most famous Greek bronze

67a. Young musician. Hellenistic period, bronze. Bibliothèque Nationale, Paris; Cabinet des Médailles, Inv. 1009. (Photograph courtesy of the Bibliothèque Nationale.)

67b. Young musician, Hellenistic period. Frontal view. (Photograph courtesy of the Bibliothèque Nationale.)

68. Statuette of young athlete. Hellenistic period, bronze. Metropolitan Museum of Art, New York, Rogers Fund, Inv. 18.145.10. (Photograph © Metropolitan Museum of Art. All rights reserved.)

69. Statue of young orator. Bronze fragment, 2d or 1st cent. B.C. Archaeological Museum, Bodrum, Turkey. (Photograph courtesy of Institute of Nautical Archaeology.)

statues is the *Spinario,* or Thorn-Puller (Fig. 70), whose body follows the conventions of the fourth century whereas the head is fifth-century classical and incongruous with the posture of the statue as the hair, for instance, does not fall forward. We do not know when the two pieces were combined, but if it was done as early as Hellenistic times, it may have been yet another factor that contributed to the many parodic takeoffs on this subject. One of these is a first-century B.C. statuette of a young Negro (Fig. 71). It is not a vicious burlesque; there is the usual Hellenistic realism of portraiture, emphasizing such facial aspects as wrinkles on the nose and brow, puckered lips, puffed-up cheeks, and squinting eyes. We find the same kind of gentle and yet pointed humor here that characterizes literary parodies of the period, and the subject is rendered with sensitivity, charm, and wit rather than facile caricature.[28] The problem with the original's hair, for instance, is obviated by the use of a cap.

In sum, the portraiture of blacks does not constitute a case of artistic apart-

70. *Spinario* (Thorn-Puller). Bronze, 3d? cent. B.C. Capitoline Museums, Rome. (Photograph courtesy of German Archaeological Institute, Rome.)

71. Parody of *Spinario.* From Priene, 1st cent. B.C. Antikenmuseum Berlin, SMPK, Inv. TC 8626. (Photograph by Ingrid Geske-Heiden; © Antikenmuseum, Staatliche Museen Preußischer Kulturbesitz.)

heid but is part of the mainstream of Hellenistic art. Frank Snowden's summary is concise and to the point: "The popularity of the Negro in Hellenistic art, the understanding of the life of this non-Greek people in alien lands, and the care and skill with which blacks are portrayed, reflect the cosmopolitanism of the age and prompt the inference that the sentiment of the kinship of all men as expressed by Menander and later by Terence—'I am a man; I consider nothing human foreign to me'—was not limited to philosopher or dramatist."[29]

This is not to say that intercultural relations in the Hellenistic age were a love feast. There was plenty of resistance to Hellenism among the Eastern natives, and many Greeks—most of them not philosophers and writers, but traders and military both active and retired—preferred to keep to their own ways, centered on the Greek institution of the gymnasium in the various Eastern cities. At the same time, we now have evidence, for instance, of non-

Greeks participating in the Olympic Games and Greeks becoming function-
aries of Egyptian temples. We need to look at the whole panorama from the
perspective of world history, i.e., in relative terms;[30] absolutes are the privilege
of the ahistorical. There was cultural hermeticism, but there was also a truly
multicultural inclusiveness. That was the attitude which was to prevail in the
Roman world.

Rome

In his national epic, which is characterized, as we saw earlier, by a blend of
Roman and universal perspectives, Vergil offers a remarkably concise definition of the Roman character (*Aen.* 6.847–853). Other nations may excel, he
writes, in the fields of science, the arts, and rhetoric, but the Romans' mission
is to establish the Pax Romana, to spare the conquered and war down the
proud. Although the Romans did in fact produce superior works of art and
literature, they, unlike the fifth-century Athenians or the devotees of Greek
gymnasia in the Hellenistic East, never developed a cultural superiority complex that would interfere with their cultural interactions with other peoples.
Being non-Greeks and, alas, "barbarians," they had from the very beginning a
very non-Greek perspective on cultural and ethnic diversity. There were several contributing factors.

One is that the main characteristic of the Romans' origin in both legend and
reality was the fusion of peoples. Early Italy was inhabited by numerous
peoples of whom the Latins were only one. Under Rome's mythical founder
Romulus, they took Sabine wives and soon totally mixed with the Sabines;
Romulus had a Sabine coruler, and the second Roman king, Numa, was Sabine
also. Even after the Roman conquest of the Italian peninsula (early 3d century
B.C.), the other populations, such as the Oscans and Etruscans, retained their
cultural identity and dialects while the normal process of intermarrying gradually produced a common culture. It is not until the first century B.C., however,
after all Italians obtained Roman citizenship, that we can speak of a generally
Roman culture in Italy. It was a mixed culture; the Etruscans, for example,
significantly contributed to Roman religion and the social role of Roman
women, and the Oscans shaped the more rambunctious nature of Roman
comedy. Equally extensive were the mythological versions that ascribed to
Rome descent from Troy. The Trojans could be viewed either as Asiatics—
Dido's African suitor Iarbas describes Aeneas unflatteringly in such terms
(*Aen.* 4.215–217)[31]—or Greeks, and the myths of Trojan ancestry were
melded in numerous ways with the native Italic myths both of Latinus and of
Romulus and Remus. While the speculations in Greece about the Pelasgian
and other multiracial origins of the Greeks may have been "regarded as remote
intellectual curiosities . . . devoid of practical influence,"[32] that was not the
case in Rome where, aside from Vergil's *Aeneid,* much of the earlier historical

and epic writing centers on the Romans' multicultural descent and traditions.

A second factor was the Roman system of slavery. While it was color blind, as always in Greco-Roman antiquity, it differed from the Greek by the frequent emancipation of slaves, especially the urban slaves, at the end of their useful life or before. Usually, the right to intermarry, if not outright citizenship, would result within two generations. The result was that the Roman citizen body was constantly enlarged by the inclusion of non-Romans. That attitude shaped the Romans' treatment of their former subjects who were integrated in a gradual fashion into the Roman citizenry until Caracalla's edict in A.D. 212 granted all denizens of the Roman Empire citizenship en bloc. We should be careful, incidentally, not to view this action of a Roman emperor of North African descent as being motivated by an overriding concern for civil rights; the principal motive was to prevent noncitizens from escaping inheritance taxes. The gradualism and pragmatism characterizing the whole process of slave emancipation and extension of citizenship is paralleled by a differentiated and nuanced terminology of references to foreign peoples, *barbari,* and non-Romans, which depend on the individual social, political, or historical context.[33]

In contrast to Greece, then, there was never any overriding Roman/barbarian antithesis. "The Romans themselves," as one observer has aptly pointed out, "were not a static people intent on preserving their own identity. The Romans of the Social or Italian War at the beginning of the first century B.C. were very different from those of the early empire, and even the Romans of Augustus' day were different from those of the time of Hadrian. Since Roman society itself was so mobile, the accommodation of former subjects was hardly a problem."[34] Accordingly, Seneca and Tacitus comment favorably on the empire's sound policy of intermingling conqueror and conquered.

Roman law exemplifies the institutionalization of the recognition of cultural diversity. The Romans did not destroy the legal systems of the peoples they conquered. Sometimes they even borrowed from them, administering law in the provinces on the basis of local law, and they promoted the holding of dual citizenship; members of a Berber family, for example, who were made Roman citizens in the second century A.D., explicitly were not exempted from the law of their tribe.[35] Since 242 B.C., the Romans elected one (and later, more) of their chief judicial officials, the praetors, "to give justice between peregrines," and they established the notion of the *ius gentium,* i.e., "those legal habits which were accepted by the Roman law as applying to, and being used by, all the people they met, whether Roman citizens or not." On a more theoretical level, *ius gentium* came to be identified with "natural law," i.e., the concept that some provisions are common to the legal systems of all nations they knew.[36] Such tendencies were enhanced by the continuing teachings of the Hellenistic philosophies, especially the Stoics, on the unity of mankind. They are voiced both by philosophers, such as Cicero and Seneca, and by others like Pliny the

Elder, who defined Rome as "the one fatherland of all nations in the entire world" (*una cunctarum gentium in toto orbe patria; N.H.* 3.5.39). This notion went hand in hand with the Pax Romana and explained its continuing obligation; obviously, more was involved than mere military might.

Unlike the Greeks, the Romans were not held back by assumptions of cultural superiority from taking a serious interest in other peoples and their cultures. It was they who systematically encouraged ethnography, and they employed Greeks for the task.[37] The same Polybius who mused about the decline and fall of nations[38] traveled at the Romans' behest and under their protection in Gaul and was the first to describe the interior of Spain. With Roman help, he also explored the coasts of Africa; we do not know how far he reached because those portions of his work are lost. Somewhat later (late 2d cent./early 1st cent. B.C.), Posidonius spent several years of his life exploring Gaul, Spain, and North Africa. His work remained a major source of information for decades—he left a detailed account of the Druids, for example—and was used extensively by Julius Caesar. There were ulterior motives on the part of the Romans for all this research: they went on to conquer those very lands. But, as previously noted, many other conquerors never took the interest or trouble. The Romans' curiosity, however motivated, certainly is a far cry from the procedure of Greek historiographers in the sixth and fifth centuries who stayed home and simply invented mythological linkages. And once conquest was over, it was time for assimilation. An appropriate postscript on the exploration of Celtic culture is Emperor Claudius' speech on the admission of Gauls to the Roman Senate. He pointedly reminds the senators of the multinational origins of their ancestors, goes on to say that the Gauls now are "united [the actual Latin word is *mixti*, "mixed"] with us by manners, education, and intermarriage," and concludes with an equally Roman and pragmatic argument that "they might as well bring us their gold and their wealth rather than enjoy it in isolation" (Tacitus, *Annals* 11.24.6). Integration of other cultures and Roman self-interest could be combined. The senators, I should add, accepted Claudius' argument.

Hellenistic civilization, as we saw earlier, did not practice cultural imperialism. It did not have to: in the West, it was embraced ardently by the Romans beginning with the Roman conquest of Greece, which was complete by 146 B.C. The Romans seized on this already-flexible and diverse culture, revitalized it further by adaptation and innovation, and combined it with their own traditions into a remarkable synthesis. It is these dynamic reasons that account for the longevity of Roman culture and its influence. As might be expected, many of its protagonists were not Roman natives, but before we look at some examples, a brief comment is useful on the process itself in the light of the current issue of acculturation.

"Why the Romans," as one modern scholar has remarked so aptly, "threw themselves into the difficult business of absorbing the culture of one foreign nation just when they were involved in exhausting wars with another foreign nation [i.e., Carthage in the 3d cent. B.C.], remains one of those puzzles which characterize nations in their most inscrutable and decisive hours. . . . The assimilation of Greek language, manners and beliefs is indistinguishable from the creation of a national literature which, with all the imitation of alien models, was immediately original, self-assured and aggressive."[39] The realization that cultural identity can be achieved by the creative adaptation of an alien culture rather than by its rejection is a useful perspective for today's debate about multiculturalism. The Romans had it both ways: they took the best from another culture without railing against its hegemony and without giving up their own traditions. The difference is that they were secure in these traditions, which were less sophisticated but well defined and vital, and their own value system.[40] A contributory sociological reason was the strength and intact nature of the Roman family at the time; a sound family structure, as we know from social psychology, is a far greater factor in building self-confidence and self-esteem than any attempts at self-esteem elevation by artificial means. Further self-assurance, as is clear from the example of a variety of Romans, comes from individual achievement and the creative continuation rather than the mere awareness of a tradition. Cato the Censor, for instance, who often is wrongly profiled as the stereotype of a crusty Roman isolationist abjuring the evils of Hellenism, in reality stood for the proper balance in the process of acculturation. He did not want the Romans to lose sight of their own ways amidst the appeal of a far more advanced culture, but inter alia, he initiated the study of the Celts—he even gave them credit for their wit—and he learned Greek. Most educated Romans did so, too, whereas the knowledge of another language was not the common practice in the Hellenistic East, let alone in pre-Alexandrian Greece.

Terence, the former African slave, was a contemporary of Cato's and a paradigm of humane multiculturalism, as I have already noted. While writing at Rome, his comedies were more in the Greek vein, and yet, as a recent critic has commented, "Terence's primary place is among the seminal figures of *Latin* literature. . . . Terence became the last pioneer of the ancient stage."[41] Similarly representative of diverse cultural traditions was Apuleius (2d cent. A.D.), the author of the only surviving Latin novel. Augustine calls him *Afer* ("African"),[42] as he was born in Madaurus (in today's Algeria). He was educated at Carthage, Athens, and Rome. After some eventful travels to Egypt and Libya, he returned to Carthage, where he taught rhetoric and Platonic philosophy. Although he is known today chiefly for *The Golden Ass* (it contains the famous story of Cupid and Psyche and ends with the protagonist's salvation by Isis), his prolific writings in both Greek and Latin included works on agriculture, astronomy, and arithmetic as well as philosophical and rhetorical treatises. He enjoyed tremendous renown and was honored with an appointment to the priesthood of the imperial cult and with many statues. Or, to mention just one other major writer: Martial, who was born in Spain around A.D.40, prided himself on his Celtic and Iberian descent. He moved to Rome and, basically creating the modern epigram, wrote more than fifteen hundred short poems, which give us a vivid picture of Roman society and everyday life. His focus, like Terence's, was on man (10.4.10), and because of this human concern and his stylistic brilliance, wit, and descriptive powers, his influence on later centuries was just as strong as that of his well-known fellow Spaniard (though of Italic stock) and contemporary, the tragedian Seneca. Another contemporary, Quintilian, who wrote the most influential treatise on rhetoric—and rhetoric was at the center of Roman education—in all probability also was a Spanish native. And the foremost Roman orator of the second century, Fronto, who pioneered a highly innovative style, came from Numidia.

As we saw earlier,[43] Gibbon could call the years A.D. 96–180 the most happy and prosperous period of mankind because the Romans then decided to set aside the hereditary system of succession and instead had the emperor chosen on the basis of merit. It is anything but surprising that two of the best emperors of the period came from Spain. Trajan's ancestors probably were from Italy but are likely to have intermarried with the natives. His administration (A.D. 98–117) set a standard for those to come, as can be seen from the formula with which the senate in the late Roman Empire acclaimed any new emperor: "May you be luckier than Augustus and better than Trajan." There was some "imperial overstretch" as the Roman Empire under Trajan reached its largest size ever, but besides being effective, his rule also was humane, as exemplified by his attitude to Christian persecutions ("they are not in the spirit of our century") and a public alimentary program for Italian municipalities on the model of private foundations.

The family into which his successor Hadrian (A.D. 117–138) was born had been residing in Spain for more than 250 years, and again intermarriage with natives is more than likely. I have already cited Hadrian as a counterexample to the notion of decline and fall,[44] and he was certainly one of the most gifted and creative Roman emperors ever. Like few others, he consciously addressed the issues of cohesiveness and centrifugalism that come with geographic and multicultural diversity. His administrative solution was to go out to the provinces as often as possible instead of staying in Rome. His cultural solution was an emphasis on Hellenism as the unifying force. This was not cultural imperialism because a flexible Hellenistic culture, with all its Roman and other regional adaptations, was in fact one of the strongest existing commonalities of the empire and did not need to be imposed, but Hadrian expected similar openmindedness and willingness to assimilate from all nations of the Roman world. Multiculturalism was meant to be reciprocal. Accordingly, he perceived the cultural and military resistance of the Jews as a threat, and the results were the massacre following the Bar Kochba rebellion in the early 130s, the denationalization of Judaea, and the beginnings of the Jewish Diaspora. Outside of Rome, Hadrian's so-called Villa, which is really a complex of diverse buildings, mirrors his interest in the various architectural traditions of the empire (including Egypt), and it is easy to understand why this congenial example of free-style classicism has been a frequent inspiration to postmodern architects.[45]

Marcus Aurelius, the Stoic sage and last of the emperors appointed on merit, made the mistake of reverting to the hereditary system. His incompetent son Commodus (A.D. 180–192), who fancied himself another Herakles, was finally murdered, and a struggle ensued that ended with the ascent of the African dynasty of the Severi, whose best and longest-ruling member was Septimius Severus (A.D. 193–211). As the first African emperor (the family was from Leptis Magna in Libya), he attracted more hostility from Eurocentric historians than from his own subjects, and it didn't help that his wife was Syrian. The discussion, not always enlightened, even reached the floor of the U.S. House of Representatives in 1963.[46] It was, as so often, Edward Gibbon who started it two centuries earlier.

While Gibbon was aware of the complex causalities of Rome's decline and fall, which justified the extraordinary length of his treatment of the subject, he could on occasion startle the somnolent reader by proffering just one simple explanation. His accentuation of "immoderate greatness" is a famous example.[47] Another is his point-blank identification of Septimius Severus as "the principal author of the decline of the Roman Empire." A plethora of historians, though by no means all, took their cue from him, with German, French, and British scholars leading the charge. Septimius was seen as the destroyer of the culture of the Mediterranean, as Hannibal's revenge, as planting "the despotism of the East in the soil of the West." Such phrases as the "mongrelization of manners" that allegedly took place under his rule are unsubtle references to his racial origin that are still found in American textbooks. Other historians tried to rescue him essentially by making him into a white man and arguing, unconvincingly, that he really may have been of Italian stock.

In Septimius' own time, race was not the issue. He became emperor after a bloody struggle, which Rome had not seen since the death of Nero, against other contenders and proceeded to execute some senators sympathetic to his rivals—an action that the U.S. Constitution forbids the president from taking, though one not uncommon in world history. In the course of his reign, he also shifted more power from the senate to other classes and governing entities in the empire. Because many historians in ancient Rome came from senatorial circles, all this engendered a hostile tradition that modern historians have tended to follow, but even in antiquity it was by no means universal. Although not another Hadrian or Augustus—Septimius' acknowledged model was Marcus Aurelius—he was a strong emperor who was not without vision. He had courage, spent much of his time going to the provinces, led military campaigns on both the Near Eastern and the British frontier, had a relentless capacity for hard work, left a budget surplus despite being afflicted with an edifice complex in Rome, and balanced his toughness with the promotion of equitable and humane concerns in the administration of justice: three of the most influential Roman jurists, including Papinian and Ulpian, both probably from Syria, worked in his administration.

There is no evidence that he packed the senate with Africans, Syrians, and Illyrians nor that he favored his homeland at the expense of other parts of the empire. If he surrounded himself with trusted advisers from there, the custom has plentiful parallels in the history of the American presidency. There is no question that he was a man of considerable accomplishment, and his redistribution of powers, far from the despotic tendencies of some of the later emperors, even prompted one modern historian to conclude that "it is not excessive to say that the Roman Empire and—in general terms—the Mediterranean world were never more democratic"[48] than under the rule of this African emperor. A painting on a wood medallion from Egypt shows him and his family around A.D. 200 (Fig. 72); the face of the younger son was obliterated after he fell into disfavor after Septimius' death.

This must suffice as a sample of Hispanics and Africans who were leaders in Roman letters, education, and government; others, like Augustine and Tertullian, could easily be added. A detailed study of the multicultural aspects of the Roman world could fill an entire book, which is testimony to their richness and pervasiveness. Two final questions may be posed, however. How did this multiculturalism affect the Roman Empire, and what was its relation to Romanization?

Let me take up the second question first. As we have seen, Roman culture was a mixed culture. It was an evolving form of Hellenism: religious syncretism advanced, and so did the Hellenistic philosophies with their emphasis on cultural and racial toleration. The representation of blacks continued unabated and without denigration in Roman art, and the material culture, as evidenced by the architecture of temples, theaters, and other public and private buildings, was an amalgam of Greek and Roman characteristics. As we saw in the discussion of Augustan culture, such a synthesis was anything but un-Roman, a misconception that is still found all too frequently in modern historical writing. Again, parallel to what we observed earlier about the Hellenistic world, such cosmopolitan attitudes, although they now appear on an even grander scale, were not universal, and we find the usual share of xenophobia and racist slurs, the satirist Juvenal (2d half of 1st cent.–1st half of 2d cent. A.D.) being a prime example. Some native Romans, just like some of our contemporaries, felt threatened by the equality of opportunity for foreigners and members of other races, and they were not shy about venting their dismay. Conversely, Tacitus could hold up the Germanic tribes as models for emulation.

In approaching the first question, we should note again that the Romans

72. Septimius Severus and his family. Antikenmuseum Berlin, SMPK, Inv. 31329. (Photograph by Ingrid Geske-Heiden; © Antikenmuseum, Staatliche Museen Preußischer Kulturbesitz.)

generally left local cultures alone and even respected them as is shown, for example, by their judicial practice. They imposed the Roman/Hellenistic culture as little on other peoples as Hellenistic culture had been imposed on them. The distinction between the imposition of Roman *rule*—and here the Romans brooked no resistance—and the imposition, if any, of Roman *culture* is vital.[49] The degree of their Romanization, then, depended mostly on the initiative of the natives; in contrast to the Greek cities in the Hellenistic East, no attempt was made to keep foreigners from participating in the Roman culture. Unless it was accompanied by military nationalism, multiculturalism was not a significant threat to the empire's cohesiveness. It could have been if hermetic attitudes had prevailed, but the Roman world exemplifies that multiculturalism is a two-way street: even Egypt, that supreme example of impermeability, finally opened up to Hellenism in Roman times.[50]

In fact, the acceptance of Romanization in some provinces, including Spain, may be of great discomfort to those who today define multiculturalism in terms of the rigid maintenance of separate cultural identities. It also raises the final, important issue of the relation between material and spiritual Romanization or, for that matter, acculturation. Within a century of Augustus' rule, the art and architecture in Spain and Gaul had taken on a decidedly Roman cast, and there were only a few remainders of native traditions, such as smaller shrines.[51] Regardless of where the impulse lay, it has been well observed that "the concern was to generate a visual image of Romanness that could give encouragement to the idea of assimilation and promote a sense of common unity and shared values in a heterogeneous mix of peoples."[52] The same undoubtedly could be said about many of the Greek foundations in the East during the Hellenistic period, and yet, most remained mere enclaves whereas Romanization in Gaul and Spain, for instance, was pervasive. It was more than a material veneer "covering stronger native and tribal sensibilities. Roman identity replaced the older concepts of self." The success of Roman acculturation, in the final analysis, was based not on the superiority of a material culture but on the acceptance and voluntary espousal of values and attitudes that different races and cultures could share. We saw earlier that the articulation of such unifying values is essential to the concept of transforming leadership and that such leadership, in turn, was essential for the vitality of the Roman Empire.[53] At the same time, those values could be shared by many cultures because the Romans were a multicultural people and more open to other cultures than most nations in history.

Multiculturalism Then and Now

Multiculturalism is a subject that deserves to be studied seriously (and with intellectual rigor rather than "special methodologies" that imply its absence) instead of being reduced to crude politicization. The United States, in Walt Whitman's words, is a "teeming Nation of nations," and so was the world of Greece and Rome at least since the time of Alexander the Great. The multicultural experience of these civilizations provides, as history always does, some perspectives that are useful for today.

First, it is amply documented—and I had to restrict myself to mere samples—that the Greco-Roman beginnings of Western civilization are the product of many different races and cultures. Race and culture were not equated—nor is there any evidence today that they should be—and such terms as "racism," "race prejudice," and "color prejudice" are irrelevant and anachronistic for the discussion of Greek and Roman attitudes.[54] Multiculturalism was alive, but the race issue, which is so explosive today, has no counterpart in classical antiquity. As Anna Quindlen has put it, "anyone who has ever faced discrimination knows that bigotry begins when race [and] ethnicity are applied as sole definitions."[55] Greeks and Romans could live without such bigotry, and the current multiculturalism debate would be improved by its absence.

Secondly, there was from the very beginning an awareness of commonality transcending ethnic origins and cultural affiliations. The search for it was an organic process that increased in intensity and never resulted in the sort of bland homogeneity of the modern International Style against which postmodern architects rebelled for the sake of humanness and cultural diversity. Hellenization and Romanization were the result not of cultural imperialism but of the ability to meld cultural contributions from variegated groups and heritages into ideas and customs that could be shared by all. That did not mean the end of other traditions, which persisted to varying degrees and coexisted with the cultural *koine*. Because the peoples of the Hellenistic and Roman world were heterogeneous and kept evolving, the Hellenistic and Roman culture did too. It did not remain static.

This opens up several aspects on the current debate. As William Raspberry has pointed out, the "search for community" and "appeal to commonality" were hallmarks of the civil rights movement until recently. More generally, a core of shared ideas and beliefs, centering on liberty and democracy (both coming from the "Western" tradition), has traditionally been at the center of American culture, providing transcendent commonalities amidst all the heterogeneity. Against this stands the cultural tribalism of much of the multicultural movement, stressing the unassimilable nature of individual groups (rather than cultures, strictly speaking) and suspiciousness of people unlike one's own.[56]

These are regressive attitudes merely from the historical perspectives I have sketched. One difference emerges by way of explanation: in Greco-Roman times, cultural traditions of any sort were organic and ongoing. That, in turn, led to confident attitudes in confronting and assimilating other cultures. By contrast, the traditions of African Americans, whose ancestors did not come to this country voluntarily, were interrupted to varying degrees and given little attention. Accordingly, even while a major effort is under way to recover these traditions, there is a great deal of defensiveness, perhaps because of some all too imaginative reconstructions. It has resulted in attempts at curricular imperialism—the revision of New York State's history curriculum is a prominent example[57]—which make the absence of Greek and Roman cultural imperialism look even more benign by comparison.

Besides, and this is one final lesson from the experience of multiculturalism in Greece and Rome, such artificial measures are neither necessary nor workable to achieve cultural identity. Rather, as both the Greco-Roman experience and the new classicism in postmodern architecture make clear, we attain such identity by availing ourselves of existing cultural traditions, regardless of their origin, and keeping them and ourselves vital by our own, distinctive contributions instead of treating them as static entities or immovable inheritances. The ultimate commonality is creativity.[58]

Selected Bibliography and Suggestions for Further Reading

Because this is the first overview of multiculturalism in the field of classics, I have listed a fuller bibliography than for the other chapters. It should be noted that the entire Sixth International Congress of Classical Studies in 1974 was devoted to the topic of "Assimilation and Resistance to Greco-Roman Culture in the Ancient World." The many contributions to that subject were edited and published by D. M. Pippidi (Bucharest and Paris 1976).

Avi-Yonah, M. *Hellenism and the East: Contacts and Interrelations from Alexander to the Roman Conquest* (University Microfilms International 1978).

Baldry, H. C. *The Unity of Man in Greek Thought* (Cambridge 1965).

Bochner, S. *Cultures in Contact: Studies in Cross-Cultural Interaction* (Oxford 1982).

Bowersock, G. W. *Hellenism in Late Antiquity* (Ann Arbor 1990).

Burkert, W. *Structure and History in Greek Mythology and Ritual* (Berkeley 1979).

Diller, A. *Race Mixture among Greeks before Alexander*. Illinois Studies in Language and Literature 20.1 (1937), repr. 1971.

Crook, J. A. *Law and Life of Rome, 90* B.C.–A.D. *212* (Ithaca 1967).

Green, Peter. *From Alexander to Actium: The Historical Evolution of the Hellenistic Age* (Berkeley 1990).

———. "Greek Gifts?" *History Today* 40 (1990) 27–34.

Kuhrt, A., and S. Sherwin-White, eds. *Hellenism in the East: The Interaction of Greek and Non-Greek Civilizations from Syria to Central Asia after Alexander* (London 1987).

Lawrence, A. W. *Greek Architecture*. 4th ed., rev. by R. A. Tomlinson (Penguin 1983).

Lewis, Bernard. "Other People's History." *American Scholar* 59 (1990) 397–405.

Martin, L. H. *Hellenistic Religions: An Introduction* (New York 1987).

Momigliano, A. *Alien Wisdom: The Limits of Hellenization* (Cambridge 1975).

Pollitt, J. J. *Art in the Hellenistic Age* (Cambridge 1986).

Ravitch, Diane. "Multiculturalism." *American Scholar* 59 (1990) 337–354.

Reverdin, M., ed. *Grecs et barbares: Entretiens sur l'antiquité classique* 8 (Geneva 1962).

Robertson, M. L. *A History of Greek Art* (Cambridge 1975).

Saddington, W. B. "Race Relations in the Early Roman Empire." In H. Temporini, ed., *Aufstieg und Niedergang der Römischen Welt* II.3 (Berlin and New York 1975) 112–137.

Snowden, F. M. *Blacks in Antiquity* (Cambridge, Mass. 1970).

————. "Iconographical Evidence on the Black Populations in Graeco-Roman Antiquity." In J. Vercoutter et al., *The Image of the Black in Western Art* 1 (New York 1976) 133–245, 298–307.

————. *Before Color Prejudice: The Ancient View of Blacks* (Cambridge, Mass. 1983).

Thompson, L. A. *Romans and Blacks* (Norman 1989).

Walcot, P. *Hesiod and the Near East* (Cardiff 1966).

West, M. L. *Early Greek Philosophy and the Orient* (Oxford 1971).

VI

Rome, America, and the Classics in America Today

America and Rome

Comparisons between Rome and America have been popular from the time of the colonial period and, especially, the beginning of the American Republic. Such analogies fall into two categories of inspiration. Some are based on direct and conscious cultural continuity as in the areas of education, law, government, city planning, and neoclassical architecture. The second mode of the classical tradition is less direct but just as vital. It is the discovery of affinities; we use various aspects of Roman (and, for that matter, Greek) history and civilization as paradigms "not because," in the words of a recent writer, "they were perfect models that must be imitated [nor] because they are the source of either the perfection or the problems of western civilization . . . but because they challenge us to imagine, to argue, to become more fully conscious, and to think what otherwise would be unthinkable."[1] These two strands of the classical tradition in America are not always separate: the resurgence of classicism in postmodern American architecture, for instance, exemplifies the convergence of both. The study of the first, centering chiefly on direct influences and the practice of classical learning, has been revitalized in recent years mostly due to the efforts of such scholars as Meyer Reinhold and is not my primary concern. Rather, I want to bring together some major affinities, which we have already seen in evidence throughout the preceding chapters, between contemporary America and Rome and make a final comment on them before proceeding to a brief assessment of the role of professional classicists from that perspective and others.

Let me begin with an example of historical influence. It pertains to the U.S. Constitution, whose making the English-born Alfred North Whitehead praised as follows:

I know of only two occasions when the people in power did what needed to be done about as well as you can imagine its being possible. One was the framing of your Constitution. They were able statesmen; they had access to a body of good ideas; they incorporated these principles into the instrument without trying to particularize too explicitly how they should be put into effect; and they were men of immense practical experience themselves. The other was in Rome and it undoubtedly saved civilization for, roughly, about four hundred years. It was the work of Augustus. . . . Somehow, he found a way to call in, first . . . the "new men" of new ideas, then, as the centuries went on, came the provincials, people like the Spanish Caesars.[2]

Whitehead's recognition of the true importance of the "Augustan revolution," which involved the active participation of poets like Vergil in the formulation of the guiding ideas,[3] is most welcome; few scholars have been so discerning. So is his opinion of the merits of non-Roman emperors. What about the American Constitution as a similar paragon of the combination of practicality and high principles?

We pride ourselves today primarily on the system of checks and balances that it embodies and that were characteristic especially of the Roman constitution. As is clear from *The Federalist Papers* and many other contemporary sources, the delegates to the Constitutional Convention, who assembled "at a time when influence of the classics was at its height,"[4] were conversant with models unknown even to culturally literate Americans today, such as the Amphictyonic League and the Lycian confederacy, while the center of the debate was held by the pertinent writings of Aristotle, Polybius, and Cicero. The delving into classical precedents, enhanced by the appointment of the classics instructor James Wilson as a researcher, became so pronounced as to be satirized, and since the delegates were practical men, they also realized that all antecedents came from states and nations that had declined and fallen, or so Benjamin Franklin reminded them. Thus they came up with their particular mix, and Richard Gummere summed up the issue of "classical influence" very well by stating that "these classical experiments in government did not convince the delegates of 1787, but they did serve to promote intelligent discussion." As can be seen, we are dealing mostly with the second of the two aspects of the vitality of the classical tradition in this case. The framers of the Constitution used the extensive Greek and Roman tradition not to establish Rome on the Potomac but as a challenge to argue and become more fully conscious of their undertaking.

It is important, therefore, for us today not to be obsessed with the system of checks and balances but to put it in perspective. The Roman example—and the distribution of powers and checks there was arranged in a somewhat different manner, which is not essential to the argument—makes it clear that it is the spirit behind the system that matters, and not the letter and its concomitant technical provisions; for good reason, the Roman constitution was never actually written down. The Romans established checks and balances not to paralyze government but as a challenge for all those involved to work together and resolve any disputes by goodwill and assiduous cooperation. To the modern observer, the multiple veto powers of Roman consuls and tribunes are mind-boggling, and so is the absence of a genuine bicameral system: decrees passed by either the senate or one of the assemblies did not have to be ratified by the other. That the system worked for so long during the Roman Republic is a tribute to the political and cooperative skills of the Roman leaders. The end of the Republic came when that spirit ceased to exist, and in that sense, Augustus, who did not abolish the constitution, could claim without hypocrisy that he had saved the Republic from the tyranny of a faction and restored it.[5]

The point is that our system of checks and balances should not serve as an excuse for our government today for not getting on with the business of governing. The issue has been injected, inevitably, into the current debate about decline with a few envious glances being cast in the direction of parliamentary democracy. A correct perception of the classical tradition in this instance helps us realize that the problem is not the immobility of the system but the absence of the qualities of leadership and concern for social responsibility, which, as we saw earlier, sustained the Roman commonwealth for a remarkably long time. Whitehead and others well observed that the genius of the American Constitution lay in the emphasis on principles rather than explicit particularization, and the same is true of Rome. It encouraged the exercise of creativity, imagination, and flexibility—the same characteristics we have seen time and again as being vital to the continuity of any cultural tradition—rather than the filling of the void by an infinite number of statutes.

Not only does James MacGregor Burns' distinction between transactional and transforming leadership[6] come from such a context but so does the American aversion to ideologies and dogmas; while there are exceptions, such as in literary theory, pragmatic attitudes prevail by and large in real life. For good reason, therefore, Plato's writings on government never figured in the discussions at the Constitutional Convention because he was the most doctrinaire of the ancient authorities. The parallel with Roman attitudes readily suggests itself.

In tune with the long-standing predisposition of American classicists for things Greek, it is the Greek "influence" that has been emphasized rather than the Roman. Outside of such academic discussions, however, another affinity between America and Rome has been part of the discourse at least since the Constitutional Convention: the recognition of the far greater complexity of the Roman world. The *Aeneid,* as we have seen, reflects that: it is a complex work of literature trying to do justice to its time and ours. That meaning is not lost on our students; increasingly—and I have heard this from colleagues all over the country besides experiencing it in my own teaching—they prefer and appreciate that dimension of the *Aeneid,* while the Homeric epics, the *Odyssey* in particular, are easier to digest.

Part of that complexity was the cultural synthesis that was Rome. As we have seen, its multidimensionality is a useful and intrinsically necessary perspective on Roman civilization. Renewed interest in its study may come from current, external impulses, such as the concern with multiculturalism and its definition, but the pertinence of the Roman experience, which incorporated Hellenism, is another testimony to the richness and utility of the classical tradition for purposes of comparison and for helping us achieve greater consciousness.

We have seen throughout this book that study of some aspects of the ancient world often stems from concern with contemporary issues, and such study is legitimate unless it lapses into anachronisms. It is but one example of "that variety, vitality, and richness of the classical tradition which has made it possible for the classics to surmount all artificial supports, to find constantly new interests, and to contribute to American life in ways undreamed of earlier."[7] That realization should be both comforting and challenging for American classicists. It is also a useful springboard for some opportune questions. What, in fact, do the classics today contribute to American life? Is such a contribution one of the considered missions of the classics profession? What demand is there and how is it being met? And how do the profession's inherent strengths and limitations and its self-perception relate to such endeavors?

The Role of the Classics in America Today: Some Observations

Life beyond Academe

The vitality of the classics in the broadest sense is a concern not limited to the classics profession these days. Architecture, as we have seen, provides an instructive parallel: for decades, the dehumanizing Modernist Style of Mies van der Rohe (a Platonist, at that) and others reigned supreme to the point of dogma, and any humanist aspirations, expressed, for example, by decorative and historicizing tendencies, virtually vanished during this period of the "Protestant Inquisition." Less than twenty years ago, classicism in architecture was not just in a crisis, but dead in concrete and steel due to the reigning orthodoxy of the International Style. It took courage, conviction, and individual creativity to bring it back: we are dealing, clearly, not with neoclassicism but with a pluralistic variety of idiosyncratic practitioners.

That, in essence, is also true of academic classicists in American higher education today. Instead of being institutionalized, as it was by virtue of the nineteenth-century curriculum, the classics discipline today increasingly lives by the wits of its practitioners. This accounts for the diversity of their orientation, activities, and initiatives. Another characteristic shared by them and their classicizing colleagues in architecture is the creed that brought the classical mode in architecture back from virtual extinction: "Classicism," as Robert Stern has put it, "offers the architect a canon as a guide, but what a liberal and tolerant canon it is. It proposes models of excellence in composition and detail. It does not set out on a singular route but points out various ways. . . . classicism has flexibility and built-in tolerance."[8]

This is the authentic voice of a classicist, articulating an attitude with which most academic classicists identify today because it is self-definition in these creative, pluralistic, tolerant, and humane terms that justifies the existence of our discipline, explains the demand for the classics in our country, and insures their continuing vitality. The terms of Stern's definition, in fact, are very similar to those used by Walter Agard in the 1950s in his survey of American classical scholarship.[9] The contrast could not be more marked with many of the views expressed in the recently published *Classics: A Discipline and Profession in Crisis?*[10] where entropy and self-commiseration—two attitudes always dear to academe—prevail and surprisingly little attention is paid to the historical development of the discipline in the United States, nor the many successful models in existence, nor to discernible future challenges. It all amounts to a kind of closing of the classical mind at a time of unprecedented opportunities.

Such opportunities, which require resourcefulness and adaptability instead of the conventional recourse to the cant of crisis, lie both within and outside academe. Most of them involve outreach and expansion. This is not a matter of mere tactics but a strategic goal in view of the vitality of the classical tradition, as defined above, in America. More than twenty-five years ago, the historian of the American Philological Association, Professor Lucius Shero, commendably emphasized the desideratum of "disseminating reliable information about the ancient world to a wider public."[11] This was only the logical extension of a development that had culminated in the 1950s when classics departments increasingly started offering courses in ancient civilization, history, archaeology, and the like to appeal to the general student rather than to the dwindling number of those who wanted to study Greek or Latin. It was, alas, a matter of survival. Nineteenth-century philology had become an end in itself rather than proceeding to raise "questions of more general significance about literature,"[12] and that solipsistic orientation, in conjunction with some external factors, led to the understandable diminution of the classical curriculum. By coincidence, the National Endowment for the Humanities was chartered in the same year (1964) in which Mr. Shero stated the expanded objective and has supported several successful outreach projects undertaken by classicists. They and others illustrate that ample and grateful demand for appropriate instruction in the classics exists both in the larger context of individual colleges and universities and in the public and private sectors. They also illustrate that the only limiting factor is the extent of initiative on the part of the classicists themselves.

Cooperation with the elementary and secondary schools is a good example. By the early 1980s, jeremiads about the state of secondary education in particular had become commonplace. This is not to detract from their validity, but there was something self-servingly Olympian about the often hyperbolical plaints of university professors who declared their students' "illiteracy" to be the fault of the high schools without proffering any help. Significantly, the initiative to offer summer seminars for high school teachers through NEH did not come from the humanities profession, which was content with looking to NEH primarily as a provider of research funds, but from its chairman at the time, William Bennett. It was, at last, a matter of putting the money where the mouth was, and the program, expanded meanwhile to accommodate teachers at all levels, has been immensely successful. It found natural allies among classicists because many university and college programs had cultivated supportive relations with the schools long before it became fashionable to do so. Another model of a successful response to an existing need is collaborative programs between a local university and school district to strengthen humanities areas like world literature. Many English teachers have a background in American literature and some English literature (this side of Chaucer); the demand is there to provide instruction, through summer institutes and other organized activities during the school year, in other literatures and cultures.

Demand often exceeds supply. This has been true particularly of the need for Latin teachers for almost a decade.[13] With the disappearance of the cafeteria curriculum of the 1960s and because of the renewed emphasis on tough subjects, Latin enrollments have increased again and are kept from increasing further only by our inability to train more Latin teachers. That is not due to a lack of responsive and successful initiatives. One such remedy, for instance, has been to offer certification programs to teachers who are already certified in other subjects and welcome a change without changing careers. As for the elementary level, established programs in inner-city schools in Philadelphia, Detroit, and Los Angeles, among others, have made a mock of the supposedly elitist nature of Latin. The same is true of "the classics": three eminently successful summer institutes at Georgetown and Miami University in Ohio on Homer's *Odyssey,* Vergil's *Aeneid,* and mythology (anchored by Ovid's *Metamorphoses*) responded to an obviously existing demand, have had a lively impact, and were given due recognition in such broadly based publications as the American Federation of Teachers' *American Educator.*[14]

A few other projects may be singled out to illustrate the range of possibilities. They include curricular programs at two-year colleges. The splendid example of Richland College in Dallas and its cooperative classics concentration is a good model for further initiatives of this kind. So is the involvement of faculty from four-year institutions in the development of such programs. With the help of an NEH grant, the Richland program established a coordinated classics program with participating faculty from humanities and social studies.

Guidance was provided, especially through two summer institutes, by classics faculty from the University of Texas at Austin, Southern Methodist University, and the University of Texas at Arlington, who were attentive to the special needs of community colleges. The same kind of outreach has been successfully demonstrated by classicists within larger institutions. One of the largest NEH awards ever was made to the University of Florida, under the direction of Gareth Schmeling, for integrating humanities into the curricula of the professional schools. Similarly, Brooklyn College under the leadership of Ethyle Wolfe received one of the largest NEH grants for curricular development in the humanities.

The list could be expanded, but the basic point is quite clear. At a time when Western-civilization bashing commands a great deal of artificial attention, interest in Greco-Roman civilization exists as strongly as ever. Much of it goes beyond usual classroom routines and therefore has been met by academic classicists not in any systematic way, but mostly as a result of individual efforts and initiatives. The same is true of the area of adult education, which often percolates into fund-raising. For that sector, we have reliable statistics for future growth instead of the pseudoscientific guesswork that is employed in projecting the job situation for classicists. To quote John Brademas: "Enrollments in adult-education classes are increasing three times as fast as the U.S. population and represent the area of greatest growth in postsecondary education. Serving this large number of older, part-time students is the next frontier of American higher education."[15] The maturity of this clientele is another plus for classics. It includes many professionals who are desirous, in their leisure time, to recoup a liberal education and who do not mind being cultivated as patrons. Efforts to reach such people are by no means a prerogative of "elite" schools; I have seen successful endeavors of this kind by classics departments at inner-city and rural state universities. An established tie-in at many institutions is alumni tours or continuing education for special target clienteles, such as doctors, lawyers, or numismatic collectors.

As these examples show, it is salutary for classicists to go beyond academe and communicate with constituencies other than themselves. Other academic disciplines, in fact, do this routinely. It is not a matter of either/or: traditional academic activities, such as teaching and publication, on one side and greater efforts to promulgate an appreciation of the classics on the other. Rather, it is time that all of these activities be recognized as constituent professional functions and become part of the horizon of expectations for the profession. The present situation is an extension of that encountered several decades ago when classicists began meeting the demand for courses needed by a wider clientele. Then as now, resistance on the grounds of not compromising high standards turned out to be a mere mask for inertia. Then as now, such attitudes are the greatest limiting factor for satisfying the interest in the classics that demonstrably exists in many quarters of the population, even if that may not include one dean's office or the other. The very schizophrenia of the multicultural movement is yet another indication of the recognition of the centrality of Greece and Rome in the history of civilization: on the one hand, there is the rhetoric about the oppressiveness, injustice, and imperialism of the West; on the other, the effort to claim that all Western achievements ultimately are based on those of African Egypt, the assumed mother of Greek and Roman culture.

Replete as it is with such contradictions, the continuing debate about multiculturalism is a good example of the opportunities that constantly invite active participation from classicists in the public arena. The topic should be of obvious interest to any student of Greek and Roman civilization, and the intellectual level of the debate needs all the help it can get. The public may be puzzled by the reluctance of academic classicists to speak clearly to the issue. That reluctance can be usefully approached through their ambivalent attitudes to the related phenomena of the Stanford curriculum, William Bennett, and Allan Bloom.

The issues raised by this triad pose an obvious dilemma for classicists in this country. Do they want to pull the rug from under themselves by agreeing that the importance of Greco-Roman culture should be diminished? Are they then prepared to relinquish some of their few faculty positions to African-American studies and the like? The perceived dilemma, inflicted by the usual limiting dichotomies, seems to be that as a proponent of Western civilization, one is *nolens volens* allied with Bennett and Bloom, an impression any humanities professor concerned about being politically correct wishes to avoid, of course.

There is, as always, plenty of middle ground. Even with all the hype endemic to the self-absorbed milieu of academe, the revisions in the Stanford curriculum and the protestants' doggerel about Western civilization simply do not merit any further overreaction. By all accounts, the reality is that nothing much has changed. The same people still teach pretty much the same courses with pretty much the same books. The so-called canon never was monolithic in the first place. So far from being a momentous educational breakthrough, the revisions, such as they were, fall into the common category of administrative expediency of managing (minority) student unrest by PR.[16] Concerns for moral high ground or social responsibility were as little in evidence here as in Stanford's concomitant overcharging of the federal government in the manner to which major defense contractors have become accustomed.

The real lesson, drawn from Stanford as well as the experience of many successful classics programs, is that in the curricular free-market economy typical of many of our colleges and universities, classics can do very well indeed. Since there are few institutions with mandatory classics or Western civilization courses, the coercion of mandating courses in other cultures must be resisted, unless such requirements include both Western and non-Western cultures. Besides, as the phenomenon of multiculturalism in Greece and

Rome illustrates, the traditional boundary lines between "Western" and "non-Western" need to be reevaluated. Justice Brennan once wrote, in a famous court case, that university classrooms are the marketplace of free ideas. They are also the *free* marketplace for such ideas, and in such a free market, classics will do better than many others because the classics and the tradition in which they are taught are incredibly rich and substantive. While insisting on high standards, they are, as we have seen in the previous chapters, undogmatic, adaptable, and susceptible to many approaches and interpretations. Bloom and Bennett represent one aspect of the latter, though by no means the only one. This is not the place to discuss their merits and demerits at length, but it is useful to highlight two central reasons—the forest instead of the trees, really—why they have found so much resonance within academe and, especially, outside of it. We could do worse than learn from them.

The formative event for Bloom, conveniently ignored by his critics[17] because his outlandish characterizations of today's students and working mothers offer easier targets, was the quick capitulation of the Cornell administration and social science/humanities faculty to student protests and threats in 1969. The lack of resolve to uphold, in actuality, the very moral and intellectual qualities that humanists constantly like to profess does invite legitimate contempt from an outside world where most jobholders are not protected by tenure. In practical terms, more backbone in tenure and curricular decisions, for instance, will only benefit our discipline. Bennett, as previously mentioned, deserves a great deal of credit for broadening out NEH programs beyond recipients in academe. The rapport he had with these clienteles, such as high school teachers, was based on genuine respect rather than just good "communication" and therefore was authentic and substantive, as I was able to observe firsthand. It is deplorable that the pool of classicists willing to direct the kind of projects he initiated is still far too small.

Given the complex evidence with which classicists—whether they specialize in literature, history, or archaeology—deal on an almost daily basis, they can put their sense of nuance to good use and transcend the simplistic dichotomies within which the current discussion of both academic and public issues is wont to operate. I have chosen the debate about multiculturalism as only one of several possible paradigms because of the opportunity it presents classicists both on their own home turf and in the public realm. They should not simply use the excesses of such movements (another good example is contemporary literary theory to which I will return shortly) as an excuse to stand aloof from them in complete disdain. Instead, they should identify those aspects that cry out for the kind of substance classicists can well provide—it is time to lead and act rather than react. As we have seen, ancient civilization in Hellenistic and Roman times was multicultural as it comprised diverse cultures, races, religions, artistic and architectural traditions with varying degrees of commonality. Some of the most prominent statesmen, philosophers, and writers were of Near Eastern, Hispanic, and African descent. We do not need to resort to flawed and resentful scholarship, à la Martin Bernal,[18] for a multicultural pedigree for Greco-Roman civilization; that pedigree already exists. It presents us with an opportunity for studying these cultures from a fresh perspective and, by doing so in an academically honest way, for providing substance rather than doctrine and patronizing to multiculturalism in the curriculum.

A similar opportunity is the attentive study of the role of classical trends in contemporary American culture. To return to the example I gave earlier: the emergence of classicism in postmodern architecture has been accompanied by a lively debate analogous to the academic debate about classics (in the larger sense) in the curriculum. The resilience and broad perspective of these practitioners are something from which academic classicists can learn a great deal. Classicists are not the only keepers of the classical tradition and there is a need for mutual encouragement and alliances.

Classics in Its Academic Setting

One of the many merits of the late A. Bartlett Giamatti—Renaissance scholar, president of Yale, and commissioner of baseball—was that he had an upbeat view of the humanities at a time when many of its academic practitioners found it infectious to wallow in a communal malaise. With a view to the humanities in general, he sounded the encouraging and correct note that "if humanities faculties face their responsibilities and take the lead, they will be able to change and grapple with their futures."[19] For good reason, he saw classics programs as models for the humanities in general. For by nature, classics is an interdisciplinary field,[20] encompassing all aspects of ancient Mediterranean civilization (I deliberately choose this term to get away from the red herring of Eurocentrism). More than any other discipline in the humanities, classicists have been successful in counteracting the fragmentation, endemic to academic bureaucracies, of the study of whole cultures into history, language, literature, philosophy, archaeology, religion, linguistics, etc. The modus operandi can be either departmental (which is preferable), such as at Berkeley, Austin, and Princeton, or interdepartmental or even interinstitutional (the Massachusetts Consortium, centered on Amherst and environs, is a fine example). One benefit is intrinsic: in such a context, one gets to appreciate the breadth of our discipline, the variety of methodologies, and the diversity of new discoveries and approaches. Another plus is that such programs have a far greater vitality, and capacity for renewal, than others that are more limited in outlook.

In other words, the purely academic diversity, range, and heterogeneity of the classics profession are among its greatest strengths. They are a necessary counterpoise to the quantitative limitations of most departments and the resulting risk of stagnation. The appropriate training of classicists involves more than language and literature. This versatility has kept classicists vital, even in adverse locales, by giving them the regenerating ability to offer a variety of courses and to develop themselves, and their programs, in an active fashion over the period of their appointment, even if it is forty years. For our discipline, faculty renewal is even more crucial than for others; the breadth of our field provides us with the appropriate opportunities.

This is all the more important because one central fact of classical life is that most departments are small—two to eight faculty members. Most of the problems besetting classics departments result from this basic determinant, rather than from more far-fetched causations such as "elitism," the failure to appreciate the difference between *langue* and *parole,* or the overblown vicissitudes of the Stanford curriculum. The continued vitality of classics departments thus comes down to some very practical matters: so much more depends on the contribution made by individual faculty members and on their vitality, imagination, and creativity, in addition to their cooperative interaction—in short, the "chemistry" of a department. Conversely, if there is just one dysfunctional tenured member, or someone who needs to be "worked around" constantly, the impact is far greater than in typically larger departments, such as history or English, where the capacity for regeneration has a broader base.

The advantage is that there is far more latitude for experimentation and creativity than there is in many other disciplines. The prevailing character, especially of larger universities as higher education's answer to theme parks— a result of the lack of a meaningful core curriculum—is a help rather than a hindrance in this regard. There is ample room for a variety of strong, highly personal, and even entrepreneurial contributions; again, the parallel with architects working in the classical mode today comes to mind. As has been the case at universities throughout history, it is people, not concepts, that make or break a program. I am confident that these opportunities will continue to attract resourceful individuals to our profession, although the contention of Columbia's president, Michael Sovern, that the humanities and academe in general basically lost a whole generation of the best talent to other professions[21] cannot be taken lightly, as is indicated by such countermeasures as the Mellon Fellowships in the Humanities; one of the deterrents is the inordinate length to which graduate study has ballooned (see below). But one of the joys of being in classics these days is that there is so much opportunity, merely at the practical level, to build effective programs and develop the kind of activities that I described earlier and for which there is a great deal of demand. Such efforts exemplify the realistic condition on which the health of the classics profession in the United States is based and that lies outside any schematic, let alone ideological, matrices: the best we can strive for is to have practitioners who are in touch with the special character and clientele of their particular institutions, who can identify and fill existing needs there, and who, as they do so, can act and lead rather than react. American higher education since its inception has been characterized by innovation, adaptability, and pluralism. It is an exciting setting in which classics can prosper, despite the usual ups and downs, especially when compared to its situation in other countries.

The downside of the generally small size of classics departments is that they are more adversely affected than others by personnel problems, intramural mayhem, and faculty stagnation. Mostly for such reasons, several departments managed to work themselves into a state of minimal effectiveness, if not outright dysfunction, in the past decade alone, whereas others, precisely because they obviated such problems and precisely because of the rise of the budgetary criterion of selective excellence, were given additional positions.

Another practical observation about the vitality of classics departments readily suggests itself. As another consequence of small numbers of faculty, relative to other departments, classics departments pay a heavier price for tenured mistakes. There is simply less margin for error. It can be avoided, for a start, by insistence on truly honest assessments, both internal and external, of faculty quality in lieu of the expectation of stylized eulogies that would make even encomiasts of the Ptolemies blush and that have drastically diminished the probative value especially of outside letters in tenure and promotion cases.[22] A related point is that chairpersons cannot afford, amid their ritualistic utterances of regret over lost time for scholarship, not to be thoroughly informed about the nuts-and-bolts business of procedures. In academe in general, demonstrable procedural error, even if inadvertent, has become another avenue to tenure for faculty about whose quality one can have legitimate reservations. At a time when even the richest private universities are cutting back to allocate resources on the basis of existing strengths, classics departments that are unduly weighed down with weak tenured faculty will simply not get additional resources, and the road to recovery often is a long one. It more than behooves people who study antiquity to take the long view: a few months of unpleasantness, with open records and all, are little compared to incurring a long-term mortgage of mediocrity.

There is one significant effect of the small size of classics departments on the makeup of the profession. They usually have no room, nor do the smaller graduate departments, for scholarly interests that are other than "mainline." Ph.D.'s with dissertations in such areas as papyrology, ancient medicine, or Mycenaean studies thus depend largely on the interests of larger departments or programs to accommodate them. That need not be so, because many of these individuals are versatile classicists who can teach effectively across the discipline. They are victims of the lingering perception that scholars do not progress beyond their dissertation topic, and accordingly, they have been unfairly typed as narrow specialists. Thesis advisers have to take these market forces into account and regrettably steer Ph.D. candidates away from potentially significant topics. The situation inhibits experimentation and work on the cutting edge.

Two Current Issues: Elitism and the Importance of Theory

Academe, as is well known, not infrequently has a tendency to inflate itself at the expense of real problems; their place, moreover, is often taken by buzzwords and clichés. That is one reason I chose to focus on some actualities first. Fundamentals, as our agonistic brethren (used generically) on the coaching staffs put it, come before you practice a triple play or a reverse layup.[23] It is useful, however, to demystify briefly—certainly more briefly than such demystifications take on average in current literary theory—two notions that surface frequently, albeit in diverse ways, in the current discussion of the classics. One is elitism; the other, the importance of theory.

The label of "elitism" is applied to classics in various ways. The undifferentiated characterization, for instance, of any Ph.D.-granting classics department as elitist (a tenet held, for instance, by several contributors to the volume on the supposed crisis in the classics profession) is jaundiced rather than precise. It posits a model of utter professional statism, which ignores that many such departments, in keeping with the tremendous diversity of the American higher educational system, have multiple missions that transcend resentful dichotomies. Major graduate departments such as North Carolina, Michigan, Texas, UCLA, Ohio State, and others devote substantial resources to undergraduate education, including massive classical civilization courses, training of high school teachers (wherever we can get them), and in fact, working with and being supportive of colleagues in other, nongraduate institutions in their states, without being Big Brother. Besides, mere possession of a graduate program is not to be confused with excellence: there are first-rate classics departments or programs that are purely undergraduate, and there are mediocre Ph.D. programs.

Similarly, "elitism" defined as the elitist heritage of classics, if not liberal learning in general, is a very red herring for the classicist who wants to be a missionary—and given our small numbers, that is really what we are today. As I mentioned earlier, Latin instruction is flourishing in inner-city schools in Philadelphia, Detroit, and Los Angeles; there is a crying need for more classicists to direct NEH-funded collaborative programs between school districts and universities; classics programs can be brought even to two-year colleges; and there are thousands of students studying Latin and classical civilization at state universities all over the country. Their serendipitous state of ahistoricism makes them happily unaware that classics in the past may have served "elitist" functions. That is totally irrelevant to the way we promulgate classics in this era and can only blind us to existing opportunities.

To give another example: when my department committed itself, some seventeen years ago, to an archaeological excavation under the direction of my able colleague Professor Joseph Carter, we did not want to replicate the traditional emphasis on citadels, temples, theaters, and other urban edifices. Eighty percent or more of the Greco-Roman population lived in the countryside, and their lives had been totally neglected. Professor Carter simply went ahead with exploring the *chora* at Metaponto and pioneered a new approach in the process, which has become a much-imitated model. He went ahead directly without spouting the currently fashionable rhetoric about the marginalized and oppressed and without denouncing the demonstrable elitism of his archaeological predecessors, let alone reciting an act of contrition for their sins. Substantive change can be accomplished without such posturing.

Once more, it is useful to differentiate between myth and reality. Precisely because classics in this country has not been among the leading contributors to the discussion of literary or historical theory in recent decades, the effect of theory is sometimes overstated to the point where it is viewed as a magic wand that will ipso facto revitalize a hidebound discipline. A look at other departments of literature shows that matters are not that simple and that increased hermeticism can be one result. Or theory, as an uncreative alternative to intellectual precision or deeper spiritual values, becomes an ontological commitment rather than an epistemological instrument. Accordingly, the inscription above the entrance of the Academy today might often read May No One Without -isms Enter. The resulting intolerance is all around us; one of the laws currently operative in academe is that the amount of vociferation expended on virtues like pluralism, diversity, and inclusiveness is usually in inverse proportion to the willingness to let these very virtues govern their own implementation, such as in courses on race and gender.

The absence of a strong tradition of hermeneutic theory in classics over the past few decades has, for the most part, been detrimental. Hermeneutics, as defined by August Boeckh,[24] at a time when classics set the tone in such matters, after all provides simply an explanation of how we go about interpreting a text. The cessation of a continuing hermeneutic tradition in classics has produced such low-water marks as the continuing debate over Vergilian "optimism" and "pessimism,"[25] a kind of poor man's (and woman's) deconstructionism that legitimately makes us look like impoverished relations on the contemporary interpretive scene; even the borrowing of Harvard's halo to give "pessimism" a respectable patina cannot cover up the lack of intellectual substance. More generally, another result of this lack has been a diffidence on the part of many American classicists toward anything that smacks of theory. This diffidence in part is a reaction formation against the excessive trendiness of some of the most vocal practitioners in other fields, and against the overly schematic, one-dimensional, and ultimately boring ways in which various theories or -isms have on occasion been applied to classical authors and subjects over the past two decades.

I see considerable evidence that this is beginning to change. Many younger classicists in particular now are discerningly familiar with the contemporary discussion and its strengths and defects. They draw on various theories eclectically as part of their general interpretive strategy, providing a clear rationale, in the spirit of Boeckh's postulate, for what they are doing, and using such theoretical perspectives to lead us back to the texts. In other words, there is a clear recognition of means and ends. I have noticed this particularly in reading proposals for NEH fellowships. The classical time lag has saved classicists by and large from the trendiness, vatic cant, self-important posturing, solipsism, and dogmatism that produce fear and loathing on the theory trail. As a result, there are few "tenured radicals" in classics, and most of them are, in modern parlance, wanna-bes. Classicists have an opportunity now to be part of a more commonsensical, sophisticated, and judicious second generation that will further refine such approaches, and of the concomitant intellectual discussion that ranges far beyond literature. With their broadly humanistic and interdisciplinary perspectives, they should not be absent from shaping this discussion,[26] for in actuality, the gap between classics and modern theory often is not all that wide. Classical scholars did much research, for example, on intertextuality and interaction between author and reader long before these aspects received theoretical formulation.[27] Theory, as indicated by Boeckh, simply demands that we now should do with fuller awareness what we are already doing—a dimension missing far too often in the current interpretation of Roman poetry, for instance. Ultimately, as always, it comes down to a matter of successful models: if some interesting and substantive work is done along these lines, it will find imitators.

As in the case of multiculturalism, the palpable deficiencies and excesses of contemporary literary theory in America present classicists with considerable opportunities; for as Edward Said has observed, "in having given up the world entirely for the aporias and unthinkable paradoxes of a text, contemporary criticism has retreated from its constituency, the citizens of modern society."[28] That is precisely the clientele to whom classicists increasingly are directing outreach programs, but things begin even closer to home: if English and other literature departments become mere theoretical affiliates, the students who want to learn about authors and their times, read literature, discuss values, and study and enjoy texts will turn elsewhere, and classics departments will be among the principal beneficiaries. Again, this should not be an occasion for complacency but for practicing our craft as responsibly and creatively as we can.

Similarly, as Said notes, "in American literary studies there has not in the past quarter century been enough work of major historical scholarship that can be called 'revisionist.'"[29] Instead of providing authentic reinterpretations, the effort of modern theorists has been concentrated on redefining and repackaging an unchanged product. By contrast, serious scholarship remains the bedrock of the classical discipline. As the director of the Center for Hellenic Studies has recently pointed out, there is still so much to be done in terms of worthwhile projects.[30] This may strike the layperson as surprising, but there is very little in the field of ancient studies that is cut and dried, and there is constantly new evidence that needs to be evaluated. In contrast to classicizing architects who can be loosely inspired by classical traditions for their own ideas, classical scholars need to have a firm understanding of the first and historical horizon of the subject of their research and interpretations, no matter how modern a cast they want to give them. It is ultimately on the continuance of such substantive work that the credibility of classics as an academic field is based. By virtue of its multidisciplinary nature, classical scholarship has a strong tradition of integrative breadth, and there is no lack of desiderata for work of that kind.

It is appropriate, therefore, to conclude with some comments on an issue that is all too real, i.e., the current length of graduate study in classics and the humanities. John D'Arms, one of the numerous classicists who currently are graduate deans, deans, or presidents at major universities—not a bad record for a profession supposedly in crisis—has recently made an overdue and well-reasoned case against overly long graduate study in the humanities, which has ballooned to an average length of almost ten years.[31] I would like to add a few supporting observations, especially in regard to the classics profession.

Among many other bad results, the protracted course of graduate study has produced a mentality that (a) graduate study is primarily the acquisition of knowledge, and since knowledge in our interdisciplinary field is quite comprehensive, graduate study must therefore be correspondingly extensive; and (b) the Ph.D. is the pinnacle of long-term effort rather than the threshold of an even longer-term effort. Contra (a), graduate study, besides providing a basic knowledge, is primarily a way to learn approaches, methods, and how one goes about opening up new fields of research and interest for the prospective practitioner; the acquisition of further knowledge and development of further interests are precisely—and related to (b)—a lifelong enterprise. As we saw earlier, that attitude is essential for keeping classicists, who are handicapped by the small size of their departments, from going stale; it is anything but helped by the current system of timeserving in graduate school. Furthermore, this leads to a similarly skewed perspective on tenure: instead of being properly regarded as another way station or promissory note for continuing accomplishments and vitality, tenure all too often assumes the dimensions of the apex of a career. That is part of the mind-set behind the currently fashionable litigation involving humanities faculty.

An attendant result is the diminished willingness and ability on the part of Ph.D.'s advanced in age and sheltered by too many years of graduate life to cope successfully with the real shift—more real than any theoretical and posited paradigm shifts—i.e., the attitude at any university that classics is not owed a guaranteed existence. More is expected of departments and individuals in terms of overall activity (such as securing outside funding) than mere teaching and some publication. That is different from the state of the profession thirty years ago, or whenever the golden age occurred. The resulting resentment and frustration can lead to convenient demonologies that ignore the existence of successful solutions.

What we need, therefore, is no more than five years (at most six, if a fellowship for study abroad is obtained) of Ph.D. study and more emphasis on post-Ph.D. and post-tenure continuing education and faculty development. That is one of the purposes of the NEH summer seminars and institutes for college teachers, but universities should do more along these lines on a regular basis. Again, such programs and attitudes are a matter of course in other professions.

These comments are not meant to be exhaustive. If classics seems like a marginalized discipline today, it should not follow the currently fashionable trend of marginalized (or more correctly, self-perceived marginalized) entities toward self-pity, rancor, entropy, let alone consequent calls for empowerment by protective mandate. My basic argument is that the challenges American classicists are facing are exciting and rewarding—and can be met. In various and changing ways, as we have seen throughout this book, the Greek and Roman heritage is both a real and an inspirational part of American culture. It calls for a continuing creative, assertive, and principled response from those who teach classics in America.

Short Bibliography and Suggestions for Further Reading

Agard, W. R. "Classical Scholarship." In Merle Curti, ed., *American Scholarship in the Twentieth Century* (New York 1953) 146–167.

Astolfi, Douglas, ed. *Teaching the Ancient World* (Scholars Press 1983).

Burns, Mary Ann T., and J. F. O'Connor, eds. *The Classics in American Schools: Teaching the Ancient World* (Scholars Press 1987).

Calder, William M., III. "Die Geschichte der klassischen Philologie in den Vereinigten Staaten." *Jahrbücher für Amerikastudien* 11 (1966) 213–240.

Culham, Phyllis, and Lowell Edmunds, eds. *Classics: A Discipline and Profession in Crisis?* (Lanham, Md. 1989).

Gummere, R. M. *The American Colonial Mind and the Classical Tradition* (Cambridge, Mass. 1963).

Reinhold, Meyer. *Classica Americana: The Greek and Roman Heritage and the United States* (Detroit 1984).

Reinhold, M., and W. Haase, eds. *The Classical Tradition and the Americas*. 6 vols. (New York and Berlin: De Gruyter), forthcoming.

Urzidil, Johannes. *Amerika und die Antike* (Zurich 1964).

Notes

Preface

1. *Sacred Wood* (London 1920) 50.

2. "Recent Trends in the Interpretation of the Augustan Age," *The Augustan Age* 5 (1986) 32f.; cf., for instance, the comments of K. A. Raaflaub in K. A. Raaflaub and M. Toher, eds., *Between Republic and Empire: Interpretations of Augustus and His Principate* (Berkeley and Los Angeles 1990) 453–454.

3. "Vergil and the Formation of the Augustan Ethos," in *Atti del Convegno mondiale scientifico di studi su Virgilio* 1 (Milan 1984) 240–254.

1. Classicism in Postmodern American Architecture

1. *The Power of Images in the Time of Augustus* (Ann Arbor 1988).

2. More details in C. Jencks, *Modern Movements in Architecture,* 2d ed. (Penguin 1985) 105–108.

3. Beeby in Charles Moore and Wayne Attoe, eds., *Ah Mediterranean! Twentieth Century Classicism in America, Center* 2 (1986) 37. On the Sulzer Library, see p. 24.

4. Cf. Christopher Lasch, *The Culture of Narcissism: American Life in an Age of Diminished Expectations* (New York 1978); cf. p. 66.

5. For closer definitions see, e.g., Ihab Hassan, *The Dismemberment of Orpheus: Toward a Postmodern Literature* (Madison 1982) and *The Postmodern Turn: Essays in Postmodern Theory and Culture* (Columbus 1987). Cf. C. Jencks, *What Is Post-Modernism?* (London 1987) 29–30; Robert A. M. Stern, "The Doubles of Post-Modern," *Harvard Architectural Review* 1 (Spring 1980) 75–87; David Harvey, *The Condition of Postmodernity* (Oxford 1989); and Susan R. Suleiman, *Subversive Intent* (Cambridge, Mass. 1990) 181–205.

6. Cf. p. 82.

7. Published in English as *Art in Crisis: The Loss of the Centre* (London 1957).

8. See K. Galinsky, ed., *The Interpretation of Roman Poetry: Empiricism or Hermeneutics?* (New York and Frankfurt 1992).

9. Martin Filler, "Building in the Past Tense," *TLS* (March 24–30, 1989).

10. Robert A. M. Stern, *Modern Classicism* (New York 1988) 246.

11. *The Language of Post-Modern Architecture,* 5th ed. (New York 1987) 7f.; cf. Heinrich Klotz, *The History of Postmodern Architecture* (Cambridge, Mass. 1987) 327 and Stern, *Modern Classicism* 82.

12. Jencks, *Post-Modernism: The New Classicism in Art and Architecture* (New York 1987) 231.

13. Stern, *Modern Classicism* 76.

14. Klotz 154.

15. Jencks, *Post-Modernism* 282.

16. "Inclusive and Exclusive," in C. Moore and Gerald Allen, *Dimensions* (New York 1976) 51. The essay was originally published in a somewhat different form in 1967.

17. Klotz 129. On Schinkel's status as a forerunner of modern classicism, see also Stern, *Modern Classicism* 20–21 and M. Filler, "Free-Style Classicism: True and False," in Moore and Attoe, *Ah Mediterranean!* 111–112.

18. Filler, "Building in the Past" 296; cf. Klotz, *The History of Postmodern Architecture* 205.

19. Smith has set forth his own views in *Classical Architecture: Rule and Invention* (Layton, Utah 1988).

20. See below, pp. 35–37.

21. Jencks, *Post-Modernism* 198.

22. Jaquelin Robertson, "The Empire Strikes Back," in *Architect. Design* 7/8 (1984) 11. This whole issue of *AD* is entitled *Leon Krier: Houses, Palaces, Cities.* See further discussion in Jencks, *Post-Modernism* 190ff.; Klotz 295ff., and Stern, *Modern Classicism* 256–263; cf. Krier's own contributions in Andreas Papadakis, ed., *The New Classicism in Architecture and Urbanism, Architect. Design Profile* 71 (London 1988) 56ff.; and in Demetri Porphyrios, ed., *Classicism Is Not a Style, Architect. Design* 5–6 (London 1982) 58ff. on his influential design for a school at St. Quentin-en-Yvelines, France. Not surprisingly, he has become a sympathetic adviser to Prince Charles, whose concern for a more vital architecture is well known.

23. Stern, *Modern Classicism* 264.

24. Batey in Moore and Attoe, *Ah Mediterranean!* 89.

25. Both quotations in this paragraph are taken from Stern, *Modern Classicism* 222.

26. I am indebted especially to Jencks' observations (*Post-Modernism* 225f.).

27. A phrase coined by Paul Goldberger, who supplies detailed illustrations (*The New York Times,* May 20, 1990, sec. 2, pp. 1, 38).

28. Cf. Richard J. Betts, "Looking for America: Part 1," *ACSA Forum, Chicago* 2–3 (Oct. 1986) 14.

29. Stern, *Modern Classicism* 190.

30. *The Uses of Enchantment* (New York 1976) 194–215 where, among other things, he draws attention to classical affinities.

31. Stern, *Modern Classicism* 118; cf. Jencks, *Post-Modernism* 288–291.

32. See the concise survey by Paul V. Turner, "The Varieties of Collegiate Classicism," in Moore and Attoe, *Ah Mediterranean!* 67–73.

33. *Travel and Leisure* 19.9 (Sept. 1989) 128.

34. Stern, *Modern Classicism* 78.

35. Moore in Moore and Attoe, *Ah Mediterranean!* 123.

36. W. Iser, *The Act of Reading: A Theory of Aesthetic Response* (Baltimore 1978); cf. pp. 74–75.

37. Stern, *Modern Classicism* 78.

38. Jencks, *The Language of Post-Modern Architecture* 125; cf. Klotz 183–191. Moore's essay on Hadrian's Villa appeared first in *Perspecta* 6 (1958); reprinted in Moore and Allen, *Dimensions* (New York 1976). Cf. Thorsten Rodiek, *James Stirling: Die Neue Staatsgalerie Stuttgart* (Stuttgart 1984) 41 with n. 84. On Hadrian, see pp. 57 and 146–147.

39. Klotz, *The History of Postmodern Architecture* 189.

40. Filler, "Building in the Past" 296.

41. W. J. Bate, *The Burden of the Past and the English Poet* (Cambridge, Mass. 1970).

42. Klotz, *The History of Postmodern Architecture* 170.

43. Stern, *Modern Classicism* 266. See also the comments by Jones and Kirkland and by Robert Maxwell in Papadakis, *The New Classicism* 34–43.

44. Graves in P. Arnell and T. Bickford, *A Tower for Louisville: The Humana Competition* (New York 1982) 89–90.

45. Graves, ibid. 90–93.

46. Jencks, *Post-Modernism* 312. I am indebted to his masterful discussion on pp. 310–315.

47. Jencks, ibid. 312.

48. V. Scully in Arnell and Bickford, *Tower for Louisville* 108.

49. Ibid. 10.

50. Cf. pp. 108–112.

51. Jencks, *What Is Post-Modernism?* 12–13; cf. his chapter on "The Counter-Reformation in Architecture," ibid. 40–42, and Paolo Portoghesi on "The End of Prohibition," in *Postmodern: The Architecture of the Post-Industrial Society* (New York 1983) 14–30.

52. Porphyrios, *Classicism Is Not a Style* 53.

53. Filler, "Building in the Past" 296.

54. Filler, "Free-Style Classicism" 114.

55. As D. Porphyrios realizes in "Imitation and Convention in Architecture," in Papadakis, *The New Classicism* 14–21.

56. J. Huizinga, *Homo ludens: A Study of the Play Element in Culture* (London 1955).

57. Roger G. Kennedy, "Architecture in the Image of Athens," *Smithsonian* 20.7 (Oct. 1989) 171.

58. See p. 150 for an example in the Roman world.

59. Jean-François Lyotard, *The Postmodern Condition: A Report on Knowledge* (Minneapolis 1984).

60. Jencks, *Post-Modernism* 315.

61. See note 7, above.

2. The Decline and Fall of the Roman Empire: Are There Modern Parallels?

1. The most comprehensive study is that of Alexander Demandt, *Der Fall Roms* (almost 700 pages). Ramsay MacMullen's *Corruption and the Decline of Rome* (New Haven 1988) not surprisingly was written during the Reagan years, when corruption of government officials became an issue. Corruption, for that matter, had already been singled out by Thomas Jefferson as one of the causes for the fall of the Roman Republic (letter to John Adams of May 10, 1819).

2. For example, Jeremy Rifkin of the Foundation of Economic Trends, as quoted by Ellen Goodman in her syndicated column of April 15, 1988.

3. G. Le Bon, *Lois psychologiques de l'évolution des peuples* (Paris 1902) 122f.: immigration of inferior individuals; T. Mommsen, *Römische Geschichte* 3 (1856) 532 f.: capitalism and slavery. Cf. the contrasting attitudes of Presidents Theodore Roosevelt and Richard M. Nixon: Roosevelt (*The Winning of the West,* 1889) felt that Rome's decline held no parallel for America; Nixon (as quoted in the German news magazine *Der Spiegel* [1972] no. 33, p. 106) was less sanguine.

4. F. Fukuyama, "The End of History?" *National Interest* 16 (Summer 1989) 3–18. Mr. Fukuyama's undergraduate major was classics.

5. Polybius, *Histories* 6.57.1–2 (Loeb transl.).

6. B. Liddell Hart, *Why Don't We Learn from History?* (London 1944) 49. He goes on to say that the phenomenon is "usually combined with the consequences of exhaustion in war"—another part of the Kennedy formula.

7. Hedrick Smith, *The Power Game: How Washington Works* (New York 1988). Cf. W. Greider, *Who Will Tell the People?* (New York 1992).

8. Joseph S. Nye, Jr., "The Misleading Metaphor of Decline," *Atlantic Monthly* (March 1990) 86. Cf. his book-length study, *Bound to Lead: The Changing Nature of American Power* (New York 1990).

9. Cf. pp. 146–147.

10. Alan Cameron, "Dispelling Myths about Gays," *Record* (Bergen County, N.J.), May 13, 1984, 14.

11. "Climatic Change and Agricultural Exhaustion as Elements in the Fall of Rome," *Quarterly Journ. of Economics* 31 (1917) 173–208; excerpted in Mortimer Chambers, ed., *The Fall of Rome: Can It Be Explained?* (New York 1974) 55–61.

12. J. O. Nriagu, "Saturnine Gout among Roman Aristocrats: Did Lead Poisoning Contribute to the Fall of the Empire?" *NE Journ. of Medicine* (March 1983) 660–663; and J. N. Wilford, "A Clue to the Decline of Rome," *The New York Times* (May 31, 1983) front page, and C3; modifications by S. Bisel in *National Geographic* 165.5 (May 1984) 605 after the strictures of A. Cameron and C. Innes, *The New York Times* (June 14, 1983) A22. My remarks in the following paragraph incorporate some of Cameron and Innes' comments. On water in lead pipes, see Trevor Hodge, *Amer. Journ. of Archaeology* 85 (1981) 486–491. For antecedents of this theory see S. C. Gilfillan, "Lead Poisoning and the Fall of Rome," *Journ. of Occupational Medicine* 7 (1965) 53–60.

13. A. J. Toynbee, *A Study of History* 1–6 (London 1934–1939).

14. Cf. Nye, "The Misleading Metaphor" 92.

15. *Leadership* (New York 1978) 4. For a fuller discussion, and the application of this concept to Augustus, see chapter 4.

16. Cf. pp. 150–152 and, among current examples, H. Grunwald, "The Second American Century," *Time* (Oct. 8, 1990) 70–75, and Arthur M. Schlesinger, Jr., *The Disuniting of America* (New York 1992).

17. Frank C. Bourne, *A History of the Romans* (Boston 1966) 498. The next quotation is taken from there also.

18. John Naisbitt, *Megatrends: Ten New Directions Transforming Our Lives* (New York 1982) 97–158.

19. *The Gamesman: The New Corporate Leaders* (New York 1975). Events in the 1980s proved the accuracy of Maccoby's observations beyond all expectations.

20. Lasch, *The Culture of Narcissism* 31. On individual responsibility, especially of intellectuals, for the *res publica* compare Vaclav Havel's comments cited on pp. 86–87.

21. See, for example, B. Ginsberg and M. Sheffer, *Politics by Other Means: The Declining Importance of Elections in America* (New York 1990).

22. Herbert J. Muller, *The Uses of the Past* (New York 1957) 234.

23. Horace, *Odes* 3.6.46–48.

24. This is an additional and, I think, useful perspective on the ongoing argument between "inevitabilists" or "declinists" like Kennedy and "revivalists" like Nye. The bipolar terms, typical of academic debate, are not mine; see S. P. Huntington, "The U.S.—Decline or Renewal?" in *Foreign Affairs* 67.2 (Winter 1988–1989) 76–96 and P. Kennedy, "Fin-de-Siècle America," *New York Review of Books* 37.11 (1990) 31–40. On pp. 39–40, Kennedy comments on the limitations of the term "inevitable" and cites E. H. Carr, *What Is History?* (Penguin 1964) 96, but he goes on to point out that discussions and predictions of decline usually precede the phenomenon itself. In Rome, they did so by hundreds of years, which detracts from their probative value. A concomitant question is the definition of "decline"; cf. the following paragraph.

25. Cf. the scholarly analysis of A. Momigliano, "La caduta senza rumore di un impero nel 476 D.C.," *Annali della Scuola Normale Superiore di Pisa* 3.3 (1973) 397–418.

3. Reading Vergil's *Aeneid* in Modern Times

1. R. C. Holub, *Reception Theory: A Critical Introduction* (New York 1984); H. R. Jauss, *Toward an Aesthetic of Reception* (Minneapolis 1982).

2. "Nineteenth-Century Idealism and Twentieth-Century Textuality," in *Consequences of Pragmatism* (New York 1982) 151.

3. See pp. 167–168 and my introduction ("The Current State of the Interpretation of Roman Poetry and the Contemporary Critical Scene") in *The Interpretation of Roman Poetry* 1–40.

4. Pp. 33–34.

5. *Texas Law Review* 60 (1982) 391. For different views, see Gerald Graff's reply, ibid. 405–413; Robert Bork, *The Tempting of America* (New York 1990) 217–218; and on literary theory in general, W. J. T. Mitchell, ed., *Against Theory: Literary Studies and the New Pragmatism* (Chicago 1985).

6. For a good presentation of this view see, for example, R. D. Williams, "The Purpose of the *Aeneid,*" in S. J. Harrison, ed., *Oxford Readings in Vergil's "Aeneid"* (Oxford 1990) 21–36.

7. *From Vergil to Milton* (London 1945) 34. The legacy ranges from Dante to Joe Paterno (see *Paterno: By the Book* [New York 1989] 40–46). Mr. Paterno's understanding of the *Aeneid* strikes me as superior to that of many scholars.

8. *Virginia Quarterly Review* 38 (1962) 13.

9. See p. 69.

10. See pp. 99–101.

11. For various literary adaptations see K. C. King, *Achilles: Paradigms of the War*

Hero from Homer to the Middle Ages (Berkeley and Los Angeles 1987); W. B. Stanford, *The Ulysses Theme,* 2d ed. (Ann Arbor 1963); and G. K. Galinsky, *The Herakles Theme* (Oxford 1972).

12. Otto Rank, *The Myth of the Birth of the Hero,* ed. R. Freund (New York 1959) 1–96, a notion central to the writings of Joseph Campbell.

13. Kunstverein Wolfenbüttel 1982; see V. Pöschl, ed., *2000 Jahre Vergil* (Wiesbaden 1983) 55 n. 85.

14. See the next chapter with reference to the works of Sir Ronald Syme and A. von Premerstein.

15. "Homer and Vergil: The Double Themes," *Furioso* 5 (1950) 52.

16. Quoted by Ezra Pound, *The ABC of Reading* (New Haven 1934) 31.

17. *Manhood in the Making: Cultural Concepts of Masculinity* (New Haven 1990). The quotations are from pp. 229, 225, and 223. Gilmore demonstrates throughout the similarity between men and women in terms of ends; men simply do things differently as a result of cultural, and not biological, conditions.

18. *Congressional Record,* Feb. 21, 1990, S1315.

19. For an overview see D. Earl, *The Moral and Political Tradition of Rome* (London 1967). Cicero, too, urged intellectuals not to shirk participation in actual politics (*Rep.* 1.5–6).

20. See the excellent analysis by D. C. Feeney, "The Taciturnity of Aeneas," in Harrison, ed., *Oxford Readings* 167–190, esp. 186–187.

21. C. J. Mackie, *The Characterisation of Aeneas* (Edinburgh 1988) 219–220.

22. *De Oratore* 2.178.

23. Euripides, who was reacting against the Sophists, achieved the same effect by having many of his characters speechify relentlessly at the expense of real communication.

24. Cf. R. P. Hart, *The Sound of Leadership: Presidential Communication in the Modern Age* (Chicago 1988).

25. Defined concisely by R. Heinze, *Vergils epische Technik,* 3d ed. (Leipzig 1928) 281.

26. I have followed the translation of C. Day Lewis, with some modifications in the last three lines.

27. For more detail on this aspect and others see my article, "The Anger of Aeneas," *Amer. Journ. Phil.* 109 (1988) 321–348.

28. R. Novaco, *Anger Control* (Lexington, Mass. 1975) 3. The most comprehensive discussion, including a historical survey, is J. Averill, *Anger and Aggression* (New York/ Berlin 1982); further, Carol Tavris, *Anger: The Misunderstood Emotion* (New York 1982); F. R. Stearns, M.D., *Anger: Psychology, Physiology, Pathology* (Springfield, Ill. 1972); L. Madow, M.D., *Anger* (New York 1975).

29. In the preface to *Animadversions upon the Remonstrant's Defence against Smectymnus* (1641).

30. N. Elias, *The Civilizing Process* (New York 1979); T. Parsons, *Essays in Sociological Theory* (Glencoe, Ill. 1954) 397.

31. "The Creation of Characters in the *Aeneid,*" in *Latin Poets and Roman Life* (London 1985) 195.

32. W. Clausen, *Virgil's "Aeneid" and the Tradition of Hellenistic Poetry* (Berkeley and Los Angeles 1987) 99.

33. See p. 51; cf. Peter Green's study of the Hellenistic world *From Alexander to Actium: The Historical Evolution of the Hellenistic Age* (Berkeley 1990).

34. For more detail see my chapter on "Hercules in the *Aeneid*," in Harrison, ed., *Oxford Readings* 277–294. Cf., on the heroism of the Sophoclean Herakles, P. Holt in *Journ. Hell. Studies* 109 (1989) 78–80.

35. *The New York Times Book Review* (June 10, 1990) 40.

4. Leadership, Values, and the Question of Ideology: The Reign of Augustus

1. See my article "Recent Trends in the Interpretation of the Augustan Age," *Augustan Age* 5 (1986) 22–36, and the collection of essays edited by K. A. Raaflaub and M. Toher.

2. See p. 76.

3. H. Weinbrot, *Augustus Caesar in "Augustan" England* (Princeton 1978). The quotations that follow are taken from p. 86. For Alfred North Whitehead's very different view of Augustus, see pp. 154–155.

4. *Journ. of Roman Studies* 30 (1940) 77. On Syme's portrait of Augustus, see also the chapters by H. Galsterer and Z. Yavetz in Raaflaub and Toher.

5. See P. Zanker, *The Power of Images in the Time of Augustus* (Ann Arbor 1988); T. Woodman and D. West, eds., *Poetry and Politics in the Age of Augustus* (Cambridge 1988); and J. Griffin, "Augustus and the Poets: 'Caesar qui cogere posset,'" in F. Millar and E. Segal, eds., *Caesar Augustus: Seven Aspects* (Oxford 1984) 189–218.

6. James M. Burns, *Leadership* (New York 1978) 20, 40.

7. Thomas J. Peters and Robert H. Waterman, Jr., *In Search of Excellence* (New York 1982) 82–83 with references to further studies of leadership.

8. Details in *Cambridge Anc. History* 10 (1934) 425–464; cf. my article, "Augustus' Legislation on Morals and Marriage," *Philologus* 125 (1981) 126–144.

9. Cassius Dio 56.1–10.

10. The writers of the television movie *Masada* recaptured this essential Roman argument very well in the dialogue between the Roman commander Flavius Silva and the leader of the Zealots, Eleazar Ben Yair.

11. For details see T. P. Wiseman, *New Men in the Roman Senate* (Oxford 1971) 107ff.

12. Suetonius, *Augustus* 89.2.

13. Cf. Griffin, "Augustus and the Poets" 204.

14. Gordon Williams, *Tradition and Originality in Roman Poetry* (Oxford 1968) 578.

15. Woodman and West, *Poetry and Politics* 195.

16. The fundamental article still is E. T. Salmon, "The Evolution of Augustus' Principate," *Historia* 5 (1956) 456–478.

17. As defined, for example, by H. Arendt, *The Origins of Totalitarianism,* 2d ed. (London 1961) and K. Minogue, *Alien Powers: The Pure Theory of Ideology* (New York 1985).

18. José Ortega y Gasset, *The Revolt of the Masses* (New York 1932) 30.

19. G. W. F. Hegel, *Lectures on the Philosophy of History,* trans. J. Sibree (London 1857); on Fukuyama, see p. 54.

20. J. M. Burns, *Leadership* 287.

21. Cf. p. 78.

22. Details in Zanker, *The Power of Images* 143–145.

23. The concept, a familiar one in Roman poetry, has been well discussed for English literature by W. J. Bate (p. 173, note 41).

24. *Annals* 1.2: *cunctos dulcedine otii pellexit.*

25. See pp. 86–87.

26. (Durham, N.C. 1990.) The quotations are from pp. 58 and 59, and his call for moral education in chapters 3 and 4 strikes a positively Augustan note. Cf. further D. Kanter and P. Mirvis, *The Cynical Americans* (Boston 1990).

27. *Metamorphoses* 15.834.

28. Cf. A. Wallace-Hadrill, "The Golden Age and Sin in Augustan Ideology," *Past and Present* 95 (1982) 35; G. Lichtheim, *The Concept of Ideology and Other Essays* (New York 1967); J. Larrain, *The Concept of Ideology* (London 1979) and the works cited in note 17, above.

29. Full documentation in E. T. Salmon, "The Evolution of Augustus' Principate."

30. See Colin Wells' pioneering study *The German Policy of Augustus* (Oxford 1972).

31. *Nat. Hist.* 7.147–150.

32. P. 60.

33. See p. 41.

34. P. 49.

35. Dionysius of Halicarnassus, *On the Ancient Orators* 1–3. All this highlights the liability of Aeneas' Eastern descent; see p. 80.

36. Full discussion in Zanker, *The Power of Images* 239ff.

37. Cf. Zanker, ibid. 171, German edition (Munich 1987); this essential paragraph was inexplicably left out of the English version.

38. Zanker, ibid. 265–295.

39. Cf. p. 82. The distinction is ahistorical: in the very first sentence of the *Res Gestae,* for example, Augustus refers to the long tradition of a *privatus* coming to the aid of the *res publica.* Similarly, the commingling of private and public spheres is typical of the Roman house; see A. Wallace-Hadrill, "The Social Structure of the Roman House," *Papers of the Brit. School in Rome* 57 (1988) 43–97.

40. F. Fukuyama, *The End of History and the Last Man* (New York 1992).

41. See the discussion by E. Gabba, *Dionysius of Halicarnassus and the History of Archaic Rome* (Berkeley 1991) 42–45; for many of the ancient sources, see H. Fuchs, "Der Friede als Gefahr," *Harvard Studies in Class. Philol.* 63 (1958) 363–385.

5. Multiculturalism in Greece and Rome

1. The case made recently by Martin Bernal, *Black Athena: The Afroasiatic Roots of Classical Civilization,* vol. 1, *The Fabrication of Ancient Greece 1783–1985* (New Brunswick 1987), is somewhat different: the assumption is that Greece in the Bronze Age was heavily influenced by and perhaps was even a colony of Egypt and/or Phoenicia. The main problem is the lack of continuity between Bronze Age Greece and archaic Greece; for that issue and others, including the misleading title, see D. Gress in *New Criterion* 8 (December 1989) 36–43, the special issue of *Arethusa* entitled *The Challenge of "Black Athena"* (1989), and M. Poliakoff, "Roll Over Aristotle: Martin Bernal and His Critics," *Academic Questions* 4.3 (1991) 12–28. The situation is not changed

by the "evidence" Bernal presents in vol. 2 (1991); see the review by John Baines in *The New York Times Book Review* (Aug. 11, 1991) 12f. For diverging assessments of the reliability of Herodotus' attribution of Greek customs to Egypt, see, for example, A. B. Lloyd in *Entretiens Fondation Hardt* 35 (1990) 229ff. and W. Burkert, *Museum Helveticum* 42 (1985) 121–132. Cf. Diane Ravitch, "Multiculturalism," *American Scholar* 59 (1990) 342–348 for a discussion of ethnocentric multicultural views.

2. See F. M. Snowden, *Before Color Prejudice: The Ancient View of Blacks* (Cambridge, Mass. 1983) and L. A. Thompson, *Romans and Blacks* (Norman 1989) 1–56.

3. J. D. Gurney, *Times Lit. Supplement* (March 11, 1983) 241, reviewing *The Muslim Discovery of Europe;* cf. Bernard Lewis, "Other People's History," *American Scholar* 59 (1990) 397–405.

4. Herodotus 1.56, cf. 2.51, 8.44. For detailed discussions, see A. Diller, *Race Mixture among Greeks before Alexander,* Illinois Studies in Language and Literature 20.1 (1937), repr. 1971, 35ff.; and H. Diller in M. Reverdin, *Grecs et barbares* (Geneva 1962) 66–68.

5. It is to this second group to which Isocrates' (4th cent.) often-quoted pronouncement applies (4.50) "that the name 'Hellenes' suggests no longer a race, but an intelligence, and that the title 'Hellenes' is applied rather to those who share our culture than to those who share our blood." This is usually misunderstood as being enlightened and pertaining to the barbarians' ability to qualify as Greeks.

6. Antiphon, *On Truth,* fragment 44B, col. 2, in H. Diels and W. Kranz, *Die Fragmente der Vorsokratiker* 2 (Dublin and Zurich 1966) supplemented with *P. Oxy.* 3647; for the context, see *Oxyrhynchus Papyri* 52 (1984) 1–5.

7. H. Diller (see note 4, above) 68 with reference to Herodotus 4.56–80. For an informative study of barbarians in Greek tragedy, see E. Hall, *Inventing the Barbarian: Greek Self-Definition through Tragedy* (Oxford 1989).

8. Ch. 16; trans. J. Chadwick and W. N. Mann. It is curious that a less-refined variant of the climatic theory has resurfaced in the modern multicultural debate.

9. Details in E. Bickerman, "Origines Gentium," *Class. Philology* 48 (1952) 65–81.

10. *Hesiod. Theogony* (Oxford 1966) 31, with further discussion; cf. P. Walcot, *Hesiod and the Near East* (Cardiff 1966).

11. See W. Burkert, *Structure and History in Greek Mythology and Ritual* (Berkeley 1979) 80–98; the quotations are from pp. 94 and 83. For Herakles' later development, see my book on *The Herakles Theme* (Oxford 1972).

12. Jencks in Papadakis, *The New Classicism* 23–24, and in Moore and Attoe, *Ah Mediterranean!* 11 (both listed in the Bibliography to Ch. 1). See also A. W. Lawrence, *Greek Architecture,* 4th ed., rev. by R. A. Tomlinson (Penguin 1983).

13. Jencks in Papadakis 23.

14. M. L. Robertson, *A History of Greek Art* (Cambridge 1975) 39.

15. Ibid. 29.

16. An example is M. L. West, *Early Greek Philosophy and the Orient* (Oxford 1971); cf. the comments of A. Momigliano, *Alien Wisdom: The Limits of Hellenization* (Cambridge 1975) 123–129.

17. See especially the book (Ch. 19 in particular) and article by Peter Green listed in the Bibliography to this chapter.

18. Lewis, "Other People's History" 401.

19. Details in Momigliano, *Alien Wisdom* 74–122. The story of *Joseph and Aseneth,* for example, probably written in the 2d cent. B.C., may be rightly considered the oldest Greek novel in existence.

20. M. Avi-Yonah, *Hellenism and the East: Contacts and Interrelations from Alexander to the Roman Conquest* (University Microfilms International 1978) 188; I have substituted "Hellenistic" for "Hellenic."

21. L. H. Martin, *Hellenistic Religions: An Introduction* (New York 1987) 10.

22. Avi-Yonah, *Hellenism and the East* 35.

23. As documented by G. W. Bowersock, *Hellenism in Late Antiquity* (Ann Arbor 1990). For the cult of Isis, cf. F. Solmsen, *Isis among the Greeks and Romans* (Cambridge, Mass. 1979).

24. See M. Colledge, "Greek and Non-Greek Interaction in the Art and Architecture of the Hellenistic East," in Kuhrt and Sherwin-White 134–162.

25. J. J. Pollitt, *Art in the Hellenistic Age* (Cambridge 1986) 86.

26. Cf. Momigliano, *Alien Wisdom* 63.

27. F. M. Snowden, "Iconographical Evidence on the Black Populations in Graeco-Roman Antiquity," in J. Vercoutter et al., *The Image of the Black in Western Art* 1 (New York 1976) 188.

28. Cf. Snowden 206 and B. Fowler, *The Hellenistic Aesthetic* (Madison 1989) 44.

29. Snowden 210.

30. As S. K. Eddy, *The King Is Dead: Studies in the Near Eastern Resistance to Hellenism 334–31 B.C.* (Lincoln 1961), astutely observes, it was resistance to change in general rather than resistance to Hellenism specifically that often was a primary motivation.

31. Cf. p. 80.

32. Diller, *Race Mixture among Greeks* 56.

33. See especially W. B. Saddington, "Race Relations in the Early Roman Empire," in H. Temporini, ed., *Aufstieg und Niedergang der römischen Welt* II.3 (Berlin and New York 1975) 115–119.

34. Saddington, ibid. 135.

35. See J. A. Crook, *Law and Life of Rome, 90 B.C.–A.D. 212* (Ithaca 1967) 39–40. The quotation in the next sentence is from Crook 29.

36. Cf. H. F. Jolowicz, *Historical Introduction to the Study of Roman Law* (Cambridge 1932) 100–105.

37. Further discussion in Momigliano, *Alien Wisdom* 64–73.

38. See p. 54.

39. Momigliano, *Alien Wisdom* 17.

40. See pp. 86, 96–101, and 106–108.

41. S. Goldberg, *Understanding Terence* (Princeton 1985) xii, 220.

42. The word was frequently used to denote a negroid type; see F. M. Snowden, *Blacks in Antiquity* (Cambridge, Mass. 1970) 16 and his long note on Terence (270 n. 3).

43. P. 57.

44. P. 57; he also remedied Trajan's "imperial overstretch" (62).

45. Cf. pp. 35–36.

46. *Congressional Record for the Year 1963,* 11498 and 12197–12198. The subject

was the qualifications of African governments. For much of my discussion of Septimius, I am indebted to the sane book of Anthony Birley, *Septimius Severus: The African Emperor* (London 1971).

47. See pp. 61–62.

48. G. Charles-Picard, *La civilisation de l'Afrique romaine* (Paris 1959) 145.

49. A point well made by Saddington, "Race Relations" 133–134. Cf. R. MacMullen, *Enemies of the Roman Order: Treason, Unrest, and Alienation in the Empire* (Cambridge, Mass. 1966).

50. See Bowersock, *Hellenism in Late Antiquity* 55–69.

51. In the north of Gaul, however, and in Switzerland, Germany, and Britain hybrid forms prevailed; see P. D. Horne, "Roman or Celtic Temples? A Case Study," in M. Henig and A. King, eds., *Pagan Gods and Shrines in the Roman Empire* (Oxford 1986) 15–24.

52. W. Mierse in Raaflaub and Toher (see the Bibliography to Ch. 4) 325; the next quote is taken from there also. Cf. L. A. Curchin, *The Local Magistrates of Roman Spain* (Toronto 1990) 85, 102.

53. Cf. pp. 95–96; cf. pp. 62–63.

54. On this point see especially L. A. Thompson, *Romans and Blacks* (Norman 1989) 11–12. Cf. the argument of Molefi K. Asante, *The Afrocentric Idea* (Philadelphia 1987) 124, who rejects the view of W. E. B. DuBois that race, and not culture, is a prime determinant.

55. *The New York Times* (August 12, 1990) E21.

56. Cf. C. E. Finn, Jr., in *Chronicle of Higher Education* (June 13, 1990) A40; the quotations from Mr. Raspberry are also taken from there.

57. The curriculum revision prompted the concerns of a wide variety of historians of different political persuasions; see D. Ravitch and A. Schlesinger, Jr., in *The New York Times* (August 12, 1990) E7.

58. Cf. Francis Ford Coppola, "Here Comes a Creative American Era," *Internat. Herald Tribune* (Nov. 14, 1988) 15; the most recent adaptation of Homer's epics, for example, is set in the multicultural milieu of the Caribbean (Derek Walcott, *Omeros* [New York 1990]). All this contradicts a tendency of the new ethnic histories to subscribe to what a European observer has aptly called "the static notion of eternal groups" (W. Sollors in S. Bercovitch, ed., *Reconstructing American Literary History* [Cambridge, Mass. 1986] 19).

6. Rome, America, and the Classics in America Today

1. W. R. Connor in *American Scholar* 59 (1989) 541.

2. L. Price, ed., *Dialogues of Alfred North Whitehead* (Boston 1954) 161, where he also attributes the brilliance of the Greeks to racial mixture.

3. See pp. 100–102.

4. R. M. Gummere, "The Classical Ancestry of the Constitution," in *The American Colonial Mind and the Classical Tradition* (Cambridge, Mass. 1963) 174; the next quote is taken from p. 183.

5. *Res Gestae* (see Bibliography to Ch. 4) 1.1; cf. p. 102.

6. See pp. 95–96 and pp. 62–63.

7. George A. Kennedy in Meyer Reinhold, *Classica Americana: The Greek and Roman Heritage and the United States* (Detroit 1984) 349.

8. Stern (see the Bibliography to Ch. 1) 283.

9. W. R. Agard, "Classical Scholarship," in Merle Curti, ed., *American Scholarship in the Twentieth Century* (New York 1953) 166–167.

10. P. Culham and L. Edmunds, eds., *Classics: A Discipline and Profession in Crisis?* (Lanham, Md. 1989). The definition of "classics" is unduly limited, as classical archaeology, art history, philosophy, etc., seem to be considered separate disciplines.

11. *The American Philological Association: An Historical Sketch* (Philadelphia 1964) 43–44.

12. G. Graff, *Professing Literature: An Institutional History* (Chicago 1987) 35.

13. See R. A. LaFleur, ed., *The Teaching of Latin in American Schools* (Atlanta 1987).

14. Spring 1990, 35–40 ("Classics Are for Kids").

15. *Chronicle of Higher Education* (May 2, 1990) B1. By contrast, the brave attempt at demography in Culham and Edmunds ("Taking Classics into the 21st Century: A Demographic Portrait" 14–23) could have benefited from consultation with statistical and demographic experts, as several variables are ignored.

16. See, for example, I. D. Barchas, "Stanford after the Fall," *Academic Questions* 3.1 (1989–1990) 28, and John Searle in *New York Review of Books* (Dec. 6, 1990) 38–39.

17. Except, for example, for Sidney Hook in *American Scholar* 58 (1989) 126–127.

18. Cf. Ch. 5, note 1.

19. *The University and the Public Interest* (New York 1981) 57.

20. Cf. my remarks in Douglas Astolfi, ed., *Teaching the Ancient World* (Scholars Press 1983) 1–11; *ADFL Bulletin* 13.1 (1981) 29–30 and *Humanities* 2.3 (1982) 1–4.

21. "Higher Education—The Real Crisis," *The New York Times Sunday Magazine*, Jan. 22, 1989, 24ff.

22. Cf. my comments in *Chronicle of Higher Education* (Feb. 21, 1990) B4.

23. The only recent writer to attempt a broader (and by now somewhat dated) comparison between modern America and Greco-Roman antiquity was a German-speaking Czech; he singles out the principle of competition (*agon*), including its function in athletics, as such a parallel (Johannes Urzidil, *Amerika und die Antike* [Zurich 1964] 72).

24. August Boeckh, *Encyklopädie und Methodologie der philologischen Wissenschaften*, ed. E. Bratuschek (2d ed. [Leipzig 1886, repr. Darmstadt 1966]) 76–77.

25. Cf. p. 82.

26. Such as the debate comprised by the essays in W. J. T. Mitchell, ed., *Against Theory: Literary Studies and the New Pragmatism* (Chicago 1985); it would be too complacent for classicists to argue that in a world without theory such a debate would not have been necessary in the first place. For its application to the U.S. Constitution, see pp. 75–76 with note 5.

27. As Gerald Graff (note 12, above) reminds us (esp. in Ch. 15), traditionalists or "conservatives" differ from the new theorists only in not having realized or systematized their presuppositions.

28. *The World, the Text, and the Critic* (Cambridge, Mass. 1983) 4. I have discussed these issues in greater detail in *The Interpretation of Roman Poetry* 1–40.

29. E. Said (note 28, above) 167.

30. Z. Stewart, "Changing Patterns of Scholarship as Seen from the Center of Hellenic Studies," *Amer. Journ. of Philology* 111 (1990) 263.

31. *Chronicle of Higher Education* (Jan. 17, 1990) B2. At the time of this writing, a six-year limit (i.e., students—in all disciplines—who do not complete the requirements for a Ph.D. in six years will not be given financial aid) was announced by Deans Pollitt and Kagan at Yale, drawing predictable howls of protest (*The New York Times*, July 23, 1990, B4); both deans are classicists.

Index